Our Own Years

OUR OWN YEARS

What Women over 35 Should Know about Themselves

Alice Lake

A Woman's Day/Random House Book
New York

*Grateful acknowledgment is made to the following
for permission to reprint previously published
material:*
Houghton Mifflin Company: Excerpt of poetry by
Anne Sexton.
McCall Publishing Company: Excerpt of poetry by
Felicia Lamport. Reprinted from the November 1977
issue of *McCall's* by permission of the McCall
Publishing Company.

Library of Congress Cataloging in Publication Data
Lake, Alice, 1916–
    Our own years.
    "A Woman's Day/Random House book."
    Bibliography: p.
    1.   Middle aged women—United States.   2.   Middle
aged women—Health and hygiene—United States.
3.   Women—Psychology.   I.   Title.
HQ1221.L28   301.43'4   79–4801
ISBN 0–394–50620–0

Manufactured in the United States of America
98765432

For the three significant
women in my life

Elsie (1890–1978)
Dorothy
Ellen

Acknowledgments

Although over the years I have interviewed countless physicians, psychologists and sociologists in the course of writing medical articles for magazines, I am still pleasantly surprised by their generosity in allotting time to a writer's questions. A sense of responsibility for helping to inform the public accurately appears to counterbalance the exigencies of a crowded schedule. I am grateful for a chance to say thanks to the many experts who gave willingly of their time during the preparation of this book. They include: Anthony Albanese, David Arenberg, William Adler, Sidney Arje, Uriel Barzel, Judith Brandenburg, Leonard Flom, Edward Graber, Reva Greenberg, Beth Hess, Florine Livson, Leonore Luftman, Marvin Moser, Willibald Nagler, Norman Orentreich, Mary Parlee, Anna Rand, Emmanuel Rudd, Barbara Sang, Stephen Scheidt, Arthur Seligmann, Bernard Simon, Muriel Stone, Edward Tonna, Lillian Troll, Louise Tyrer, Tilla Vahanian, Virginia Watts, Patricia Wolman, Marc Weksler.

Just as valuable as the expert is the expediter: the assistant, the information specialist, the person who knows where the elusive bit of fact is buried. My special thanks to the courteous and patient men and women who helped far beyond what the job required: Nancy Durr, Robin Elliott, Marjorie Hoagland, Adele Paroni, Daniel S. Rogers.

And a special word of thanks to a woman who may be unaware of the boost her articles give to the research of others: Jane E. Brody, medical writer for *The New York Times*.

Despite all the expertise, a book on middle age in women needs the glue essential for binding it together—the experience of women themselves. Several score of women gave up hours of their time to talk about how the middle years looked to them. For the sake of their privacy, I have changed their names, and thus must express my gratitude to Anonymous.

Rita McCann and Marcia Dillon brought order out of chaos, turning each of my messily typed pages into a neat, professional-looking manuscript.

I reserve my deepest gratitude for the last. As an editor, Charlotte Mayerson is immensely knowledgeable on a bewildering variety of topics, has a sure eye for turning the ambiguous sentence into a model of clarity without ever showing disrespect for the writer's concept. Dina von Zweck and Geraldine Rhoads also helped keep my ego intact during the early months when it faltered.

My husband, Leonard M. Lake, did absolutely everything that could be helpful to this book's preparation. He gave up vacations and social engagements, suffered late and sketchy meals, endured moodiness and quick temper without complaint. Most important, he listened, and gave cogent advice only when it was asked for.

Contents

OUR OWN YEARS

I
Years
of Freedom

Middle age is a new invention, and ours is probably the first generation to enjoy it.

Chances are that your grandmother had no middle age, no period of life when she was a vigorous woman shorn of the responsibilities of child-rearing. Born in the late nineteenth century, she was fifty-five when her last youngster married, and widowhood and death were not far away. Our mothers did have a middle age, but probably didn't know what to do with it except more of the same—washing, cleaning, cooking, mothering and grandmothering, caring for a husband who was older than she was, and possibly sick as well.

But for us it's a brand-new script. Statistics show that the average woman now in her middle years married at twenty, bore her first child at twenty-two, and her last at thirty or thirty-one. In grandmother's day the children remained at home until they married. Now youngsters are likely to leave at nineteen. If you are that average woman, you will be forty-nine when you wave goodbye to the youngest, with almost two-fifths of your life lying ahead. Eighty years ago a woman and her husband could expect two years alone together after the last child married. You can look forward to thirteen.

There is a dazzling variety of options. There's better than one chance in two that a middle-aged woman will be working for pay. She may be attending school—for a course in crafts or self-improvement, to get a college degree or perhaps a doctorate. And even if she is less venturesome in terms of education, she will be busy playing tennis, learning yoga's lotus position, grubbing in the vegetable plot, painting or potting or running the League of Women Voters.

Fearful at first that it's the beginning of the end, most women soon discover that the middle years are the best of their lives. "Finally I have my head together," one told me. She is forty-three, a musician, jogger and tennis player. "I was draggy during my thirties—three kids to raise, a house to run, a husband with a scratchy ego. Now I feel a new sense of self, a confidence that is like a shot in the arm. I no longer live through the children or through my husband. Yet there's more love now, and even more fun in bed."

There are those with a darker view. "After forty," one woman told me, "it's nothing but patch, patch, patch." Another, who moved with her child back to her parents' home after a divorce, refused to talk about the middle years. "It means gaining wrinkles and losing a chance for a husband. What's there to discuss?"

Who is right? That's what this inquiry is all about. It intends to explore the pluses—the expanding ego, the newfound independence—without ignoring the minuses—breasts that sag, hair that grays, skin etched with lines. The best way to deal with middle age, advises Dr. Robert Butler, director of the National Institute on Aging, is: "Don't try to pretend that it isn't happening." This report intends to follow Dr. Butler's advice, and look at it squarely, warts and all.

But what is middle age? When does it start and end? When they are asked, women choose wildly diverging chronological limits. "I expect it to start at fifty-five, although I know intellectually that most will pick forty," says one woman. Although she is forty-two, she still has a four-year-old to raise. Others relate it to their state of mind or body. "For me there was a reawakening at thirty-five when my youngest went off to kindergarten," says one. "It starts when you realize you're a person, not a puppet of your parents or husband," says another. And from a woman of thirty-six—"I've had the first sign. My skin needs a moisturizer now."

The poet Felicia Lamport offers this reckoning:

> Middle age is very difficult to chart
> Since no one really knows when it should start

But a simple calculation gets the figure down pat:
It begins a decade later than wherever you're at.

Psychologists frequently use the ages from forty to sixty to define the period, although they caution against arbitrary chronological labels. This inquiry extends it from thirty-five to fifty-five. Middle age at thirty-five? This needs some explanation. If one views woman as a reproductive animal, thirty-five marks the age when childbearing becomes more hazardous for her and contraception more urgent; as a social animal, it marks the time when she waves her youngest child off to kindergarten and gains a modicum of freedom. If thirty-five is not yet midlife, it is certainly the prologue. Nor is fifty-five its end, but perhaps the beginning of the end—a time when a woman and her husband (he nudging into the Social Security years) begin talking retirement or even acting upon it.

Nevertheless, if middle age is also a state of mind, its beginning and end depend on other facets of a woman's role. The woman who marries at thirty and bears her last child at thirty-eight places herself at a different stage in the life cycle from one who marries at twenty and ends childbearing at twenty-five. If she embarks on a career at twenty-two and remains childless, if she divorces at thirty-two, or is widowed at forty-two, her life experience will diverge from the typical pattern of marriage, children and *then* the midlife reawakening.

The significant word is *dynamic*. Social scientists used to think of growth and development as the prerogative of youth, followed by a stable plateau in adulthood and then a decline in old age. Now they know that restless change throughout the cycle is the norm rather than the exception.

The 1978 meeting of the American Association for the Advancement of Science featured a symposium titled "Aging from Birth to Death." This illustrates another concept—that aging is a continuum that cannot be boxed into a single stage of life. From the moment of birth, we suffer loss as well as gain. A female infant's ovaries contain more eggs—potential offspring—than they will ever again in her lifetime. An ability to hear extremely high-pitched sounds begins to decline at two and is gone by twenty. Precise muscular coordination starts to fail at twenty-five, and basal metabolism to fall after thirty. Some organ systems begin an early downward spiral, some late; others perform adequately throughout the life span. Individual experience compounds the diversity; your heredity and what you do with your body help determine the speed of its aging.

In other words, middle age is *not* the beginning of the end of bodily vigor. There is no single period of life when the body functions on an even keel, and no single magic age at which deterioration sets in. At forty, you are squarely in the middle of an average woman's life span; you can expect to live about thirty-nine more years. If you are thirty-five, more than half of life lies ahead, with death predicted for seventy-nine. If you have reached fifty, your life expectancy is now eighty, and at sixty, it rises to eighty-two.

What a woman makes of these years is her own choice. But before she embarks on her journey, she should throw away some excess baggage, the myths and stereotypes about loss that make the trip appear fearful. Among them:

• Expect to suffer a midlife crises, likely to be negative in character. The dust jacket of a book published a decade ago listed typical symptoms of this alleged crisis: boredom, emotional instability, irrational fear of aging, hypochondria. Of course, some women at some time experience some of these symptoms, but are they common? Not one of them. They are based on an invalid thesis that two events of a woman's middle years—the menopause and the children leaving home—are perceived by her as tragic loss. With the menopause she loses her fertility, and with the empty nest, her role as mother, the two central reasons for female existence. It is hard not to hoot at that idea.

In the past decade women scientists have exploded this myth. Their research studies reach a unanimous conclusion: when menstruation ends and the children leave home, most women shout "Hurrah!" Dr. Bernice Neugarten, University of Chicago psychologist, was the first to interview large groups of women about these two events. "I'm so happy about not menstruating any more, I could dance with joy," one told her. Asked to pick the worst thing about middle age, only nine percent thought it was the empty nest. Asked what they personally disliked most about being middle-aged, a bare two percent replied, "Feeling useless." "Rather than being a stressful period," wrote Dr. Neugarten and co-author Nancy Datan in one report, "the empty nest was associated with a somewhat *higher level of life satisfaction* than were the other family stages. It is an inaccurate view that middle age constitutes a crisis period."

When Dr. Reva Greenberg, a social gerontologist, recently interviewed seventy-five suburban women, aged forty-one to seventy-four, she received even blunter comments about the empty nest. "I wouldn't want to be a full-time mom again," said one woman. "It's nice when they come and it's nice when they go." And another answered, "At first there was a void when the children left, but now I get annoyed when they come home and make a mess."

• At middle age you lose your looks and your ability to attract a man. This is perhaps less myth than misemphasis. It is predicated on the popular belief that youth is beauty, and ugliness marks its waning. The poet Anne Sexton wrote differently.

> Once I was Beautiful . . .
> Now I am myself.

If one considers only physical attributes, and not the serene inner beauty that comes with maturity, it's true that neither crow's-feet nor puffy circles under the eyes make a female prettier. Yet nature is far from cruel. As youth's vivid coloring fades, paler skin tones blend subtly with graying hair, and the facial palette shifts to soft pastels.

Is this ugly? It is if you think so. But not everyone agrees. One observant writer noted, "She was old; her ugliness had faded." And a woman of thirty-five made an honest assessment—"Sure, I know my skin will sag, but I was never so beautiful that I expect to lose much." Gypsy Rose Lee took it in stride—"I have everything now that I had twenty years ago except it's all lower."

As for sexual attractiveness, whose measure are you using? The workman who no longer wolf-whistles as you walk down the street? As they become older, some men do choose younger women to date and to marry, but isn't that often related to their own fears of waning sexual powers? A woman is different: she is at her sexual peak at midlife. Enjoyment comes easier; orgasm is more frequent; technique more smoothly skilled to enhance a partner's pleasure and her own. "There are plenty of men who are scared to take a young chick to bed," a fifty-two-year-old widow observes. "They hate the pressure of having to perform as if they were seventeen."

If at forty-five you think you're past your physical prime, why isn't your husband, with his paunch and balding head? Why are a man's graying temples "distinguished" and his facial lines signs of "character," while your hair is mousy and your wrinkles repulsive? The answer is that you've been conned. You've been conned by the advertising industry, by the media and by Hollywood into believing that for women alone, young is the only way to be. Susan Sontag exposed the cruel myth a few years ago in an essay titled "The Double Standard of Aging." "It is particularly women who experience growing older (everything that comes *before* one is actually old)," she wrote, "with such distaste and even shame. Society is much more permissive about aging in men."

In the teens most of us bought the sexist package about the crucial importance of female appearance: we were certain that only the pretty girls went to the prom and caught the rich husbands. And the majority who were ordinary-looking suffered agonies attempting to re-create themselves in the image of Miss America. We think we know better now; we recognize that warmth and maturity and self-reliance are more enduring rocks on which to stand than youthful beauty. But old habits die hard, and in the middle years it is women themselves who are most negative about their physical image. We accept pejorative terms like "fat and forty." "A kind of self-hatred infects most women," Susan Sontag says. "Like men, they find old age in women 'uglier' than old age in men."

A few straws in the wind indicate that the emphasis may be shifting. We appear to have come a long way from the days when *every* woman over forty lied about her age. Jane Fonda says openly that she is forty-one; Beverly Sills, forty-eight; Betty Ford, sixty; and most consider all three attractive. Imagine proclaiming how old you are on the front page of *The New York Times?* That's where one husband inserted an ad last year to wish his wife a happy fortieth birthday. One company, Clairol, now advertises a silver hair tint in which a gray-haired woman, face etched with lines, appears under the heading, "Free, gray and fifty-one."

Yet the bulk of television commercials still favor the woman whose skin, hair and hands are just like her daughter's. Women should stop buying this myth. Unless the high point of your own life came at the junior prom, you're better off looking like yourself.

• In middle age a woman starts to slow down mentally and physically. Anticipating what we fear—physical and mental decrepitude—most are inclined to exaggerate the changes that occur at this time, to gloss over those that happened earlier, and to predate those that still lie ahead. These facts should be borne in mind:

Whether women are physically healthier or not, they visit the doctor *less* often in their middle years than when they were younger. Up to the age of forty-five, women account for almost two-thirds of all medical visits, but for only fifty-five percent between forty-five and sixty-five, and fifty percent after sixty-five.

Many report a fresh surge of physical energy once the menopause has passed. I know one woman of fifty-three who during the summer plays three sets of tennis before lunch, two sets after, and then swims for half an hour. Another rises at six-thirty, arrives at school, where she is a librarian, at eight. She belongs to a gourmet cooking club and often works until one in the morning preparing a dish for the group's next meeting. Casually she mentions the sports she still enjoys—golf, tennis, horseback riding, swimming, skiing.

We assume that we are shrinking in size, but a decline in height occurs mostly after the age of fifty, accelerating only after fifty-five, according to recent studies. You may end up about two inches shorter, but not until your seventies, and exercise may help to diminish the loss.

As for mental capacity, although memory may start to flag and reaction time to slow in the middle years or earlier, the ability to solve problems usually persists undiminished until the seventies. When women return to school at middle age, they frequently get better grades than when they were young. "It's easier to learn," says a forty-year-old, "because I know what's important to me and why."

There are still huge gaps in our knowledge about the middle years and the process of aging, areas in which research is barely out of its infancy. And women must be wary of the findings thus far, because most scientists have studied only males, and then extrapolated the results to include females. The story of the Gerontology Research Center in Baltimore, a federally sponsored project, is a case in point. Since its founding in 1958, the center has been engaged in an intensive study of the aging process. It has enrolled some 650 subjects, ranging in age from the twenties to the nineties, who are given thorough checkups at least every two years. The catch is that before 1978 *all the participants were men.*

Now a research arm of the National Institute on Aging, newest of the eleven National Institutes of Health, the GRC, somewhat embarrassed, is finally also enrolling women. "Women have been badly neglected in terms of studying the aging process," admits Dr. Butler, who heads the NIA. He believes that men and women experience aging differently during the middle years, but says, "We don't really know why. Most studies on aging have been done with men."

In many ways, the difference between the sexes is dramatic during the middle years. Because the female bears and raises the children, it is she who experiences the most profound change in life focus when this job ends. For men, in our society at least, there is no such sharp break, no surge in self-realization. These are the fresh satisfactions that women report:

A new sense of freedom. In recent interviews, the change that women mentioned most often was a sense of increased freedom. One woman, whose youngest has just left for college, says, "For twenty-six years I was very conscious of having to be home by four. The children were the single most important thing in my life. But I have a feeling of freedom now, of being a bird again about to fly."

An enhancement of identity. No generation has invested more in their progeny than ours. We created the baby boom, knelt at the altar of togetherness, changed more diapers, made more peanut butter sandwiches, chauffeured more miles than others before or since. Now we are learning with joy that a woman's ego does not rise or fall on a child's popularity, a husband's success, the height of a chocolate soufflé. "I feel a strong sense of myself. It's a sense of power," says one woman. And another, a re-entry student, reports, "The praise from my teachers is rebuilding my badly battered self-esteem." But applause for achievement is a secondary gain. "I've thought it through," says one woman, "and I've decided against looking for a job. I've achieved what's important—I no longer feel driven. I'm the driver now."

An ability for self-assertion. Although many are flocking to assertiveness-training classes, others find with delight that now it all comes naturally. A forty-four-year-old divorcee says, "After years of being compliant, I can say, 'What do *I* want?'" And another terms it the major plus of the middle years: "Finally I've learned to ask for what I need. Though it still comes hard, I can ask for help, for support, for sexual stimulation, and even for a raise. I used to think the feminine way was by indirection and subterfuge, but being open and direct is better."

This change is apparently not new to our generation or even to our culture. Almost fifty years ago Carl Jung, the Swiss psychiatrist, developed the theory that the roles men and women filled in early parenthood, he as breadwinner and she as nurturer of the young, were necessary to protect the offspring and continue the species. But in the twilight of parenthood, he said, parts of the personality that were once suppressed for this purpose are allowed to resurface. In middle age, says Jung in effect, all women are free to fulfill themselves, and men to cultivate the nurturing side of their nature.

More recently Dr. David Gutmann, a University of Michigan psychologist, has reported that the phenomenon of emerging androgyny—or unisex—occurs in a variety of cultures, as the sharp divisions between both the functions and the pleasures of the two sexes become blurred. "With their children grown, wives become less needful . . . of male assertion, more ready to recognize and enjoy such energies in themselves," he writes. "A massive turnover of sex roles takes place . . . Particularly for women, aging brings new beginnings."

Although this may sound idyllic, midlife is not without problems. One arises from the frequent reversal of dependency between aging parent and middle-aged offspring. "Woman is the family kin keeper," says Dr. Lillian Troll, who heads the psychology department at Rutgers University in New Brunswick, New Jersey. As responsibility for her children lightens, it becomes heavier for her parents—and often also for her parents-in-law.

And for some couples the newfound years of second honeymoon may turn out to be grim. "It's a delightful, different world since the children left. It's a gift to be alone together," one woman reported. But another said, "It's hard for my husband and me to find interests together now that we are alone. He wants a lot of attention. He wants to be babied."

Some women themselves fail to make the transition to independence and self-identity. There are the super-Moms, unable to shift gears from a life of sacrificing self for the children. Sociologist Pauline Bart described them in "Mother Portnoy's Complaints," a study of depressed middle-aged women in a mental hospital. "I didn't think of myself at all," one said. "I was just someone who was there to take care of the needs of my family, my husband and children."

If you are entering the middle years, the professionals who are now studying this turbulently joyous period have some advice to guide you in transition and in meeting the new challenges. They suggest:

Now is the time to cut, ever so gently, the psychic umbilical cords that bind a woman to her husband, to her parents, and to her children. This means abandoning dependency, but not love, raising one's consciousness of self without lowering one's concern for others. "Isn't that selfish?" some may ask. But it's time, too, to accept selfishness as the opposite of selflessness, to practice a measure of egocentricity instead of drowning in self-abnegation.

Women should adopt a new motto: Use it or lose it. This applies equally on the tennis court, in the college library, and in bed. Muscles atrophy, orgasms fade, minds decay unless they are exercised vigorously. If physical and mental risks are not taken now, they never will be.

Involvement is the name of the game, and one should plan for it early. This is particularly pertinent for the woman in her late thirties who stands on the threshold of middle age. In her interviews with suburban women, Reva Greenberg reports that she found a significant difference between those who made their own choice before the children left home, and those still struggling to make it later. Dr. Greenberg, a suburban matron of forty-two, has herself practiced what she preaches. "I'm the perfect product of coming of age in the fifties," she says. She was graduated from college in 1958, spent a year earning an M.A. as a teacher, married a lawyer, became pregnant, and ended her career before it had started. Until eight years ago, when her third and youngest child turned six, "I was content superficially but not happy, if you know the difference." Without a goal in mind, she began to take courses at a local college, and drifted into social gerontology, the field in which she now has a doctorate. Her advice: "Whatever you may do, it's time you started doing it and doing it well."

Be flexible. As you grow older, there's an insidious pull toward rigidity. Unless you watch out, limbs will creak, muscles harden, and the mind will set into a psychosclerosis that parallels the hardening of the arteries. Once you defend an action—"this is the way I've always done it"—then it's time to try a different way. I know a woman aged fifty-two, accustomed to carrying matched luggage in luxury-hotel-hopping with her husband, who died recently. "I'm going to Greece next summer," she told me, "but no more suitcases. I'm borrowing a backpack, carrying a duffel, and wearing blue jeans. I intend to look like an eccentric old lady, and I expect to have a ball."

It's not always necessary to throw out the luggage, only the excess mental baggage that may cramp one's style in midlife or later. Dr. Robert Butler, asked whether he recommended growing old gracefully, replied, "I don't think that's the way to go . . . being sweet and nice, not making any noise . . . I would recommend growing old candidly, open-mindedly and flexibly."

Although this report hopes to anticipate some of the problems of growing old, its major focus will be on the unique experience of the middle years that stretch for two decades from thirty-five to fifty-five. Over twenty-four million American woman are now living through this time, one-third of all those over twenty-one. This book hopes to serve them by enhancing the highs and ameliorating the lows of the period, by telling them what to expect in changes of mind and body, and by pointing out ways of coping with such changes.

Some developments may throw you into a panic—blotchy brown spots on the hands, fat that thickens the torso, fear of cancer, or of crippling that destroys independence. These must be faced. It is ignorance that nourishes fear, and knowledge that foreshadows free choice. Women should know about their bodies in the middle years in order to choose whether to mask, to alter or to accept the changes that will occur; they should know about their psyches, and how to stretch them for the greatest fulfillment.

If you face these years with trepidation, if you suspect that there's nothing ahead but "patch, patch, patch," ask yourself if you would prefer to wave a magic wand and be a teen-ager again (a period that most women judge the worst), or even to relive the sour-milk-and-soiled-diaper days of young motherhood. Few really want to turn back the clock. "There is a difference between wanting to *feel* young and wanting to *be* young," one woman told an interviewer. "I would not trade the vigor and appearance of youth for the authority or the autonomy I feel—no, nor the ease of interpersonal relationships or the self-confidence that comes from experience."

Billie Burke summed it up best. "Age is something that doesn't matter unless you're a cheese."

II

Still Feminine

Among President Carter's ten senior advisers working in the White House, there is only one woman, and she is middle-aged and until recently was a housewife.

Her name is Anne Wexler, and her age is forty-eight. She married two weeks after her college graduation in 1951, and soon became pregnant. Until eight years ago, she was a full-time suburban mother, living in Westport, Connecticut, with her husband, a doctor, and two young sons. Although she dabbled in politics as a volunteer, she did not hold a paying job until she was forty. She made it a rule always to be home before the boys arrived from school. "I enjoyed my kids. I was a very traditional person," Mrs. Wexler says. "And I don't regret an instant of it."

In 1970 Anne Wexler managed the unsuccessful campaign of Joseph Duffey for the Senate. (Four years later, after they both got divorces, she married Duffey, head of the National Endowment for the Humanities.) She worked her way up from local to state to national politics, becoming known as a skilled political operator.

Although she is unique—smarter, smoother, more competent, and probably luckier than most men or women—whatever made Annie run is motivating millions of other midlife women. Their lives have changed drastically, as has hers, and the difference is only in degree. "I'm happier now than I've ever been," Anne Wexler says, and others in her age range echo the sentiment. Among two groups of home-oriented women—one in the late forties, the other in the late fifties—middle age was the time of life most often chosen as the best. One suburban housewife, aged forty-three, says, "The older I get, the more secure and confident I become. It comes from liking myself more and being happier with my life."

Whether a woman goes to work in the White House, becomes a six-mile jogger or merely cultivates her own garden, she changes at midlife. A growing number of professional studies attests to this; and my own informal depth interviews with several score of women, ranging in age from thirty-five to fifty-five, agree. Many get paying jobs for the first time, or go back to school to learn a profession, or just have fun flexing long-unused mental muscles. Although the shift from fierce concentration on the growing children is often easier for such women, those who continue to center their lives on the home change too. Most experience some problems in the switch from mothering to greater autonomy—one psychologist has dubbed it nestitis—but only a few fail to make a successful transition. For most, the move is toward expansion of personality, increased potential and self-realization. These are the significant changes that occur:

A woman becomes herself, more deeply and intensely realized as a person. In a real sense, those who marry young and first devote themselves to raising their children finally grow up at midlife, completing the search for identity that started in adolescence. No longer defined as her husband's wife and her children's mother, a woman begins to respect her own worth. "I even sign my name more boldly," one says.

One happy byproduct is a lessened concern for the opinion of others, and a slackening of the sharp self-criticism in which women typically engage. "Females in our culture have lower self-esteem than do males," says Barbara Turner, a University of Massachusetts psychologist. "Women are also more self-critical than men." But by late middle age, she adds, "Women stop knocking themselves so much."

"In my twenties I thought I had to look like an expert on wines and gourmet foods," says Polly, who was a swinging single until thirty, and at thirty-five is a wife and mother, with a brand-new Ph.D. in nutrition. "Now I feel liberated from a lot of those things that used to worry me." Dinah, forty-four, who has three children and a divorce, doesn't worry any more "whether I serve the greatest soufflé or master a thousand recipes. I'm learning to reinvent myself in a way that makes sense for today's life." And there's Trudy, forty-five, who no longer follows with bated breath the rise and fall of hemlines: "If someone says that my skirt is too short, I couldn't care less. It's time to dress and act the way you feel comfortable. For the first time I don't give a damn about what other people think."

A woman gains control of her own life. There's no baby to wake her at night, no child with the sniffles to keep her home from work, and the interminable series of children's orthodontist appointments have ended. "I finally realized a dream," says a pianist, aged forty-five and the mother of three. "I took the summer off and studied in New York. It was a little hard on my husband, but I figured—it's my turn now."

"I can hardly wait," says a dental hygienist. She has one child away at college and two nearing college age. "I might even just close the front door and enjoy being all by myself for a month." "But what about your husband?" she is asked. "I haven't thought about him yet. I'm very interested in myself."

Many shed the old need to feel safe and protected and learn for the first time to dare, to take risks, even though the idea may be terrifying at first. At forty-five, one woman had just acquired her own small sailboat. "It was a blowy day. I still don't know what made me do it, but I took the boat out alone, just for ten minutes. I was scared stiff, but I felt so proud later." Widowed at fifty, this same woman returned to college to get the degree she had abandoned at nineteen when she married. "At first I was petrified. When they passed out the blue books for an exam, I wanted to start crying and go home." Five years later she graduated magna cum laude.

Many renew a long-buried need to achieve. A former social worker, Sarah quit her career when she became pregnant, only returning, tentatively at first, when the youngest of her three children was eight. Now forty-five, she works full time in a social agency and also has a small private practice, seeing patients at night. It is a heavy schedule and she and her husband have no urgent need for the extra money. "I'm more ambitious than when I was younger," she explains. "I was never sure before that I was good enough to treat patients privately. Now I know I'm able— I just have more confidence."

Sarah's ambition is not unique. Psychologist Beatrice Gilmore tested more than three hundred women who ranged in age from eighteen to fifty, trying to ascertain how important achieving was to each, and how strongly each feared success. (Earlier studies have suggested that fear of success—of besting a man at the job— is a common problem for women at school and at work.)

The results showed that the older women, aged thirty-five to forty-eight, were the most eager to achieve, and those aged twenty-five to thirty-four were the least. Among those with traditional attitudes about the feminine role, three out of four younger women appeared to fear success, but only one in four among the older. A woman in the middle years, Dr. Gilmore concludes, "is perhaps both more interested in achieving and less concerned about losing femininity through doing so . . . It seems possible that the older women, having met the standards of their sex roles— i.e., having married and had children—are now more comfortable with the idea of achieving."

(This also appears to hold true on the tennis court, an arena in which men traditionally prevail, even though the "little woman" may purposely have to serve double faults to accomplish it. A number of women in the middle years told me of fierce tennis rivalry with their husbands, to the point where both became so ruffled that they had to stop competing against each other. "My husband has played for ages, and I only started a few years ago," one confided, insisting that I not use her name. "But now I beat him and he can't stand it." "Why don't you just let him win once in a while?" she was asked. "Now what would be the point in that?" she answered.)

Thus, underlying the other changes at midlife is the most fundamental of all: *a new concept of being feminine.* Psychologists used to believe that as males and females grew up, it was important for each to accept a sexual identity—active, assertive, confident for a male; warm, sensitive, charming, but also pliant for a female. They also once thought that these stereotypes endured without change through life, serving each sex well.

Now, while feminists are questioning the worth of the feminine stereotype at any age, psychologists have learned that its strength wanes naturally during the middle years, when women become more assertive and men more tender. This concept of androgyny or unisex has been mentioned earlier as a theory first propounded by Carl Jung almost fifty years ago. Right now psychologists (mostly women) are confirming Jung's idea and even expanding it. They are discovering that midlife femininity need not mean being timid and compliant. On the contrary, it is likely that those women who continue to cling rigidly to the feminine stereotype make the worst transition to midlife.

Marjorie Fiske Lowenthal heads a group of investigators at the University of California who have been studying how ordinary people of different ages face life's transitions. Their subjects are high school seniors, newlyweds, couples just prior to the empty-nest stage, and couples on the edge of retirement, and they have written about them in a book, *Four Stages of Life.* As part of their study of the concept of self, the researchers used each person's own description of himself or herself to rate the subjects on a standard index of femininity and masculinity.

The findings were surprising: although men became neither more nor less masculine, according to the stereotypes, over the forty-year span, women became a little less traditionally feminine at each age, until among the oldest, those in their late fifties, there was no great difference between the sexes. The high school girls viewed themselves as helpless, and were looking for a man to manage their lives; the brides felt dependent on their husbands; the women close to the empty nest were in flux, ambivalent about their spouses. But in the pre-retirement stage, the women seemed finally to hit their stride, to resolve problems with confidence, to regard themselves as competent. "I don't have the fears I had when I was younger," one said. "I can say what I feel. I'm not embarrassed by many things any more, and my personality is better."

Florine Livson, a California psychologist, has been observing the problems of midlife transition among forty women, all of whom are now aged fifty. These women, mostly middle-class housewives (although some hold jobs), have been interviewed intensively at four periods of their lives—the beginning of junior high school, during senior high school, at the age of forty, and again at fifty.

Using psychological tests, Dr. Livson has divided the women into two groups, twenty-four of whom are now emotionally healthy and sixteen who are not. One of her conclusions: the healthy women, still warm and nurturing, are also more assertive and analytic, with personalities not very different from those of healthy men of the same age. The unhealthy have not changed. They are as dependent, compliant and timid as when they were young girls. "Unhealthy women are the only group who do not develop opposite-sex characteristics by fifty. And of all groups, they are the most anxious."

Thus the style a woman uses to cope with life's problems, particularly the transition to middle age, is crucial to her emotional well-being. If in the mothering years she is passive and conforming, she gets along, because there is a reasonable fit between her personality and her role. But later such a woman finds herself incapable of taking her life in her own hands. Although she develops in superficial feminine ways—she may be attractive, pay attention to her appearance, be chatty, even vivacious—deep down she is fearful, unable to grasp the opportunities that await her.

Most of us know an occasional woman like this. Her helplessness in performing simple tasks, like uncorking a wine bottle, charming in a girl, is irritating in a mature woman. She is too agreeable and unassertive. One woman I interviewed, forty-six, with a strong but deeply devoted husband, a married son, and a daughter in college, seemed to cope splendidly during her thirties but appears to be floundering now. She is traditional in outlook; when she held a full-time job as a legal secretary, "I always made sure that my husband's dinner was on the table when he got home." Her boss died a few years ago, and although she plans to get another job, she keeps vacillating. "I've become lethargic. I manage to devote a whole week to taking a sports jacket to the cleaner." She finds it harder than ever to make decisions—"and once I do make up my mind, I need my husband's approval." She uses feminine guile: "I cater to him. I get more for myself that way"; and enjoys being catered to—"I like having a man do things for me. It makes me feel so feminine." Yet she is fearful of this dependence: "If anything should happen to him, I'd just die."

Mary Anne Sedney, a psychologist at Providence College, has discovered another flaw in a continuance at middle age of the traditional feminine response—it serves a woman badly in managing stress. She talked with forty women, aged forty-five to fifty-seven, to learn how they coped with a stressful event, ranging from losing a job to losing a husband. One of these started to create a lively life for herself after divorce, but was stymied when her ex-husband turned up every night, drank her liquor, watched TV, ate the food that "she hadn't the heart" not to fix for him. She went out to dinner with him weekly, planning to discuss the problem, but he never brought it up, and she couldn't bring herself to. Furious at his sabotage of her independent life, she still kept relying on the old feminine strategies—waiting and hoping.

"The femininity and masculinity that were learned in childhood do not always serve adults well," Dr. Sedney concludes. "Even the positive aspects of femininity—warmth, tenderness—are not necessarily the most adaptive . . . response in certain situations . . . To accept and express both one's femininity and masculinity may be an important part of maturity."

Many observers of a woman's middle years believe that if she has a major interest outside the home—work or school—she makes a smoother transition to a new non-mothering role. Shortly before she became sixty, Elizabeth Janeway wrote of her own creative work, "I didn't have much confidence in myself when I was young . . . Through [my work] I gained self-confidence and a sense of self, of being a person who has some value. That is what everyone wants."

Women who classify themselves as housewives, psychologists say, have a low sense of self-esteem, particularly after the children have grown. But once they bring home a paycheck there is a surge of independence, and also a sense of pulling their own financial weight. "I was absolutely thrilled. It was the first money I'd ever earned in twenty-seven years of marriage," one woman says. "It makes me feel good to take the financial pressure off my husband," says another.

But Florine Livson's research has convinced her that getting a job is not a woman's only path to a successful midlife transition. Among the twenty-four women whom she judges to be emotionally healthy at fifty, she has found two distinct types: a traditional woman who remains stable emotionally, moving smoothly and without apparent change into the middle years; and an independent woman, who takes an emotional nose dive around the age of forty but rebounds by fifty into a life that fulfills some long-suppressed dreams.

Dr. Livson's traditional prototype is a woman who has always been friendly and sociable, warm and nurturing, conventional in outlook. Although her two married daughters now live far away, "either they're running up here or we're running down there . . . it seems there are eighteen cousins all my girls' age that love us . . . They drop in . . . our house is filled with people all the time."

The independent woman is quite different. She gave up a promising career in order to marry at twenty-four. Although she has never regretted it, her pattern of life while raising three children seemed to accentuate a dependent, fearful aspect of her personality. She became overweight, depleted of energy, shy about venturing out alone, hesitant about asking her husband for money. But within two years after the youngest child left home, she lost thirty pounds; her migraines and high blood pressure vanished. Now she looks and feels attractive, has a happier, more egalitarian marriage, and an interesting administrative job. During the decade from forty to fifty, she appears to have been transformed, says Dr. Livson, into "a competent energetic woman with high self-esteem."

The key factor is the fit between a woman's life style and her personality. Home and family are a traditional woman's turf. She may hold a job or not after the children are grown, but she always finds someone to mother. The independent woman, a doer rather than a giver, suppresses part of her personality during her mothering years and pays a temporary price in irritability, ill-health and conflict. A new role at midlife fits her personality to a T. "Life expands at fifty—for non-traditional women who live traditional lives," writes Dr. Livson. "More traditional women move smoothly into middle age with little change in life style."

There is a lesson here for other women entering midlife—choose a life style that matches the essence of your personality. Right now it may be a hard lesson to learn, for ours is the generation that reached adulthood and then, as one woman said, "they changed the rules on us." We grew up when husband and home were glorified as a worthy life goal for a woman. In 1955 Adlai Stevenson told the Smith College graduating class that their life task was to create good cultured homes for their active, ambitious husbands. This was only eight years before the publication of Betty Friedan's seminal *The Feminine Mystique*. Since then most members of the class of '55, according to a recent study, have flip-flopped with the times, raising large families and then belatedly becoming lawyers, librarians, teachers.

Often they are delighted with the new feminist thrust, but some still feel comfortable with an earlier goal: "I do not knock the satisfaction of home and family," says one.

Many who are less talented and less privileged than the Smith students are bewildered and a bit dismayed by the "careers" they feel the feminist movement expects them to embark on. Sociologist Lillian Rubin reported last year on one aspect of a research study on midlife women for which she interviewed in depth 160 women, aged thirty-five to fifty-five. Their early goal had been "to find an appropriate husband, I guess." But now one says, "I never saw past the age of forty-two, which is where I am now. Now what?" And another characterizes herself: "I'm fifty-two years old and I was brought up to be Betty Boop!"

When a woman doesn't know where she's heading, the anticipation of middle age can be disturbing. Among those I interviewed, the younger women—particularly if their futures were unsettled—were most apprehensive, regarding each birthday as a millstone instead of a milestone. At forty-two Paula is still in practical terms a "young" mother; her oldest child is eleven, her youngest only four. "My thirtieth birthday was bad, but forty was really disastrous," she says. "I've always walked around wondering what I'll do when I grow up. Finally I've had to confront reality—that I'm not a kid any more."

But Gail, now fifty-three, a professional woman with an active social life, says, "Do birthdays bother me? Not really. I thought forty was going to be the end of the world. But as a matter of fact, it turned out to be fine. It's more like the beginning of self-assertion and doing your own thing. Then fifty looked like the end. But I have no less energy now. I'm freer to do and say what I want. There are liberating aspects."

It's a standard joke, always good for a laugh, that all women lie about their age. Many women do, of course, but, in my depth interviews with close to fifty women, I noted another trend— flaunting one's age in order to garner compliments on a youthful appearance. "When I joined a consciousness-raising group," one woman told me, "I told everyone, 'Hi, I'm Juliet. I'm fifty.' I wanted them all to drop dead, to say, 'Oh, you're not!' Why would I tell them otherwise?"

This strategy, it seems to me, pays almost as much obeisance to the idolization of youth that permeates our society as the straightforward fib. What such a woman is saying is, "I look attractive, so I must be exceptional, different from other women. For if I looked my age, I'd be old, and everyone knows that old is ugly."

Some women have come to terms more realistically with the passing years. At forty, Natalie says, "I look at other women my age who aren't as physically active, and I'm pleased with the way

I look." And Sarah, forty-five, told me, "I don't care about not being twenty-five. In some ways I like it better. I was never beautiful. I didn't lose that. Right now *I just want to look as good as I can for forty-five.*"

Sarah has come to honest grips with the cult of youth, and even thumbed her nose at it. Women have been acquiescing too long in the youth worship that typifies our culture. We have been tricked into believing that once a woman is no longer young, she is old, and therefore sexless, and even a worthy subject for ridicule. Every comedian's repertoire includes a standard mother-in-law joke. A man's June–December affair is acceptable, even romantic, but when a woman turns up in public with a younger man, there are snide remarks about a gigolo, as if she couldn't attract him except with cash.

When women react to the word "middle-aged" as an insult, they are not responding with an appraisal of this stage of life, but merely accepting the false judgment of the youth cult. We are particularly vulnerable because it is the female sex alone that has been brought up to believe that looking youthful is not the best thing, it is the only thing.

One way to combat the twosome that is so wounding—ageism (prejudice against getting older) and sexism (prejudice against women)—is to stop judging ourselves through others' eyes, and to start looking through our own. One woman recognizes and is shocked by the fact that she is getting older when the pimply boy who carries out her groceries at the supermarket no longer tries to flirt, and even addresses her as "ma'am." Others lie about their age—and lose dignity in doing so—not because they are trying to fool themselves but to fool others.

At the 1977 National Women's Conference in Houston, some participants flaunted a button that read, "How Dare You Assume I'd Rather Be Young?" The writer Francine du Plessix Gray recently suggested a companion slogan, "I Shall Not Be Defined by Anyone but Myself." These are appropriate mottoes for the twenty-four million women who are now enjoying their middle years.

III

Intimate Relations

As a woman changes in the middle years, she makes waves that shake and sometimes even topple the delicate structure of family equilibrium. Relations with others—husband, children, parents, friends—are profoundly altered because she is different from what they have come to expect.

She becomes more of an equal to her husband. "I am no longer half a person in someone else's shadow," says a Boston woman in her forties. "I have my own opinions. I can succeed on my own."

She becomes less of a mother to her children. "I'm still very much bound up with the kids, but sometimes I resent all I do for them," says Carol, forty-six, who has three daughters in their teens. "I guess I've become more concerned with myself."

As her parents age, she starts shifting roles with them. She becomes the mother, they the dependent children. And sometimes she is boxed in the middle between the demands and the needs of the generations on either side.

Hers is not the only psyche in flux. Just at the time as a wife grows more confident, a husband's *macho* self-image may be faltering. His son starts beating him at tennis; at work, he keeps running to stay in the same place, with retirement just around the corner. The rocket that launched the children from the home fizzles out: a daughter's marriage may be on the rocks; a son expects an unpaid sitter for his new baby.

Practically every woman in our generation got married—ninety-six percent, the highest rate ever. Two-thirds of these marriages remain intact; husband and wife can expect to live together for forty-four years, and to spend almost one-third of that time, about thirteen years, as a couple with no children at home. But eight percent of the women of this age group are divorced, and the breakup of twenty-year marriages is on the rise. Because our husbands' life spans are shorter, because they were older than we were at marriage, widowhood lies in our future, most likely during our late sixties or early seventies.

Husband and Wife

Marital relations are central to a woman's emotional equilibrium. Most observers believe that they hit rock bottom just before the youngest child leaves home, and then start to shoot up, achieving a level rivaling your days as a bride as you approach retirement. "It's a totally new thing," says one wife. "There's more privacy and freedom to be yourself. We can even sit down and have a conversation."

What goes wrong, and how does it improve?

You fight over the children. Teen-agers are poison to marital bliss. "It's probably the number one thing we argue about," says one mother, with two youngsters in college and one in high school. In the book *Four Stages of Life*, the authors report that the middle-aged couples they interviewed "appeared anxious for an end to parenting and a return to spousing, which they regarded as antithetical."

Yet when the moment arrives, the wife and her husband experience it differently. Her gain of freedom is sometimes perceived by him as loss. One researcher reports that the fathers "often had no time for the kids when they were young. Suddenly the kids are gone and Dad's left with regrets."

You've lost contact, no longer know how to communicate. "It's the boredom between us that we didn't face before," one wife explains. "With the kids at home we found something to talk about, but now the buffer is gone. There are just the two of us, face to face."

Sexual communication may also be at a low. Accustomed to viewing each other as parent and not as lover, some men and women start searching elsewhere for sexual enjoyment. "Men have always done this, and now women are starting to," says Virginia Watts, a psychoanalyst at the Postgraduate Center for Mental Health in New York.

You have changed and he feels threatened by it. You're out in the world—at school, on the job: and the milkman and butcher are no longer the only males you talk with. (It was middle-aged wives who started the female exodus from home into the labor market. By 1973 more than half the women aged thirty-five to fifty-five were working for pay, a percentage only recently equaled by younger women.) The more insecure a husband is, the more frightened he becomes by a wife's change in status. "Every step a wife makes to gain power is a husband's loss," says Tilla Vahanian, a New York City psychotherapist. "You don't give up power without a fight."

Some men even forbid their wives to work or go to school, and make it stick. Others tighten the purse strings, refusing to pay for tuition. In her report, "Mother is a Freshperson," psychologist Barbara Brooks tells of several such marital battles. One woman stole the tuition money from her husband's pocket when he came home after a night of drinking: "I would just go in and take out twenty, forty, fifty dollars at a time. He would never even know it was missing." Another defied her husband directly: "I've told him that if he refuses to pay tuition, I'd walk out and that's it. I gained more self-confidence. I still don't have much, but I gained some." Another study concludes that one out of three marriages is strained by the seemingly innocuous decision of a woman to go to school.

One husband, unruffled when his wife worked as a part-time receptionist, became deeply disturbed when she was asked to assume responsible full-time work managing a doctor's office. Although he didn't object openly, their sex life stopped. Then he expressed concern that she was getting too thin—though she was at least thirty-five pounds overweight. "He's worried that I won't be the same person," said the wife. "And I'm not."

Although these distraught husbands may not represent a majority, there are enough of them to create problems. Other husbands are proud of a wife's expanding opportunities. Most are aware that for better or worse, relations within a marriage have profoundly altered. At a 1977 conference of fifteen American fam-

ilies chosen as typical, a husband said, "We had this gold standard in our family—I brought home the gold and I set the standard. But now my wife works and we share the authority."

Even when all seems serene on the surface, resentments often
smolder over a wife's new status. One husband kept complaining
that his dinner wasn't ready on time. Another wrote to the dean
of the college his wife attended, commending him on her progress, but adding that she would not be returning: "She hasn't
kept up with sewing buttons on my shirts, and I think we'll keep
her home for a while."

Wives also become angry when, after a full day's work in the
office, they are still expected to assume single-handed a full day's
chores at home. Yet a surprising number of middle-aged women
are reluctant to see a husband don an apron. "Splitting household responsibilities with him would be perfect, but it wouldn't
work for me," one explained. "My own guilt would come up. And
many men over forty still feel women should take care of the
home." Another wife was opposed to a husband in the kitchen,
but not to a son. "I've tried to bring my boys up differently," she
explained, "because they're going to live in a different kind of
world."

This attitude is often not limited to household chores. Researchers point out that for many working wives, perhaps a majority, home and family remain the first priority. "School is my
pleasure," a fifty-year-old graduate student said. "The family is
my responsibility."

*Husband and wife are temporarily out of phase with each
other.* As her horizons are expanding, his may be contracting.
During their forties and fifties many men are bored with their
jobs, and concerned only with not rocking the boat until retirement comes. This is the time when they question the value of the
rat race in which they've been running since early manhood.
"He keeps asking—have I accomplished what I wanted to?" says
the wife of a man of fifty-two. "And he worries about the future—
he's more concerned with money than ever."

Just as she is starting to dare, to take risks, he is finished with
such concerns. She needs his support to calm her anxiety; he
needs hers to sustain him in his new worries about aging. Yet both
are often too preoccupied to give generously to the other. In her
study of suburban empty-nest women, Reva Greenberg reports
several complaints about increased demands from a husband.

"Since the children left, he has gotten more time-consuming," said one. "He likes me to travel and play golf with him. He feels I can have more time for him because there are no children around."

Sometimes the two are out of sync in bed. At the time when she is beginning to realize her full sexual potential, his sexual drive, which peaked in late adolescence, may be starting to wane and this may lead to a husband's Don Juanism.

Planning for retirement is often sharply out of time phase for husband and wife. More men than ever are retiring at sixty or sixty-two, and starting to talk about it by their early fifties. Their wives, a few years younger, may have just entered the labor market. One of these was forty-nine when she went back to school to become a practical nurse. A few years later her husband turned sixty-two, and retired from a job at the post office. Now she works and he doesn't, and she is constantly furious that he ignores the chores that a housewife would do automatically. Her nursing hours are from three in the afternoon to eleven in the evening. "He eats his dinner at a restaurant, and that's expensive," she says. "You'd think he could at least learn to cook."

Researchers used to believe that retirement represented no great trauma for a woman because her primary interest remained in the home, but now many admit they were wrong. Women retire younger than men, often because the timing better matches their husbands' retirement, and many don't like it. "In some respects retirement is a greater loss for women than for men," says Dr. Pauline Ragan, a California sociologist.

Observers suggest that after a few stormy marital years, couples reach a calm again in late middle age—almost as if they were honeymooning. But many women point out that something new has been added, a mellowing with maturity, a sense of emerging battle-scarred but stronger.

Marjorie, forty-nine, a tall redhead with freckles, discussing her marriage's new serenity, believes that the rough period began when her older daughter, then in high school, started to challenge her opinions. "She's very positive, like my husband. She knows everything. I found this very shattering. I crumbled completely. I used to be too unsure of myself to state anything positively.

"But as you try to clarify who you are in dealing with the children, you do start to state things more positively, and you and your husband disagree. My God! You fight much more, I think.

I used to be shocked when people got divorced after twenty years together, but when I was married twenty years, I could understand it. There comes a time when you're unhappy or angry, when you ask yourself, 'Do I want to stay with someone who makes me feel bad?' It's a choice then about whether or not to dissolve your marriage. At that point you make a commitment which is much stronger than your original marriage vows. You continue to have fights, but they're different now, less relevant to the strong core of the marriage."

Yet a painful clash is not always necessary in order to reach a happier new plateau. These are the suggestions from marriage counselors that are good insurance for couples approaching the postparental years:

Start making practical plans now for the time when you will become a twosome again. At forty-six, Carol is a second-grade teacher, with a husband three years older who is already talking about retirement. She is learning new sports, developing hobbies that she hopes the two will eventually enjoy together—tennis, biking, contract bridge. "I'm looking ahead. It's a good thing to build these things up for us both."

Learn to communicate again by feeling empathy for what stage the other is in. Once the children have gone, there's time to devote emotional energy to one's spouse, says Dr. Harold Feldman, professor of Human Development and Family Studies at Cornell University. He quotes a wife as saying, "My husband and I had drifted apart . . . I just wasn't aware that he needed me . . . I'm glad I found out in time."

For another couple, the wife's return to school and her new enthusiasm for amateur theatricals resulted in "a loss of marital innocence," according to a *New York Times* report. Both are forty-seven. He is a Baptist minister in a Southern city, and she, until recently, was merely the minister's wife. Now she is busy five or six nights a week in little-theater productions, making new friends, male as well as female, whom her husband has never met. Both recognize there is risk, but believe that talking it out honestly will lessen it. "Even if I seem less dependent," the wife assures her husband, "I need you emotionally more than ever." "I know she's right," he says, "but in my gut—well, I've had such a good life style before that it's hard."

Get rid of the last vestige of authoritarianism—the male "I'm the boss" sort of pose—and make your marriage a democracy based on mutual regard. Overwhelming each other with togetherness isn't necessary, says Tilla Vahanian—"that's been overdone." But when you split for a favorite activity, make it clear that you're not abandoning him. "This is a husband's deepest fear about his changing wife."

According to the *Four Stages of Life* study, a shift in marital dominance occurs gradually over the years. Among the brides, only eight percent considered themselves the boss, compared to thirty percent of the women in their late forties, and fifty percent of those in the late fifties. A surprisingly low fourteen percent of the older women concurred with the statement, "Marriage doesn't give me enough chance to be the person I want to be." With the shift to egalitarianism in late middle age, a wife becomes more maternal toward her husband, and he in turn seeks out her tenderness.

This growth in marital intimacy carries a significant side effect: It helps to buffer a couple from the stresses connected with aging. One expert says, "The achievement of . . . intimacy . . . acts as a critical intervening factor in surviving various stresses in later life."

Adult Children

The empty-nest syndrome must be laid to rest. It does not exist in the vast majority of women. Most do not go into a tailspin of depression when their children grow up and leave home. All research studies within the last decade agree that, on the contrary, they greet the development with relief.

Researchers in the *Four Stages of Life* study compare a group of women in their late forties who still have children at home with another group who don't, and conclude that the empty-nesters have a better self-concept. Those whose children are still in high school show more self-pity, touchiness, self-criticism. For them the anticipation may be disturbing, but the reality turns out to be sheer pleasure.

Nor is this reaction confined to those who are busy with new activities like a job or further schooling. Housewives are no more apt to get depressed after the children leave home than they were before, according to Lenore Radloff of the National Institute of Mental Health. Citing a study of some three thousand adults in Maryland and Missouri, she adds, "If anything, they were *less* depressed."

If the clock is turned back, if children once considered launched return home to demand their mother's time and attention, a woman reacts with consternation, even barely concealed anger. One mother said: "You do miss your kids when they grow up and leave the nest . . . but after a short time you get used to them being away . . . Then the kids come back and visit and you have a lovely time. When they go off, you miss them again for about a week . . . If they stay a little too long, you simply can't wait to get rid of them."

Concern is mixed with resentment when the divorced daughter comes back, or the son who can't get a job. Partly it's the return to yesterday that's so upsetting—the blaring hi-fi, the rooms strewn with shoes and sweaters, just as they were when the children were in their high school days. Partly it's the interference with a mother's rewarding new cultivation of self that causes the upset.

Florence Rush, a feminist writer, describes years of frustration in which she shuttled between her own new career and her three children's late-adolescent crises. First there was Bob, the oldest, back from college with an injured knee, who remained in traction at home for six weeks while his mother had to quit her job in order to care for him. Next there was Bill, the youngest; when school counselors insisted that he needed to attend an expensive private school, his mother had to cancel her own plans for further schooling in order to work and pay for his tuition. Finally there was Anne, miserable in her first job after college, who "moved back home, let her frustration out on me, and we fought constantly." It took several years after she moved away for mother and daughter to become friends again.

Even if they don't return home, a woman apparently can turn her emotional attention away from her children to focus on herself more easily after she feels they are well launched, settled in job or marriage and reasonably happy. But a mother has no control over the outcome of her children's problems and this compounds her anxiety and frustration. Her feeling of maternal success, say the *Four Stages of Life* investigators, depends upon the children's actions and decisions, just at a time when her influence over such decisions has sunk to a new low. Even in late middle age, the University of California group reports, grown children continue to be a source of deep stress for their mothers. One woman categorized an unhappy period as "that was when my daughter left her husband . . . it nearly killed me."

For many women this becomes a time when the tables are turned—or at least tilted—and a daughter becomes her mother's role model. Women envy their daughters' expanding career opportunities, their independence, and wish they could emulate them. One mother, forty-four, who is Jewish, told me, "My daughter went away to college, but I didn't. I lived with my parents until I married. She married a non-Jew, even though she knew we disapproved. I admire her strength, her ability to cope. I wish I could be that way."

But some yearn for the old days when a married daughter lived down the street and brought new joy with the grandchildren. "I did all the right things," says one mother ruefully, "pushed my child from the nest, helped her become independent. Now I'm the casualty. She's too busy at her job to go shopping or have lunch with me. I'm not a grandmother, and it doesn't look as if I ever will be."

But is grandmothering a coveted goal for today's middle-aged women? There is increasing ambivalence. Recent research suggests that the bliss of being a grandmother, like the misery of the empty nest, is for many women an overly romanticized stereotype. "It's a joyous role," says Joan Robertson, of the University of Wisconsin, who has studied 125 grandmothers in a midwestern city. "Young grandmothers say that they prefer it to parenting, because they have all the goodies without the responsibilities. Yet while they speak about the role in highly laudable terms, most grandmothers are not overly identified with it."

Because many women now in the middle years bore their children early, they become grandmothers just when they're happily moving away from being mothers. In Dr. Robertson's study, the average woman was forty-six when her first grandchild was born, and four-fifths were grandmothers by their mid-fifties. These women are not eager to rush into a role they have just abandoned. One fifty-four-year-old grandmother said: "I wasn't too happy at first because I felt I was much too young for that. Now I'm glad to be young and healthy enough to do things with [the grand-children] when I can. *I don't have much time though. I work, and we have so many things to do ourselves.*"

Mothering the Parents

A woman may bow out of baby-sitting for the grand-children, and frequently does, but she has no such choice when it comes to her own parents. In our society it's axiomatic that if there's a daughter in the family, she's in charge. "It's the middle-aged woman who is faced with the responsibilities of caring for an aged parent or parent-in-law," says Dr. Bernice Neugarten, who regards this as a serious problem for a woman in the middle years, particularly because it hobbles the freedom she has just be-gun to savor.

When a parent can no longer care for herself, it's the daughter who takes her in. (One in five women and one in ten men over seventy-five live with a child.) If a nursing home is the solution, it's the daughter who surveys them, moves the parent, and then visits regularly. When parents remain in their own home, she tel-ephones daily, drives them to the doctor, buys and even cooks the meals. There's a call for help in the middle of the night, and she's on the plane at dawn. "We all commute to Florida," says one woman in her fifties. Despite the growing range of social services now available for the elderly, Dr. Robert Binstock of Brandeis University estimates that eighty percent of the care pro-vided for older persons comes from their adult children, usually the daughter.

Women in early middle age, torn between children and par-ents, have been called the "sandwich generation." One of these told Barbara Silverstone and Helen Kandel Hyman, authors of *You and Your Aging Parents*, "I'm like the rope in a tug of war. I always seem to be needed in two places at the same time, and I'm never in the right one . . . [and there's] that little voice inside my head crying out, 'What about me? When is there going to be time for me?' "

It's no different for those who are finally pursuing their own interests. Elaine Noble, a Massachusetts state legislator and avowed lesbian, announced that she would not seek reelection in

1978 because her father was ill and needed care. Her constituents understood, but it would have been unprecedented had she been a male politician.

Responsibility also often stretches to include *his* parents. One fifty-year-old graduate student says, "Who else would care for them? My husband has to work." Nor does divorce always free a woman, at least in her own heart, from concern for the in-laws. "They're in a nursing home and I still visit regularly," says one woman, divorced for five years.

It's hardly surprising that at best a woman's reactions are ambivalent. "It was my mother, of course. I would have done anything in the world for her," says one woman of the eight years her mother lived in the daughter's home. But "she was a burden . . . our freedom was gone." Often she feels resentful. One told me that her father-in-law had a stroke when the elderly couple were visiting; as a result they ended up staying six months. "I certainly didn't enjoy it," she said. "I'm not good with sick people. It seemed like ten years to me."

No matter how much a woman does, particularly for her mother, she often feels guilty that it's not enough. She feels she owes a debt that she can never repay. And there is another feeling that she is afraid to face—a wish that the parent would die. "When my mother had a stroke, I went to the hospital when the doors opened at ten," one woman says, "and I didn't come home until they closed at eight P.M. The house was in a turmoil, my husband was furious, but what could I do? I owed my mother at least that much."

"Dealing with elderly parents is an expression of the unfinished business of growing up," says Leonore Luftman, director of a geriatric counseling service. "Particularly in relation to her mother, a daughter is reluctant to take charge, to make plans that might interfere with a mother's wishes. Even though the roles are now reversed, she's still mother's little girl, and no daughter tells her mother what to do."

Demands from a tyrannical old lady may be endless; the daughter may despair of ever pleasing her; the whole family may be going down the drain; but many daughters are still reluctant to make changes that would relieve their own intolerable burden. "She'll telephone the agency from a pay booth or a friend's house so that her mother won't overhear and become angry," says Mrs.

Luftman. "Often she'll be unrealistic, asking only for a list of hotels for the elderly, when her mother is incontinent and incapable of self-care."

A daughter's emotions are a mixture of resentment and sadness —mixed with love. What should one do? Realize you can't say yes to every demand, if it means disruption of your own life. Face it as a family problem and not your exclusive responsibility. Sons, husbands, grandchildren and the elderly person herself must join in working out a solution. And don't torture yourself with guilt. The time you spend, the concern you feel for a parent, is proof that you are acting in a responsible and caring way.

Whether an elderly parent is independent or a burden, she is also a role model for her daughter's own aging, evoking fear or confidence for the future. "My grandmother is eighty-three and a human vegetable," Linda, thirty-five, says. "That scares me about old age. I get angry with my own mother when I see her slowing down at sixty. I'm afraid she'll be like my grandmother, and my deepest fear is that I will too."

There are important lessons to be learned from an aging parent —a sort of blueprint for the future to strive for or avoid. Natalie at forty is studying her parents-in-law in their seventies. "All they seem to do is growl and get in each other's way. My mother-in-law was a homebody. She raised five children, and that's all. She had no sports, no hobbies, nothing that can stimulate her now. That's what I'm going to avoid." Another woman notices the growing rigidity, social and emotional, of her parents, who are in their eighties. She is aware of a similar tendency in herself, and vows to guard against it, to remain flexible and receptive to new ideas as she ages.

Irene, forty-nine, is optimistic about her own future. "What most of us dread is losing our mental capacity," she says. "Well, I remember my grandmother as a sharp old lady, and my mother is close to eighty and still independent. It gives me confidence that I'm going to age well too."

When her parents die, a frequent event during a woman's middle years, she feels that the last barrier is gone and hers is the generation next in line. "I'm not as carefree since my mother died a few years ago," says Ellen, forty-four. "I have a definite feeling of my own mortality. Death used to be very amorphous. Now it really exists."

Is this morbid? Not at all. It is merely recognition of fact, and may even act as a spur to growth. "Death lurks in the background of midlife," says Dr. Robert Butler. "It says that if one is going to make a different life, it must be made now."

Women without Husbands

Although only four percent of our generation has remained single, death and divorce in the middle years swell the ranks of women without husbands. Of those in the mid-thirties to mid-fifties, ten percent are widows, the first trickle of the flood that starts to engulf women by their sixties. Spiraling dizzily upward, divorce seems at first glance to have passed our generation by. As mentioned earlier, only eight percent in the thirty-five to fifty-five age span are currently divorced.

But the figures are deceptive. Although divorce is largely a young person's game—almost two-thirds of divorcing women are younger than thirty—the middle-aged have recently started to play. Divorce has almost doubled for women in the mid-thirties to mid-fifties and eleven percent of women who divorce are now forty or older.

Traumatic at any age, divorce can be devastating at midlife, particularly for the homemaker whose employment skills are rusty, and whose nurturing talents are now unwanted by husband as well as children. "I call us discards," says one woman. "It's like being a skilled worker after automation takes over." Society is finally showing concern for these displaced homemakers. The federal government and twenty-two states have passed legislation to retrain them for employment.

"It's cold out there and it's lonesome," says one woman, describing the divorcee status. Married twenty-three years, she has now been divorced for eight. "It takes at least two years to get on your feet, and it's worse if you start out without a job," she says. But eventually this woman bounced back, like a lively tennis ball, and so do many others.

For some, the word *reborn* is hardly an exaggeration. "My world collapsed the night my husband told me he wanted a divorce," says a forty-five-year-old mother of twins. "I even thought about suicide." But three years and a master's degree later she said, "I'm feeling better than I have in years. For the first time in my life, I'm in control."

The metamorphosis of Diana McLaughlin, now fifty-eight, is astonishing. "I starved after the divorce, almost literally," she says, "and emotionally I just fell apart." When she moved back from Florida to Baltimore, where her two sons lived, "I got off the plane in the dead of winter with no warm clothes, a dollar in my wallet, and a carton of cigarettes under my arm." Two years later Diana, a handsome vital woman with gray curly hair, a high color and a youthful face, says, "I feel extremely good about myself. The divorce may have been the best thing that ever happened to me."

Married for thirty-four years to an officer in the merchant marine, Diana bore four children, the youngest now twenty. "I was a fun wife," she recalls. "I drank with him, played with him, jumped in and out of bed. I was a good time." With her husband frequently away at sea, she raised the children almost single-handed. A full-time homemaker, "I was a very independent type when I got married, but after all those years I didn't feel that way." It was a good marriage for twenty-five years, but later although she knew it was deteriorating, she could not muster the courage to do anything about it. "I believed marriage was forever. When he said he wanted a divorce, there was instant panic. Months later, as reality sank in, it was even worse. At first you only half believe he means it."

What happened next sounds like soap opera. Diana received no alimony. Support for the youngest son, about to start college, arrived only sporadically. "I had a job as security guard in a posh resort when I fell and broke my hip, a disaster. I had no hospitalization. That's when I hit bottom, six months after the divorce."

On her return to Baltimore, Diana got a job as an interne with Maryland's newly established Center for Displaced Homemakers, and has moved up steadily, displaying unusual skills at counseling other women in the same dismal plight. It was not an overnight transformation. "At first the only solution seems to be to get married again. Despite our own experience, we still think marriage spells security. I learned that you have to put your life together first, to start feeling good about yourself. Divorce chops part of you right off. You're angry and hurt, and you're guilty —it must have been your fault.

"You only start to recover when you realize that you're still a worthwhile person, when confidence revives that you'll make it, no matter what your age. Now I value my freedom. I'm more honest with people about my own feelings. I've learned patience. But the best is the pride of doing something on my own. I'm confident enough to try anything. Divorce allows you the luxury of trying something new. You face a choice of wallowing in misery or picking up the pieces and putting yourself together again."

Not every midlife divorcee fares as spectacularly as Diana McLaughlin, but most learn to walk alone, essentially passing through a late-blooming adolescence, and finally developing a separate identity. The problem is toughest for a woman whose husband walks out—"wife-shucking" is what Tom Wolfe calls it. She feels completely without control over her own destiny. If he has discarded her for a younger woman, she is likely to look in the mirror and assume the explanation lies there.

When she believes that remarriage is the only goal, and being attractive enough to compete with younger women the only path to reach it, the new divorcee becomes caught in a bind that stifles self-growth. Divorce is still increasing, but remarriage is now slowing down. Divorced women have less of a chance to find a mate than divorced men; and middle-aged women, less of a chance than young women. Four out of five women in their twenties marry again within four years; but less than half of those in their forties. For some it's because they don't want to marry again; and for others, because they can't find a husband. "Women become sexually ineligible much earlier than men do," Susan Sontag observes.

If catching another man is what life is all about, a woman will lie about her age, count every wrinkle, agonize over each gray hair, investing energies that could be better spent elsewhere. There's nothing wrong with desiring remarriage or trying to look your best; it's only if they are the sole aim in life that they're self-defeating. At a lunch counter recently, a woman sat down and started to chat with a stranger. She had dyed blond hair, long false eyelashes, too much makeup, and wore clothing suitable for a teen-ager. She was divorced, in her forties (she would not tell her exact age), and full of woe. "It's just terrible having to compete with a girl of twenty—compete for men, that is," she remarked. Another woman had her ears flattened by a surgeon after divorce: "The competition is really tough. You need everything you've got." A third stopped playing tennis. "I felt that everybody was looking at my thighs—watching them wobble."

These actions are not very different from the self-torture of an adolescent over a blemish that no one else can see.

Instead of suffering over the minutiae of aging, Dr. Helen Singer Kaplan, a leading sex therapist, suggests that women take strength from the qualities that living has enhanced. "If you are attractive to your partner at the age of fifty, it is not simply because you are gorgeous," she says, "but because you meet other human needs: sensitivity, intimacy, warmth. These are the assets which do not fade, but increase with age."

Consider another woman—tiny, pert, vivacious—in her late fifties and considering a face lift. "I just want to look better, partly because I need a job." Eight years after her second divorce, she is feeling confident and reasonably pleased with life. "I'm not an earth-mother type," she says, "and now with two grown children and no responsibilities except for myself, I'm busy learning the piano and Spanish, and enjoying living alone. If you have lots of interests, divorce can be exciting at middle age."

She belongs to a new breed, small but of growing significance, of women who recognize that their marriage is intolerable and burst out of its cocoon on their own. "I was terrified of my husband's disapproval. I acted like a puppet, doing what he said whether I wanted to or not," this woman says. "When I suggested that we separate, he told me not to expect a cent of alimony. But I did it anyway, and it made me feel I could do anything. Despite the money problems, I feel strong, and I know who I am."

"The notion that we can only survive with a man is not quite as powerful as it used to be," says Tilla Vahanian. "In the last few years the push to divorce has come from wives too. They're more confident, less dependent. Husbands used to outgrow their wives; now it's sometimes the other way round."

What gives a woman courage to take the risk? "It was my fortieth birthday," one woman explains, "and it made me stop and review the dreams that were unfulfilled. Mine was never a good marriage, and now it was in deep trouble. I cut out a story from the newspaper about a reporter who quit his job at middle age and sailed a small sloop to England. I knew I had to make a choice now or sit forever in the backyard."

There's a new spirit abroad among these women who are learning of necessity to be husband-shuckers. Perhaps it is embodied in the needlepoint motto that Betty Talmadge has stitched onto a chair seat in her Georgia library. After thirty-five years of marriage, Senator Herman Talmadge sued for divorce from his fifty-four-year-old wife in 1977. But Mrs. Talmadge is a woman of strength; she runs a successful meat brokerage business, and recently attempted a run for a seat in Congress. Needlepoint is her hobby, and she has embroidered the motto in black thread on gray: *Uppity Women Unite.*

Uppity women appear to fare better as widows as well as divorcees. Docile women, who have woven a life around being a half person, tend to do worse. In *The Menopause Book*, psychiatrist Natalie Shainess quotes a depressed widow, of about fifty: "My wonderful husband has been gone for several years . . . I keep hoping that I'll meet someone. I hope that soon I'll meet my Prince Charming." To which Dr. Shainess responds, if she's "determined to wait for her Prince Charming, I suspect that she is waiting still."

Hoping and waiting passively will not win a new husband for a widow, nor will it win her much else, either. Widows outnumber widowers five to one, and below the age of forty-five, seven to one; and their chances for remarriage are far slimmer. Less than four percent of American widows are younger than forty-five; nine out of ten are fifty-five and older. In the decade between the mid-fifties and mid-sixties, the percentage of widows doubled, representing about two out of every five women in this age range.

Nevertheless, most agree that widowhood is easier for a woman to handle than divorce. "It's over," says one widow, "and there are no second thoughts that if you'd only been more attractive, you might have kept your husband. You don't have a divorcee's feeling of failure, nor her fear of remarriage." It helps too, say the psychologists, that by late middle age many women start unconsciously rehearsing for their widowhood.

Drs. Bernice Neugarten and Nancy Datan also suggest that widowhood is more traumatic when it occurs unexpectedly. "The hardest hit are those who experience widowhood earlier than their associates . . . it is the unanticipated, not the anticipated, that is likely to represent the traumatic event." One woman, widowed twice by the age of fifty-one, points out the vast emotional difference between the two events. When her first husband died, she was forty, with three sons, the youngest only ten. "I had no interest in clothes or my appearance. I was so wrapped up with the kids and my responsibilities. For two years I had no dates, and when

I did start to date I had nothing to say to a man, and no libido to help me relate." But when her second husband died, the children were grown and supportive; she had a job that "helped me to feel new and young" and had gained strength from experience: "I knew I would survive." After the second death, "My sex urge continues to be strong, but I'm realistic about how slim my chances are for a successful remarriage. I intend to build my own life."

Once the first year of intense grief is over, research reports suggest that women adjust fairly well, and that older women adjust the best. Holding a job makes it easier for the younger. "I am convinced that having to go to work every day and act as if I were on an even emotional keel helped me back to normality," writes Lynn Caine in *Widow*. (Widows and divorcees work in far higher numbers than married women. More than three out of five of those aged forty-five to sixty are in the labor force.)

Perhaps the most difficult of a widow's problems, and, even more, of a divorcee's, is her social asymmetry. She is partnerless, a fifth wheel, and often even viewed as a sexual threat by women friends who used to welcome her as half of a couple. If being a wife was her major role, even if she also held a job, then she is emotionally unemployed. A widower usually views himself as worker and then husband; the fact that hostesses welcome him with glad little cries helps, too. Divorcees and widows living in the suburbs, where a couple is the accepted social unit, suffer this problem more acutely than those in a more heterogeneous city social life.

Many midlife widows find that they have to battle to keep from being treated like a fragile little old lady. "Everyone puts me in cotton batting," one complains. Another, fifty when her husband died, returned to school "to keep my children from hovering over me." A third, only thirty-seven and left with four young children when her husband was killed in a plane crash, fought off the solicitude of both sets of parents. "Any time I acted weak or cried, someone took over and told me what to do. If you don't prove you can handle things, you just lose control over your life."

Being bluntly honest is fashionable these days. When the emperor has no clothes on, it's as likely to be a woman as the proverbial child who will pipe up and say so. Yet even Ann Landers appeared a bit upset at a recent letter signed "Widowhood is

Great." Married twenty-eight years, widowed for three, this woman wrote, "The freedom is wonderful. I'm enjoying life now as never before. I'm glad he's dead."

Others who have loved and mourned their husbands certainly do not rejoice over his passing, but may admit that there are advantages. The woman who was thirty-seven when her husband was killed says, "I married at twenty-one, went from my father's nest to college, and then to my husband's nest. He was very protective. After his death there was a whole new life. I was the boss and I liked it. I discovered that I was more excited about living than ever before."

This woman confided something that at first seemed a shocker: "I went to bed with another man two months after my husband died. In less than a year I started an affair that lasted thirteen months." Others report similar reactions. One moved to Florida with her ailing diabetic husband in an attempt to prolong his life, and nursed him through difficult months when he lost his sight. She was fifty when he died. There was a brief period of mourning, and then "I just had a ball." Divorcees too are frequently surprised by a burst of sexual energy.

The widowed thirty-seven-year-old explains: "Losing the sexual part of life is something no one talks about. My husband and I had had good sex, and my sexual feelings returned very soon. For a brief time I went through a sort of sexually promiscuous adolescence. I didn't even feel guilty. Partly it's the feeling of having someone hold you. You realize soon that there's no one to hold you. But the need for sex is also part of the immense loneliness you feel. You're aware that there's not one soul in the world who really cares for you." Now forty-two, this woman is about to remarry. "If my husband had not died," she says, "I think I would have been monogamous and satisfied with it in the same way that I am satisfied with monogamy now."

Although women do learn to make their peace with early widowhood, is their grief necessary? Until science can learn to equalize male and female life spans, why shouldn't they consider marrying men closer to their age, or even a few years younger? As it stands now, the average woman can look forward to eleven years of widowhood—five or six because she lives longer, three to five because she marries younger. (The first husband of the twice-widowed woman described earlier was fourteen years her senior, and her second was eight years older.)

Why do we do it? Why is it socially acceptable to marry an older man, and almost taboo to marry one younger? "The convention that wives should be younger," explains Susan Sontag, "powerfully enforces the 'minority' status of women, since being senior in age always carries with it . . . a certain amount of power and authority . . . The convention is obeyed because to do otherwise makes one feel as if one is doing something . . . in bad taste."

For the first time there appear to be some signs of change, at least in the dating pattern of divorced women. Many report that they find a better emotional "fit" when they become friendly with younger men. (According to statistical data from the Kinsey studies, men in their early twenties and women in their forties are both at their orgasmic peak.) "It's hard to talk with a man in my own generation," says a divorcee, fifty-six, "because his head is not where mine is." Another divorcee, forty-four, says, "An older man needs ego support, reassurance that he's still a male. When a woman has a good job and makes her own financial decisions, she's intimidating to a man her own age. But a younger man doesn't make any demands on you."

There is yet another group of women in their middle years about whom there is little accurate information. These do not want a man of any age. They are interested in friendship, including sex, with other women. Some have been lesbians since youth, but others have married, raised a family, and are only now turning to homosexual relationships. There are no reliable estimates of how many women fall in the latter group, or even how many women are homosexual. About one in every twenty-five women is a lesbian, according to one frequently quoted estimate.

This much is known or surmised about middle-aged lesbians:

Their transition to the middle years is no more threatening than for heterosexuals. It may even be smoother for some, because the never-married homosexual has usually held a job, and faces no jolting change from home-centered to work-centered living.

Concern over appearance, the fear of looking older, may be somewhat less of a problem particularly for the lesbian in a stable relationship. "We have better bodies," said a homosexual psychologist in a telephone interview. "We've always been more into sports and keeping fit." She also maintains that lesbian women look younger: "If you saw me, you'd find it hard to believe that I was forty-one."

Her emotional relationships are far more stable than those of a male homosexual, but—despite divorce and widowhood—less so than for the heterosexual woman. According to *Homosexualities,* the Kinsey Institute's recent study of close to a thousand homosexuals in San Francisco, more than one out of three lesbians is relatively monogamous, and another quarter maintains fairly stable relationships. Mina Robinson, who has studied a small group of lesbians aged fifty and over, describes their life style as "serial monogamy." Among her group, some had only one, and none more than ten "major relationships" in a lifetime, a figure consistent with the Kinsey report.

Many lesbians are former wives and present mothers. Among those in the San Francisco study, one-third had been married and one-fifth had children. Half of the older lesbian women interviewed by Robinson were the mothers of grown children.

Although the evidence is meager, it is suggestive that a growing number of women, but still a tiny minority, having sampled marriage, are turning in the middle years to intimacy with another woman. A woman of fifty, mother of five, divorced after twenty years, explains why: "It is difficult to relearn the art of seductive flirtation, and as men begin to move closer, often they just want you to cook for them, to clean for them. I found a comfortable union with another woman whose marriage also had faltered and who had been my close friend for thirty years. For us it has been a beautiful thing . . ."

Middle-aged lesbians are either afraid to come out of the closet or are well-adjusted to their life style. In at least one major city, therapists who counsel homosexual women report that few midlife women consult them. The vast majority of their troubled patients are in their twenties and thirties.

It appears then that a lesbian woman's middle years are not too dissimilar from those of a heterosexual woman. She goes through the same physical menopause. Her children grow up, and she turns away from nurturing them to caring for others and for herself. Her skin becomes dryer and her body thicker, and the emotional impact of these changes—as with all women—depends upon how tightly her feelings of self-worth are entwined with looking youthful.

A Woman's Friends

When it comes to making and keeping friends, women are luckier—and probably wiser—than men. For despite the reports on male bonding, despite the broad significance of the word *fraternity* compared with the word *sorority*, women have more friends and share greater intimacy with them than men do. Psychologists suggest that one reason why men feel an urgent need to remarry after divorce or widowhood is that they haven't the friends to help them hack it alone.

Both the quality and quantity of friends appear to change during the middle years. The key word is *discrimination*. "We were all together in the PTA, but now everyone's off in a different direction," says Marjorie. She works part-time as a bookkeeper, and has stopped inviting twenty guests to elaborate dinner parties, concentrating instead on people she really cares about. "There's no time. We've just dropped the people we used to see twice a year." "I don't go out of my way to chat with neighbors any more," says Irene. "I'm not accumulating new friends. I'm closer to a few and less interested in having a mob of them."

One reason why women have fewer and closer friends is that their needs change. For a young mother, friends allay boredom. "When I was confined to the neighborhood with a new baby," one woman recalls, "I was happy to talk with anyone." Many used to be swayed by what a friend thought, but with a sturdier self-image, "I'm more likely to disregard a friend's opinion," another woman says. Formerly, operating in a narrower arena, women used to need friends for status or power; now they have broader resources. "With increasing age, women tend to develop deeper, more understanding, and more meaningful relationships that are also characterized by more reciprocity," wrote Sandra Gibbs Candy, in *Looking Ahead*, a book edited by Lillian Troll and Joan and Kenneth Israel.

"My husband is my best friend," a woman in her late forties told me. "We have so much fun together that I've never needed many others." But she added, "I suppose that might be bad for the future." By older middle age, others realize this. In a Wisconsin study, women aged fifty and over were asked to name the relationship of greatest significance to them. Although most put a spouse first, close to one-fifth of the married women mentioned a woman friend instead. Families—siblings, sons, and daughters—came in a poor third.

Having an intimate friend and confidante, but not too many of them, appears of increasing importance for a woman in the middle years. The slackening of competition for a man and the feminist emphasis on sisterhood have helped to strengthen these bonds. "I went through a time when I didn't really like women," says Janet, thirty-five. "Now I realize how much we help each other."

Francine du Plessix Gray, in a recent address, urged women to consider friendship as a more "ideal human bonding" than the "enchantment and possession" of romantic love. "It could bring about a minor revolution against the sexual-industrial complex, which [is] brainwashing us into the roles of temptress and seductress, estranging us from that plain and beautiful Quakerish ideal of being 'a sister to the world.'"

IV

The Years Before the Menopause

In the late thirties you really start to worry about accidental pregnancy. Your children are well launched in school. You're a student, hold a job or are perhaps considering one of these, and a baby would disrupt your life. But while your concern increases, the chance for such an accident decreases. Your fertility—the ability to reproduce—is on the downgrade. Dr. Louise Tyrer, medical director of the Planned Parenthood Federation, puts it bluntly: "As far as reproductive potential is concerned, by thirty-five a woman's ovaries are over the hill."

A woman's peak years for pregnancy lie between twenty and thirty; on the average in the United States, her age is thirty when she bears her last child. The fertility rate is well over one hundred babies per thousand women in the decade of the twenties, drops to fifty-three by the early thirties, nineteen in the late thirties, less than five at forty to forty-four, and a minuscule .3 in the late forties. These 1975 figures reflect, of course, the older woman's careful attention to contraception, but even in 1965, before effective birth control was so widespread, the fertility rate for women in their late forties was less than one per thousand, and in the early forties, under thirteen.

What is happening inside your body? The first change is an accelerated decline in the number of germ cells (potential eggs) in the ovaries. These immature eggs are actually at a peak at the moment you are born, decline until about your mid-twenties, then stabilize until the age of thirty-eight, when they start dropping precipitously. This loss is in addition to the twelve or thirteen mature ova you release each year at midpoint in the menstrual cycle and is due to the natural degeneration of the eggs. If no other changes occurred, your ability to bear babies would cease at about fifty because the egg basket would be empty.

But other changes are occurring throughout your forties, altering the complex play of hormones that prepares the uterus for nesting, as well as producing a mature egg ready for fertilization. In a female's early teens, the hormonal orchestration involving hypothalamus, pituitary and ovary was often ragged, with cues being missed and instruments playing sour notes. As a result, menstruation was irregular, scanty or heavy, long or short, without predictable pattern. For many women the premenopausal years are quite similar. "My periods are irregular. I never know when I'm going to get one," says a woman in her late forties. "It's just the same with my sixteen-year-old daughter." One gynecologist calls this a time of "endocrine chaos," when the natural balance between the production of the two ovarian hormones, estrogen and progesterone, is upset, and the other hormones that trigger their action fluctuate widely.

This does not happen to every woman; each has different symptoms at different ages; and some have none at all until the menopause occurs abruptly at an average age of fifty. Among those in the forties to whom I spoke, there were these variations: Marjorie, forty-nine, "Not a thing has changed"; Paula, forty-two, "My period only lasts four days instead of the usual seven"; Ellen, forty-four, "the flow is lighter"; Alice, forty-five, "I'm starting to become a little irregular"; Eve, forty-seven, "I stopped for six months, then flowed normally for three, and now I'm irregular again."

Many of these women are no longer ovulating every month, which paradoxically may result in scanty flow, excessive flow, brief periods, prolonged periods, occasional spotting. Some are producing subnormal amounts of estrogen, and their periods may be short or scanty, or they may spot at midcycle. Others secrete too little progesterone, the most common cause of heavy or prolonged menses during these years. And what is most likely is a varying combination of all of these.

For a woman who has been fairly regular for thirty years, this can be worrisome. Most likely there is nothing wrong except premenopausal hormonal imbalance, but the changes could be due to benign polyps in the cervix or uterus, or to a fibroid tumor, which is also benign, particularly if there is occasional flooding during a period. Cancer of the cervix or endometrium is a remote possibility (see pp. 155–58), and the years just before the menopause are when it is hardest to spot. To play safe, report to your doctor if a period lasts more than eight days, if it comes more frequently than every three weeks, if the flow is unusually heavy and full of clots, or if you bleed between periods.

The simple surgical procedure of dilatation and curettage is most frequently used to diagnose such troubles in women in their forties. Under general anesthesia the cervix is dilated and an instrument called a curette is inserted into the uterus to scrape out the lining. D and C is a tool for diagnosis, but it sometimes also cures. Merely removing excess tissue that has built up for months in the uterine lining may stop an excess-bleeding cycle. Some gynecologists now try to avoid a D and C when possible by using an instrument that sucks out cells and tissue from the uterus for examination under the microscope. This examination, though uncomfortable, can be performed without anesthetic in the doctor's office.

One problem is to strike a nice balance between over- and under-concern with the menstrual changes of the late forties. Christine, who is forty-four, has more frequent periods and flows "enormously." Her doctor shrugs and says, "That's what you can expect at your age." But when Marion, also forty-four, reports similar symptoms, *her* doctor says, "We'll have to investigate. You're too young for the menopause."

Some women in their forties explain away every change in body or mind—the onset of depression, for example—as due to the menopause. This could be dangerous. Emotional symptoms such as depression should *not* be blamed on impending menopause (see p. 81). If excess emotional tension, combined with swelling, bloating and even migraines, appears in the week before a period is due, it is probably the premenstrual syndrome, which, because it is related to fluctuation in ovarian hormones, sometimes worsens or appears for the first time in the late menstrual years.

Some women in this age group report their first sleepless nights —every month—right before they get their period. Others complain of fluid retention, pelvic fullness, sore and painful breasts, unaccountable mood swings. There is still no consensus among physicians about what causes the premenstrual syndrome, and even less about why it may intensify in the decade before the menopause, because not enough research money has ever been allocated to so-called female problems. Sleep problems before and during the menopause are, for example, probably related to fluctuations in activity of the hypothalamus gland, which influences and is influenced by changing ovarian function. Discomfort from fluid retention lessens after vigorous exercise. It is wise to remember during these years of bodily flux that psyche and soma—mind and body—are inextricably intertwined. It's not all in your mind; it's not all in your glands; both contribute to every sour or sweet note of the human orchestra.

Women should also remember that although the *average* age for the menopause is fifty, the change occurs for a number of women by the mid-forties, and for an equal number not until the mid-fifties. And in some there are no signs at all until the menses cease. In other words, don't dump every symptom into a wastebasket labeled "menopause," but don't go into a cancer panic either when signs which may be premenopausal occur. To accomplish this, you need the cooperation of a doctor who is reassuring but not over-casual, and to whom you can report menstrual changes without being made to feel foolish.

Contraception

It's all very well to talk bravely about lowered fertility after thirty-five, but when a woman in her late thirties is told, because of potential risks to her health, to stop using the Pill, her security blanket for fifteen years, statistics don't soothe her nervousness. She's just plain scared of getting pregnant. Though it is extremely rare, she has heard dark tales of menopause motherhood, and the thought of using a less potent contraceptive puts her in a panic. Even those who don't face the trauma of leaving a trusted method become jittery during the forties when a period is skipped or delayed.

Actually, this is a time when a woman trying to avoid pregnancy has a lot going for her. Not only is she less fertile, but she is likely to have intercourse less often than in the heady days of early marriage. She is also a better contraceptor; statistics show that when a woman wants to avoid pregnancy, and not merely delay it, she is twice as successful in the use of her birth-control method.

But which contraceptive to use? The age between thirty-five and forty is a time for reassessment. This is the range of methods that married women in the late childbearing years (thirty-five to forty-four) choose most frequently, according to a 1976 federal survey:

Sterilization. One out of every two women in this age range cannot become pregnant because she or her husband is sterile. Twenty-nine percent have had sterilization surgery for contraceptive purposes, making it by far the most popular birth-control method for older couples. Other surgery which incidentally sterilizes, such as removal of the uterus, ovaries or Fallopian tubes, accounts for eighteen percent; and three percent are infertile, even without surgery.

The Pill. Only eight percent use the contraceptive pill, a significant drop from a survey three years earlier.

The condom. At this age, the husband's use of a condom, the rubber sheath that covers the penis and prevents male sperm from entering the female genital tract, is as popular as the Pill for married couples—eight percent rely on it.

The IUD. The intrauterine device is the contraceptive choice of about five percent of women aged thirty-five to forty-four.

Rhythm. Four percent use rhythm, the only method sanctioned by the Catholic Church.

Diaphragm or foam. Some three percent choose either of these barrier methods, so named because both the diaphragm, a rubber cup covering the cervix, and the chemical that lays down a curtain of foam deep in the vagina act by forming a barrier to the entrance of the sperm.

Withdrawal or *douching,* the two methods (more aptly, nonmethods) widely considered to be useless for birth control, are chosen by close to four percent of women over thirty-five.

No method. Three percent are either pregnant or trying to become pregnant, and close to twelve percent use no contraceptive.

The shift away from the Pill is related to growing knowledge about its accelerating dangers to women in their thirties and forties. Although it has long been known that use of the Pill increases the risk of blood clots (and its associated diseases, heart attack, stroke and pulmonary embolism), recent statistics show that these risks shoot up for the older Pill user. But the harshest news comes for the smoker. For a nonsmoker aged forty or over on the Pill, the risk of death from the contraceptive is only one-third the risk of using *no* birth control and bearing a child at this age. But if she smokes, the hazard multiplies eightfold and is almost three times as high as the risk of getting pregnant. And for a heavy smoker who consumes more than fifteen cigarettes daily, using the Pill is almost four times as hazardous to life as chancing a pregnancy.

The Food and Drug Administration now says flatly, "Women who use oral contraceptives should not smoke." It emphasizes that its warning is particularly pertinent to smokers over thirty-five.

The Pill's hazards, although not so great for older nonsmokers, are nonetheless sobering—a sixfold rise from the time she is in her twenties until her late thirties. The increase in the Pill's dangers when used later in life appears to be associated with a rise in other factors related to circulatory diseases—obesity, high blood pressure, high cholesterol levels, diabetes. As to the Pill's association with cancer, another disease whose incidence rises as women get older, the case is not clear. But a woman should avoid the Pill if she already has cancer of the breast or sex organs, or is suspected of having one of these.

For years many doctors plugged the Pill as the most convenient and effective contraceptive. "Not being on the Pill is almost the same as driving around in a horse-drawn buggy," is the way one internist puts it. Now most are changing their tune. They are advising those of their patients who are over thirty-five—and strongly urging those over forty—to switch to another contraceptive. "We recommend getting off the Pill for many women at thirty-five," says Dr. Tyrer of Planned Parenthood. "If she has any of the risk factors for circulatory disease, use of the Pill is generally contraindicated." For those who neither smoke nor have other risk factors, Planned Parenthood believes that, once she is aware of the hazards involved, a woman should make up her own mind.

When a woman has been on the Pill for years, the first few months without it aren't always easy. Nancy, forty-two, says, "I loved the Pill and I didn't want to go off it. But my second husband, who is a doctor, insisted. Right after I stopped, I developed the adolescent symptoms—cramps, premenstrual weight gain—that I'd forgotten even existed." An occasional woman even experiences a temporary loss of hair, similar to what may happen after childbirth.

Use of the IUD during the late menstrual years also concerns some gynecologists. The trouble is that the device, inserted by a doctor inside the uterus, causes some abnormal vaginal bleeding in about one woman in three. If she should start to bleed between periods, or have an unusually heavy flow during a period, she and her doctor may blame it on the contraceptive, and postpone further investigation. This could result in failure to diagnose an occasional case of uterine polyps or even cancer of the uterus. "If you've been using an IUD and the pattern of menstrual flow that you've associated with it begins to change, particularly if the flow gets heavier," says Dr. Tyrer, "this is a danger sign that needs to be looked into." To do this, she adds, a doctor must remove the device, and even if everything checks out normal, it's wiser not to reinsert it, since the problem may well recur. The hazards of the IUD itself, however, unlike those of the Pill, do not rise with its user's age.

Although the death rate associated with the IUD is minuscule, it can cause severe cramps as well as chronic infection in the uterus and Fallopian tubes, which carry an egg from ovary to uterus. "I've always been against the Pill," Barbara, thirty-six, a psychologist, told me. "A few years ago I switched from a diaphragm to an IUD, and thought I was all set. But one coil was removed when I got an infection, and now it looks as if I'll have to have the second one taken out. We have two children, as many as we want, but neither of us feels emotionally ready for sterilization. What's next? We really don't know."

The third contraceptive method that loses its charms for a woman in the forties is rhythm. Its effectiveness, which is limited at best, is based on the regularity of the menstrual cycle. But in the years before the menopause when it's regular to be irregular, rhythm's ability to prevent pregnancy plummets. This hasn't happened yet to Natalie, who is forty and relies on rhythm, but she is becoming increasingly worried that it may. "We plan our sex life around my ovulation, and we've been very fortunate," she says. "I just hope things don't get all mixed up when the change of life starts. The youngest of our three children is fifteen, and I think I would find getting pregnant again quite disturbing. I'm not too sure what I would do. My husband's a lot more religious than I am. We'd have a hassle, that's for sure."

Of course, what Natalie is talking about, but as a Catholic won't put a name to, is abortion. When I asked Dr. Tyrer about the contraceptive options for a woman of forty, she emphasized the importance of clarifying at the outset one's attitude toward abortion. "If a woman has hangups about such effective methods as sterilization," she told me, "she should ask herself this question How would I feel if I got pregnant? Would I be willing either to bear the child or get an abortion? The contraceptive you choose depends on your answer." And if the answer is, Okay, I would be willing to get an abortion or have the baby, then Dr. Tyrer says a likely choice is a barrier method—condom, diaphragm, foam or a combination of two of these.

This may seem surprising advice from a family-planning expert, but her opinion is widely shared by others who have considered the contraceptive problems of women over thirty-five. Most agree that sterilization is the answer for a couple who are certain they want no more children. But for others, these points in favor of the traditional methods are persuasive:

• The Pill, and to a lesser degree, the IUD, have serious disadvantages for a woman in her later fertile years.

• The barrier methods are the safest for her health. Recently Dr. Christopher Tietze of The Population Council made an elaborate statistical study, in which he compared a woman's chances of dying from various birth-control methods to her chances with no method, but with the likelihood of getting pregnant and bearing a child. "At all ages, the lowest level of mortality, by far, is achieved by the use of traditional methods with recourse to early abortion in case of failure," Dr. Tietze concluded.

• The criticism that the barrier methods are ineffective in preventing pregnancy is not accurate. The main hazard is that they must be used at every act of intercourse, a time when it is particularly easy to forget. And they must be used correctly; there's more technique than there is to swallowing a pill. But if they are used correctly, their effectiveness can approach ninety-seven percent, compared with ninety-nine and six-tenth percent for correct use of the Pill, and ninety-seven to ninety-eight percent for the IUD.

Some family-planning experts hold that when a man uses a condom during sex and his partner uses foam, the effectiveness of the protection achieved is close to that of the oral contraceptive. They warn that in judging a contraceptive, one must use two yardsticks: the effectiveness of the method when used consistently and accurately; and its effectiveness under ordinary conditions, taking carelessness and clumsiness and lack of motivation into account. In method-effectiveness, the barrier contraceptives, although they don't rate quite as high as the Pill or IUD, are not far behind. But in use-effectiveness, when a random group of women of all ages is followed, they fall far short.

• Many doctors are prejudiced against the barrier methods. They put them down by describing foams and jellies as "greasy kid stuff." Dr. Gerald Bernstein, director of family planning at the University of Southern California Medical School, says, "A patient given oral contraceptives gets careful instructions on how to use them. But many private physicians don't take time to explain how to use the barrier methods, particularly those bought over the counter."

Contraceptive creams, foams and jellies, as well as the condom, appear to have a protective effect against venereal disease, and possibly also against other vaginal infections.

These are the facts women should know about how to use the various barrier methods effectively:

Condom. This sheath of rubber—it can also be made from the lining of a sheep's intestine—covers the penis. The female sex partner should also know how to use it properly, and should make sure that one is available when needed. Condoms are now made of very thin materials that lessen the validity of the common male complaint that they interfere with sensation. They can also be purchased "textured" or in bright colors, "sort of a fun thing," according to one family-planning expert. The fun aspect is heightened if the woman rolls her partner's condom onto his erect penis as a part of sex play. Modern condoms rarely break unless they have been stored for two years or longer. Some are prelubricated; for those that are not, a little K-Y jelly (not Vaseline, which makes the rubber deteriorate) may be smeared on before intercourse starts. The condom should always be rolled onto the penis *after* it becomes erect, and *before* the start of any sex play in which the penis touches the vagina. After ejaculation the man should pull out of the vagina before his penis relaxes completely, with one or the other partner holding the condom's rim in place so that it does not slip off too soon. A new condom must be used for every act of intercourse.

Diaphragm. This is a thin rubber cup that fits over the cervix, the entrance to the uterus. It must be properly fitted by a doctor, who should also show a woman how to use it. Once a year, after a substantial weight gain or loss, or following childbirth, the physician should check it again to be certain it still fits. With careful handling a diaphragm should last several years.

The trick is to *use* the diaphragm. Most pregnancies occur, not from improper use, but because it remains in the night-table drawer. "I put mine in every night when I brush my teeth," one woman told me, and this is what the experts advise. It's up to the couple to remember to use it when sex occurs spontaneously during the day. Some make it a ritual of foreplay to have the husband insert the diaphragm. Spermicidal jelly must first be dabbed on the inside and on the inner and outer rim.

Six is the magic number to remember with the diaphragm. It may be inserted up to six hours before intercourse, and *must* be left in place until at least six hours afterward. But if sex doesn't take place until two or more hours after insertion, more contraceptive jelly or cream should be squeezed deep into the vagina, using the applicator provided for that purpose. This should be repeated before each act of intercourse.

Foam and vaginal suppositories. Although all contain a sperm-killing chemical, it is important to understand that creams and jellies are effective only with a diaphragm, but foams and vaginal suppositories are barrier products that are used alone. Of these two, the suppositories are more convenient: they are small, inserted like a tampon, and do not require the additional use of an applicator, as foam does. But they are no more effective than foam, and some family-planning experts suspect they may be less so, particularly one brand that contains less spermicidal chemical than the foams. An occasional user, or her male partner, complains of local irritation or burning sensation following suppository insertion. Dr. Tyrer describes the suppositories as "unpredictable in the way they dissolve and spread over the cervix."

Foam is a white aerated chemical with the consistency of shaving cream; shot into the vagina through an applicator, it forms a mechanical barrier to the entrance of sperm into the cervix, and also has a sperm-killing action. It is available too in the form of tablets, but these are not considered as effective. "I tell women to put the foam applicator up so high that they hit something—

usually the cervix—and can't get it any higher," says Dr. Tyrer. This advice holds for the suppositories which must be inserted deep into the vagina.

Foam disperses immediately; it can be applied at the last minute before actual intercourse. A suppository should be inserted ten to fifteen minutes in advance. Both remain effective for an hour or for a single sex act; the process must be repeated each time intercourse takes place. When using either barrier method, be sure to wait at least six hours before douching.

Some women find foam messier than a diaphragm or suppository; others like the added lubrication that it gives them. Foam is a useful backup for the diaphragm (use it instead of jelly when a second application is needed), and particularly for the condom. Doctors don't consider it necessary for a man to use a condom when his partner is wearing a diaphragm, but they are in favor of a condom-foam twosome.

Abortion

According to a report from Princeton's Office of Population Research, only four percent of women who want no more children have a contraceptive failure during the first year after that decision and a bare two percent in the second. It's cheering news except for those who are among the handful of failures. In such cases, a woman must decide between getting an abortion and bearing an unwanted child. This is a personal decision, but you should know that early abortion is now safer than ever. No matter what a woman's age, an abortion performed before the sixteenth week of pregnancy is less dangerous to her life than childbirth. For those over thirty-five, with the hazards of childbirth on the rise, the difference is eightfold.

Despite tall tales about menopause pregnancies, women over thirty-five have fewer abortions than any other age group, except for those younger than fifteen. Less than five percent of the legal abortions in 1976 were performed on women aged thirty-five to thirty-nine, and fewer than two percent on women over forty. Studies show that most women feel sad and guilty only for a few hours or days. One woman who had an abortion at forty, when the youngest of her three children was a ten-year-old, told me, "I thought briefly that having another baby would solve my life for the next couple of years. I had recently gone back to work. Now I wouldn't have to worry about a successful career. But my second thoughts were more mature. Having a baby would create serious problems without solving anything. Once I made the decision, I felt fine about it—no sweat at all."

Sterilization

The news about sterilization is that it is by all odds the contraception method most frequently chosen by couples over thirty-five, and its popularity keeps rising. New techniques are making tubal ligation, the procedure for female sterilization, simpler, quicker and cheaper. This is probably why in 1977, the balance of sterilization operations shifted to a ratio of about sixty percent performed on women to forty percent on men. In the early 1970's male vasectomies represented eighty percent of total sterilizations. The enthusiasm for sterilization is greater among white couples; in fact, black men are highly suspicious of vasectomy, and rarely request it.

Increasing distrust of the various temporary methods of birth control, particularly the Pill, has been another reason for the rush to sterilization. Libby had a tubal ligation at forty-two, when the younger of her two daughters was twelve. "I just made a decision to get off that lousy Pill. It scared me, particularly when a friend developed breast cancer and blamed it on the Pill. I asked my husband to consider a vasectomy. He said, 'Absolutely not,' so I had a ligation."

Libby's friend, Paula, was thirty-eight when she had a tubal ligation soon after her unplanned third child was born. "I had tried and failed with every method of birth control," Paula says. "First I was on the Pill. When I switched to a diaphragm, I had two pregnancies and two miscarriages. Then my husband took over the contraception, and a few years later I was pregnant again. We decided to have the baby. I found a tubal ligation a lot easier to accept than an abortion. The doctor advised my husband against vasectomy. He was forty-five and the doctor thought he might have an emotional kickback.

"I enjoy my kids so much that I could be barefoot and pregnant forever, but my husband would just become unglued if we had any more. He really feels the pressure of putting aside enough money to educate them. As it is, he'll be sixty-four when our youngest starts college. It puts a very harsh burden on him."

Other women who have been sterilized told similar stories. Emily, forty-five, had three children, and then eight years later became pregnant. "It wasn't the fault of my diaphragm," she admits. "I just forgot to put it in." She had a baby girl, and two years later a boy to keep her company, followed by a tubal ligation at the age of thirty-eight. "I can get pregnant just by thinking about it," she says, "but five is plenty. I sure have loved having my tubes tied."

Other women, particularly those who have had pregnancy scares, told me they were considering sterilization, but still felt a little ambivalent. Several said with some irritation that when they asked their husband to have the operation, he had refused. Janet, who is thirty-five, explained that both her husband and her doctor were giving her trouble. "I've been asking my obstetrician since I was thirty, and he promised to let me have my tubes tied once I'd passed thirty-five. He says it's a much easier operation for a man, and my husband promises to do it, but he keeps putting it off. I'm giving him one more month. If he doesn't do it, I will."

Male and female operations are based on the same principle: that if the tubes carrying egg or sperm are permanently closed, conception will no longer be possible. Most family-planning specialists consider the vasectomy the best method (male anatomy makes it an easier procedure), but recognize that, for some men, it arouses fears of loss of manhood that, though unjustified, are very real. "If you pressure your husband and he later becomes impotent," says Dr. Tyrer, "he could blame it on you."

A vasectomy is considered minor surgery, usually performed by a urologist in his office under a local anesthetic. The surgeon generally makes a small incision through the scrotum, locates the sperm-carrying tube (vas deferens), removes about a half inch, and then seals each cut end, repeating the procedure on the other side. The procedure takes only ten or fifteen minutes, and although the patient is a little sore for a few days, he needs no convalescent period. The operation, however, does not produce instant sterility. The couple must use another contraceptive method for as long as four months, because sperm that were present in the lower end of the vas before the surgery are still capable of impregnating a woman.

Most of a man's concerns about vasectomy have no basis in

fact. Neither penis nor testicles are affected by the surgeon's knife. At climax he still ejaculates the same amount of semen; the only difference is that it contains no sperm. Blocked from moving along the vas (a passageway like the Fallopian tubes in a woman), the sperm dissolve and are absorbed into the bloodstream. Here lies the only potential problem: bits and pieces of broken-down sperm are sometimes mistakenly recognized by the body's immune system as foreign invaders, and antibodies form to combat them. The significance of this is unclear.

In a single experiment with monkeys, a group of researchers discovered recently that the animals fed a diet rich in butter fat and then sterilized developed far more advanced atherosclerosis (fatty deposits on the artery wall) than those who had the same diet but no vasectomy. The researchers believe that injury to the artery wall is related to the formation of sperm antibodies. More research studies have been started to see if this phenomenon might apply to humans. "We just don't know whether the data are appropriate for man," says Ruth Crozier of the National Institutes of Health. "The findings are unquestionable, but the numbers are small, and they refer to monkeys, not people. It's a preliminary study that needs lots of further work."

Given this potential problem, many women who want permanent birth control are deciding to undergo surgery themselves. Their choice lies between three operations: *laparotomy*, usually performed a day or two after childbirth; *laparoscopy* (the so-called Band-Aid or belly-button surgery), in which the surgeon uses a laparoscope, or lighted tube, to peer inside the abdomen and clip apart the Fallopian tubes; and *minilaparotomy* (minilap), a procedure in which a small incision is made just above the pubic hairline.

The result is the same in all three procedures: an egg matures in the ovary, but it can no longer pass through the Fallopian tubes to the uterus, and sperm can no longer swim up the tubes to impregnate the egg. Menstruation is not affected. Laparotomy, the oldest procedure, is major surgery, seldom performed any more except following childbirth or in conjunction with an abdominal operation. The other two are comparable in many ways: both take a half hour or less, require only a one- to two-inch incision, can be performed outside a hospital with a local anesthetic in most cases, and have a failure rate of less than half a percent. One disadvantage to the minilap is that it is not suitable for a woman whose lower abdomen is obese. Another is that it is new in the United States, and many surgeons still have not learned the technique. (The Association for Voluntary Sterilization, 708 Third Avenue, New York, N.Y. 10017, can direct a woman to a clinic or a surgeon for a minilap.) Its advantage over laparoscopy is that it is a simpler procedure, requiring no unusual surgical expertise, and is probably safer. Laparoscopy is usually performed in a hospital under general anesthesia (although neither is strictly necessary), and requires one or two days for recovery before the patient goes home. Most minilap patients return home after several hours. In a clinic, both operations cost upward of $350, and in a hospital, between $750 and $1,500, and a majority of Blue Cross–Blue Shield plans cover part or all of the cost. (Vasectomy is the least expensive, usually costing between $150 and $250.)

How does a woman decide whether or not to have the surgery? "She must be able to tell herself honestly," says Dr. Tyrer, " 'no matter what happens—the death of a child or a husband, divorce and remarriage—I don't ever want to become pregnant again.' " Barbara, for example, is probably wise to postpone sterilization. She is thirty-six, has two children, and a husband who refuses vasectomy. "Three years ago I told myself I'd do it once the operation was perfected, but I'm still putting it off. I'm for it intellectually, but not deep down in the gut. I keep getting a vision of both kids being killed."

Recent reports of success in reversing both vasectomy and tubal ligation have given some women the hope that they can have both a ligation and the luxury of changing their minds later. The experts advise strongly against such wishful thinking. Although reversal surgery, using microsurgical technics to resuture the vas or Fallopian tubes has had some technical success, the real test is whether the wife can become pregnant and deliver a healthy baby. This is less certain. With a reverse vasectomy, a man's chance of fathering a child is only one in four or at best one in three. Reversal of ligation through microsurgery is an even newer procedure, with barely a hundred operations performed thus far in the United States. It takes two to three hours, costs over $2,000, and has less chance for success if the tubes were blocked by cauterization in the initial surgery. Another factor is a woman's age. Some surgeons turn down women older than thirty-seven because they consider them less likely candidates for successful pregnancy.

Although reversal surgery is getting a good deal of publicity, probably only one percent or less of the women who have been sterilized seek a reversal. It is more common among men whose second wife is young and wants to have children. Few women, particularly if they are over thirty-five at the time of sterilization, have more than a fleeting moment of regret. Paula says, "The surgery just makes a tremendous difference emotionally. It takes the worry out of being close. It's like the freedom you feel when you're young, still childless, and really don't care if you get pregnant."

A woman may not regret her own sterilization, but some start to worry about a husband's sexual freedom after a vasectomy. Charlotte was thirty-seven when she and her husband decided on permanent contraception. "I would never be sterilized myself," she says. "It's a major thing, and anyway he volunteered. But sometimes I wonder. I figure he's a stud—an attractive man out in the world who doesn't have a moment of concern about getting any woman pregnant." Some husbands have a similar concern after a wife's sterilization surgery.

Hysterectomy

Many woman feel just as free after they have a hysterectomy, the surgical removal of the uterus, as after tubal ligation. One described her hysterectomy at the age of forty-seven as "the greatest thing for a woman that ever came down the pike, absolutely miraculous. I recommend it for anyone."

Don't believe her. Hysterectomy is major surgery. Although recovery takes up to six weeks, many women don't get their full energy back for six months. The surgery is often justified, but it is also the most abused of all operations performed on women. Since 1971 the annual number of hysterectomies has increased by twenty-four percent; the operation ranks second to the most frequent procedure, dilation and curettage, and first in major surgery.

Some cynics call hysterectomy hip-pocket surgery, referring to the place where the gynecologist stores his wallet, fat with surgical fees. The most frequent abuse comes from hyster-sterilization: removing the uterus in order to sterilize a woman when a tubal ligation is far simpler, cheaper and safer. It has been estimated that one in every five hysterectomies was performed merely for sterilization purposes, particularly on poor women for whom Medicaid picked up the tab (a recent HEW regulation now curtails this), and sometimes on Catholics whose doctors report a physical abnormality as the excuse for nonsanctioned sterilizing surgery. Mortality associated with hysterectomy runs more than ten times higher than with tubal ligation; the operation costs over three times as much; and recovery is far slower. One doctor describes a hysterectomy performed for sterilization as comparable to shooting a mouse with a cannon.

But physicians say it's not their fault—women demand hysterectomies. An AMA official told a congressional committee that he considered it acceptable to remove a healthy uterus if it quieted a patient's fears about cancer. And hospital residents in gynecology, seeking to practice their new trade, "sell" hysterectomy to poor patients by preying on their cancer fears. Recently a Massachusetts surgeon was accused by the state medical licensure board of performing hysterectomies as "an appropriate response to middle-aged depression and alcoholism."

About nine percent of American women have a hysterectomy during their thirties, with the incidence rising through the forties, and then dropping. A strikingly large number—over one in every four—has had a hysterectomy by the time she reaches the age of sixty. For many of these women, there are perfectly sound reasons: among them, the occurrence of cancer in the uterus or surrounding reproductive structures; severe endometriosis; or the overgrowth of fibroid tumors to the point where they cause excessive menstrual bleeding, or press painfully on other organs, such as the bladder or rectum. Fibroids are benign, smooth, muscle tumors of the uterus, more common in blacks and childless women, that appear mostly during the thirties and forties. Two out of five women probably have them, but so long as they don't cause symptoms, watchful waiting is considered the best course. One reason is that fibroids are seldom a problem after menopause, when, because of the loss of estrogen, they shrink drastically in size.

If a gynecologist recommends hysterectomy and a woman has any doubts, she should seek a second opinion. When some Blue

Cross–Blue Shield plans started urging second opinions before surgery, hysterectomy operations decreased by almost one quarter. But a woman's most important decision is the extent of the operation: along with the uterus, should she have her ovaries taken out too? Up until recently most surgeons removed the ovaries without asking a patient. "I didn't know a thing about it," says a woman who had a hysterectomy ten years ago. "The surgeon just mentioned it afterward. He seemed to think that I would care more about the bikini cut he gave me—partially hiding the scar under the pubic hair—than whether he took out my ovaries."

But removal of healthy ovaries during hysterectomy *is* important, and whether and when they should be removed is still a highly controversial topic among surgeons. When a simple hysterectomy is performed, the patient no longer menstruates and cannot become pregnant; she has no uterus as a nesting place for an embryo, and no source for monthly menstrual blood. But her ovaries continue manufacturing eggs and estrogen until the menopause starts naturally. Even then, most women manufacture some estrogen in their ovaries for the five to ten years after menopause; the decline is gradual and frequently symptomless. But if the ovaries are removed, a woman suffers a sudden surgical menopause. Symptoms like hot flashes are likely to start immediately and to be severe, because of her abrupt and complete loss of ovarian estrogen.

The rationale for removing healthy ovaries at the time of hysterectomy is the prevention of ovarian cancer, a highly fatal malignancy that gives few warning symptoms (see p. 157). "The surgeon told me it was a good idea to take out the ovaries," says one woman who had a hysterectomy to remove fibroid tumors when she was forty-seven. "It was okay with me. I just wanted the whole thing over with." But the doctor didn't tell her that without the surgery she would probably never have lost her ovaries. For ovarian cancer, although serious, is uncommon, occurring in about only one out of every five hundred women.

A second rationale is, "She's nearing the menopause anyway. The ovaries won't serve any purpose much longer." But how near is near? Among the gynecologists I talked with, in the textbooks and medical journals I read, the advice was, "Take them out if she's forty," "if she's forty-five" or "if she's forty-eight. In other words, there is little agreement on the question.

Dr. Tyrer says, "I am opposed to the routine removal of the

ovaries because of a patient's age. This is a decision the patient should be involved in." She cites the case of a woman who had a hysterectomy at forty-five, without removal of the ovaries, and went through a natural menopause at fifty-five. "If her ovaries had been taken out, she would have missed ten years of effective ovarian function." Dr. Tyrer routinely examines the ovaries for abnormality during hysterectomy. Before the surgery, she receives the patient's consent for taking out an ovary that is found to be diseased, but not one that is healthy, unless the patient requests it.

Other gynecologists, newly mindful of a woman's rights, now suggest removing only one ovary during a hysterectomy. The remaining ovary will manufacture sufficient estrogen to prevent menopausal symptoms, and the likelihood of ovarian cancer developing will be cut in half. Trudy was forty when she had one ovary removed during a hysterectomy. Five years later she has not yet had any menopausal symptoms. Other women facing hysterectomy in their thirties or forties should be sure to discuss the various options in advance with the gynecologist, and not sign a release form authorizing the surgeon to remove the ovaries unless they are diseased or this is what they wish.

When the ovaries are taken out during hysterectomy, many doctors routinely start a patient on Premarin, the leading estrogen medication, in order to control the menopausal symptoms that are likely to follow. Don't worry about estrogen causing cancer of the uterus, they tell her. You're not risking anything, because you no longer have a uterus. (See pp. 81–88 for a fuller discussion of the pros and cons of postmenopausal estrogen.) But a recent report from Framingham, Mass., suggests that a woman's risk of developing coronary heart disease increases at menopause, that surgical menopause increases it further and that the use of estrogen supplements doubles the risk.

The Framingham Heart Disease Epidemiology Study, started in 1948, is probably the only research project to chart the development from young adulthood on of heart disease in women as well as men. Aged twenty-nine through sixty-two at the start, 2,873 women were enrolled and given a cardiovascular examination every two years. By now all have passed the menopause. One out of four has had a hysterectomy, and half of these lost both ovaries at the time.

Charting the development of heart disease, the Framingham

researchers learned that removal of the uterus, either alone or with one or both ovaries, increases a woman's risk for heart disease. The change was most marked among the women who were younger—forty to forty-four—when they had a hysterectomy. Among those in their early forties who were premenopausal, only one developed coronary heart disease. But five in the menopausal group, almost all of whom had had hysterectomies, developed heart disease, and three of these five cases had had both ovaries removed. The Framingham researchers, who stressed that their findings represented only a small group, suggested that the increase was related to a change in the way the body metabolizes fat once menstruation ends.

Although the Framingham findings are preliminary and extremely complex, although heart disease in women even after hysterectomy or menopause lags far behind the disease in men (see p. 127), they suggest still another reason for not tinkering with nature by removing the uterus and ovaries unless clear evidence of disease makes this necessary.

Pregnancy after Thirty-five

Although most women older than thirty-five are desperately eager to avoid pregnancy, a few are headed in the opposite direction. Their question: Am I too old to have a baby? Some have been too busy pursuing careers to think about motherhood earlier; others have had a last-minute change of mind about being childless; and there are a few, with families apparently complete, who become pregnant inadvertently and choose not to abort or who want to keep on being mothers. Their numbers are small; only seven percent of the annual U.S. births occur to women in their late thirties, and three percent to women over forty.

If you want to have a baby after thirty-five, you should be aware of the problems:

It will be harder to conceive. According to one computation, the chance of a woman aged twenty-five getting pregnant during six months of trying is seventy-five percent; by the early thirties it drops to thirty-eight percent; in the late thirties, to twenty-five percent, and after forty, to twenty-two percent.

Pregnancy will be more difficult. A woman is likely to have decreased muscle tone and muscle reserve, more varicose veins, more relaxation of the pelvic organs if she has borne children earlier, all of which will add to fatigue and discomfort during the nine months. One obstetrician compares late pregnancy to an aging car carrying a heavy load—more things are likely to go wrong, and some may be a serious hazard.

There are likely to be more complications during childbirth, such as prolonged labor, breech presentation, premature separation of the placenta. Caesarean sections are performed more frequently. But these complications don't always occur. One woman, thirty-seven at the birth of her first child, had a normal sixteen-hour labor; labor lasted only an hour when she was forty-one and delivered her second.

Childbirth becomes more hazardous. Considering only the mother, the safest age to have a baby is between twenty and twenty-four, and the least safe after forty. During this period maternal mortality increases at each half decade, and at a quicker rate after age thirty. Yet the risk is always statistically small. Out of every ten thousand women in their early twenties having a baby, only one dies; and for women in the forties, the death rate is seven per ten thousand.

Newborn mortality rises, doubling when the mother is in her thirties, and almost doubling again if she is over forty.

Birth defects increase, and this is what worries women the most. The major concern is Down's syndrome (mongolism), the only common abnormality that seems directly connected with the mother's age. The chances of having a baby with this form of retardation are one in 600 in the early thirties, one in 280 in the late thirties, one in 80 for the first half of the forties, and one in 50 births for a mother in her late forties. In other words, until you hit the forties, the likelihood of your bearing a baby with Down's syndrome is less than half of one percent.

Doctors believe that this chromosomal abnormality occurs more frequently with age because the eggs a woman produces are even older than she is (all the ova a female will ever have—some two million of them—are present in the ovaries about two months before her birth). Down's syndrome is usually caused by the presence of an extra chromosome, an occurrence that may be related directly to aging ova or to the effects on them over the years of environmental hazards such as X-rays, drugs and chemicals.

Another possibility for a woman in her late thirties—although it certainly isn't a defect—is an increased chance for twinning.

The likelihood of producing fraternal (two-egg) twins rises gradually, peaking at thirty-seven and then declining after forty. Women over thirty-five are only slightly more likely to bear identical (one-egg) twins.

Despite this formidable array of potential hazards, the chances are excellent that a healthy, well-nourished woman past thirty-five will have a normal childbirth, without hazard to herself or her infant. Dr. Edward Graber, an obstetrician at The New York Hospital–Cornell Medical Center, says, "If she's healthy, she'll probably have no more trouble than if she were younger. I had a patient who had a fine baby after she'd passed fifty."

Doctors believe, however, that late pregnancy is more chancy for a woman with high blood pressure, diabetes, obesity or other chronic disease. There's no need to worry on several other counts: it's no more dangerous for the mother if it's her first baby or her fifth; she need have no special concern if she once had an abortion (although two or more prior abortions may possibly increase the chance of miscarriage or prematurity), or if she used the Pill as a contraceptive. Studies show that earlier use of the Pill does not increase the hazard of childbearing.

If you are over thirty-five and decide to have a baby, these actions should provide extra insurance that all will be normal:

Have a thorough physical checkup *before* you become pregnant.

At the same time get a blood test to find out whether you are immune to rubella (German measles). If you are not, ask the doctor for an injection of rubella vaccine. If you are given the vaccine, you must wait four months before becoming pregnant. A woman who develops rubella during the first three months of pregnancy may suffer a miscarriage, or deliver a baby with one or more serious birth defects. But such tragedy is easily avoided if you make sure that you are not susceptible to this childhood disease.

Change your contraception from the Pill to a barrier method (diaphragm, condom, foam) three months before you start trying to become pregnant. This will allow your menstrual cycles and hormonal balance to return to a normal pattern.

Cut out alcoholic beverages and stop smoking. The connection between drinking and a group of physical and mental abnormalities in the newborn (the fetal alcohol syndrome) was discovered only six years ago. It is now known that the extent of damage to the fetus depends on how heavy a drinker the mother was, and at what point during her pregnancy she drank. Risk of abnormality is low when one two-ounce drink of whisky is consumed daily, but rises for the moderate drinker (four ounces of whiskey or its equivalent in wine or beer), and even more for the heavy drinker, or the woman who binge-drinks occasionally. Drinking during the first month or two after conception, when many women are not yet sure they are pregnant, is particularly dangerous. The hazard applies to all women, no matter what their age.

Maternal smoking is also potentially harmful to the fetus, reducing its weight and supply of oxygen. But a woman who stops smoking during the first three months of pregnancy is no more likely to damage her child than if she had never smoked.

Any medication not prescribed by the obstetrician is suspect during pregnancy, so it's wise to be prepared and empty out the medicine cabinet during the months that you're trying to become pregnant. One medication to avoid is Valium, the most popular tranquilizer. In laboratory experiments at least, the drug interferes with fetal muscle growth and protein synthesis inside muscle cells.

Consider having an amniocentesis when you are about sixteen weeks pregnant. This diagnostic test removes a sample of fluid from the amniotic sac in which the fetus floats inside your uterus. Because the fluid contains cells shed by the unborn baby, its analysis, which may take several weeks, can detect about a hundred different genetic disorders, including all the major chromosome abnormalities (Down's syndrome and others), structural defects of the brain and spinal column and many biochemical defects. If the fetus is abnormal (only four percent are), the parents may decide on abortion. Because the amniocentesis technique may also reveal fetal sex, if the fetus is female abortion will not be necessary in diseases such as hemophilia, which are passed on only to males.

Some doctors advise amniocentesis for all pregnant women who are thirty-five; many urge it strongly for those past thirty-seven. It is usually preceded by a determination of the fetal position through the use of ultrasound, a safe, painless technique. Amniocentesis itself involves the insertion of a hypodermic needle through the abdomen into the uterus, an outpatient procedure performed under local anesthetic. The danger to the mother or fetus is considered small, though recent studies suggest some chance of miscarriage or hazard to the newborn. The cost is $300 to $500, frequently paid for by medical insurance.

Although still experimental, a fetal blood-sampling technique is now being tried in a few medical centers; when it is perfected, it will increase the number of birth abnormalities that can be diagnosed prenatally. But amniocentesis alone can assure most mothers that they have nothing to worry about. One woman who was thirty-eight (with a husband of forty-five) when her third child was born, and who did not have amniocentesis, told me, "I was terrified all through pregnancy."

But no laboratory technique can answer the most important question of all—Do I really want this baby? Honest analysis of one's motives turns up some surprising rationalizations. One woman who had her third baby at the age of thirty-seven, ten years after her second, admits, "Getting pregnant allowed me to put off any decisions about a career. In a way I was relieved." Another says, "I guess I didn't want to face an end to mothering."

And for one woman I talked with, late motherhood turned out to be a disaster. She was thirty-seven and childless, a college professor when she and her husband adopted two toddlers. She stopped teaching to care for her babies. "I know now that the decision was a bow to social conformity—everyone had children but us," she says. "By quitting work I lost identity and pride and the stability of daily routine. For me the joys of motherhood were usually overwhelmed by its concerns—we had difficult days when our children were growing up."

Having one's first baby after thirty-five, especially if it means the suspension of a meaningful job, calls for unusual flexibility and patience. Yet unlike this mother, others report that the rewards are worth it. "You know who you are when you wait," says a political scientist, childless until she was thirty-five. "You've accomplished enough so that a child is no threat to your identity." And an obstetrician whose research compared young with older mothers concluded, "The most satisfied were those who became parents after the age of thirty-five. [They] seemed to enjoy their children the most . . . They lacked physical stamina . . . but they seemed to make up for this deficiency by patience and understanding."

One older mother summed it up: "I had a child for the joy of having a child, and not to confirm myself as a woman and a mother. I think that's the best reason of all."

V

The Menopause

Long enshrouded by myth, misinformation, secrecy and prejudice, the menopause is finally being treated for what it is: a normal physiological development that ushers out a woman's reproductive life, just as menarche, the start of menstruation, ushers it in. At the outset, it is important for every woman to understand that the menopause is *not* a disease, a hormonal loss that needs replacement; nor is it the beginning of the end (one-third of a woman's life lies ahead); and certainly not a way station to the mental hospital.

Although a realistic assessment of the menopause is finally emerging, myths die hard, and there is still a long way to go. Many women still display no outward curiosity about the menopause; they seem to think that if they don't talk about it, it will, like cancer, go away. Pressed, they admit that they equate it with aging. At forty-two, Paula, weighing the pros and cons, says, "I'm sure having menstrual periods is basically a pain in the neck, but I think that I really don't want to be old," as if this were a corollary to the end of menstruation.

Myths about the menopause are only partly folklore; in large part they are the creation of male physicians who have confused real physical symptoms with psychological changes, often unrelated to the menopause, with highly unscientific abandon. "The medical literature on menopause reveals some of the most shockingly negative attitudes toward women that I have ever encountered," says Dr. Mary Brown Parlee, a psychology professor at Barnard College. In a real sense, the menopause, as it is popularly understood, is a doctor-created disease. Among physician myths:

• Like diabetes, menopause is a deficiency disease. In 1973 Dr. Francis Rhoades, president of the American Geriatric Society, called it a "chronic and incapacitating deficiency disease, that leaves women with flabby breasts, wrinkled skin, fragile bones and loss of ability to have or enjoy sex."

• It makes a woman lose her femininity. "Once the ovaries stop, the very essence of being a woman stops," writes Dr. David Reuben, a psychiatrist, in his runaway best seller, *Everything You Always Wanted to Know About Sex* but Were Afraid to Ask.* "Without estrogen, the quality of being female gradually disappears . . . Not really a man but no longer a functional woman, these individuals live in the world of intersex."

• She ages almost overnight. "I've gotten ten years older in the past two years," Dr. Reuben quotes a patient as telling him.

• She becomes tense, irritable, bitchy. At a 1971 symposium sponsored by the National Institutes of Health, with twenty-five doctors attending, not one of them a woman, gynecologist Howard Jones of Johns Hopkins Medical School described menopausal woman as "a caricature of their younger selves at their emotional worst."

• Often she collapses into depression and mental illness. Psychiatrists have long put menopausal depression into a special category which they call involutional melancholia. (Now that an excess of depression at this age has been found to be nonexistent, they have recently withdrawn the label from the psychiatric nomenclature.)

• A woman's useful life is over. Psychiatrist Helene Deutsch wrote of the menopause: "Woman has ended her existence as bearer of a future life and has reached her natural end—her partial death—as servant of the species."

Although many doctors now know better, these myths were taught in medical school, and some still appear in medical texts. As a result, a woman must be wary of occasional misdiagnosis based on physician prejudice about the menopause. One doctor, for example, explained away one patient's complaints of fatigue and dizziness as "just the menopause" until tests revealed that she had developed diabetes. A forty-four-year-old woman was referred by her family physician to a gynecologist because of menopausal "symptoms" that included chronic fatigue, sleeplessness, crying spells. Rose Oliver, a New York psychologist whom she later consulted, found out that the woman had seven children, including one who was retarded, an alcoholic husband and a sick, aging mother. *But*—her menstrual periods were still regular, and there were no physical indications of hormonal change.

Despite the medical Cassandras and their dire predictions, women in the middle years are remarkably levelheaded about the menopause. They do not regard it as a life crisis, nor do they have a sentimental attachment to continued menstruation and childbearing. About menstruation, Janet, aged thirty-five and the mother of two, told me, "Who needs it any more? I can hardly wait." And she said of the menopause, "I anticipate some inconveniences but no problems that I can't surmount. Nothing that natural frightens me."

Even in 1967, when Dr. Bernice Neugarten reported the results of her pioneering study on menopause, she found that only four percent of the women she interviewed regarded "the worst thing" as not being able to have more children. The largest number, one in four, were most bothered by "not knowing what to expect." And almost half thought that the "best thing" was no longer having to bother with menstruation.

Dr. Neugarten and her colleagues found that younger women, far from the menopause themselves, were more apprehensive about it than those close to the change. Over half of those in the menopausal age range did not expect it to affect their physical or emotional health, and two-thirds foresaw no change in sexual relations. Many admitted some concern (half said that women worry about losing their minds at this time), but looked forward to a happy ending—three out of four thought that women are usually calmer, happier and freer afterward.

One woman told the interviewer, "Yes, the change of life is an unpleasant time. No one enjoys the hot flushes . . . but I've gone through changes before, and I can weather another one. Besides, it's only a temporary condition." A decade later the women I interviewed, often too busy with their jobs to worry about an end to mothering, were even more positive. Lorna, fifty, a guidance counselor, said that she had described her menopausal symptoms to the gynecologist, and then told him, "I bet you I'm not going to have serious problems, and if I do, I won't fall with them, because it will be a small part of what I'm doing with my life."

More recent studies suggest that the menopause is viewed with melancholy anticipation only by those women who choose it as a symbol for other midlife concerns. Dr. Mary Anna Friederich, a University of Rochester gynecologist, writes: "For the woman who saw her ability to reproduce as her main reason for living and as her way to prove her self-worth, the menopause will be difficult . . . For the woman whose whole feeling of self-worth has been involved with her external physical beauty, the menopause is a severe blow." And according to a recent doctoral thesis, women in their late thirties who are homemakers are likely to have more concern than those who hold outside jobs.

A woman's life style and emotional maturity may color her view of what happens, but the menopause is basically a *physical* event, a period of significant hormonal readjustment. The time it starts, how long it lasts and the severity of the symptoms she experiences are not dependent on whether she is a feminist, an old-fashioned mother or a professional beauty.

The average menopausal age for an American woman is fifty; but normal menopause can occur over an eighteen-year span. One percent have had a natural menopause by the time they are forty; ten percent by forty-five, thirty-one percent by forty-eight. By the age of fifty-two, seventy-six percent have gone through menopause, ninety-two percent by age fifty-four, ninety-seven percent by fifty-six, and one hundred percent by the age of fifty-eight.

Why the long span occurs is unknown. Heredity certainly plays a part; if you want to anticipate your own menopause, ask your mother, aunt, older sister when theirs occurred. Smokers, it has recently been learned, tend to have an earlier menopause— heavier smokers before light smokers and lighter smokers before former smokers. At the age of fifty to fifty-one, seventy-nine percent of heavy smokers are menopausal, but only fifty-six percent of women who have never smoked. Women who have had a hysterectomy before the age of forty are also apt to have early menopause. But the time you stop menstruating appears to bear no relation to the age at which you started, nor is it affected by whether you are married or single, short or tall, thin or fat, or a mother.

What menopause means is the cessation of menstruation. But it does not represent a day etched in a woman's mind like the day she started menstruation. It is rare to have regular periods every month and then stop abruptly. What is much more common is to skip a period, menstruate regularly for several months, then stop for six weeks, and menstruate again, until an even longer gap occurs that may or may not mark the end. Doctors often tell their patients not to consider the menopause complete until a year has passed from the last period. But in *Our Bodies, Ourselves*, members of the Boston Women's Health Book Collective found that fifteen percent of the women they surveyed stopped menstruating for a full year, and then started up again.

Many women, sharp about other details of their past life, find it difficult to answer the routine medical question, "When did you have the menopause?" One, aged fifty-two, whose husband had died of cancer eighteen months earlier, told me, "I stopped menstruating two years before his death when he had the first of two operations. But a year after the funeral, a very nice man took me out and made love to me. Bango! there I was menstruating again. Have I gone through menopause? I guess so."

During the years around the menopause, ovarian function—the ripening and release of an egg, accompanied by secretion of the two ovarian hormones, estrogen and progesterone—is waning. This process usually continues for at least two years, and sometimes as long as six or eight. When production of these hormones is insufficient to cause a buildup and then a sloughing of tissue from the walls of the uterus, menstruation falters and finally ceases.

With menopause, progesterone production stops, but a small amount of estrogen is still manufactured by the ovaries, and this may continue for five or ten years, occasionally much longer. Some estrogen is also manufactured by the adrenal glands. The level of estrogen in a woman's bloodstream and how swiftly it diminishes appear to determine the character of her menopause —whether symptoms are mild or severe, and how long they last. Women who have had a surgical menopause, in which uterus and ovaries are removed, usually have the most severe symptoms, because their estrogen decline is swift and complete.

Two symptoms are known to be related definitely to the hormonal change—the immediate occurrence of hot flashes, or flushes, and later, vaginal discomfort due to thinning and drying of tissue. About three out of four women experience some degree of uncomfortable warmth, usually starting in the chest and spreading upward to neck and head. Flashes sometimes begin a year or so before the end of menstruation. The flash (the medical term is vasomotor instability) is probably caused by a wildly fluctuating hormonal balance, though the relation between estrogen and the heat-regulatory mechanism is not yet understood. For as estrogen production declines, the pituitary, the master gland that signals the ovaries to release their hormones, pours out more of its own hormones in a useless effort to force the ovary into action. It is likely that the hot flash is due to too little estrogen, too much pituitary hormone or a combination of both.

In *Everything You Always Wanted to Know about Sex . . .*, Dr. David Reuben describes the hot flash as "an unbearable sensation of heat that . . . can occur . . . every ten minutes." For most women, this is gross exaggeration. According to a government survey, at least one in six experiences no unpleasant symptoms at all. For one in ten they are severe, and for the other three-quarters they vary in intensity. "My menopause was a breeze," one woman told me. "It happened when I was fifty-three, and I never had a single flash." But some experience warmth and tingling over the entire body, break out into heavy sweats so intense at night that they leave the bedclothes soaking. Each flash lasts only a minute or two, but may recur a dozen times a day or more, particularly in the night hours.

Many women are terribly embarrassed when the hot flashes occur in public; they think that the mounting warmth is noticeable to everyone (and sometimes the face does redden in flush), and they find the perspiration, which may stain their clothes, a bit shameful. "I feel out of control," one told me. The social aura still surrounding the menopause—the belief that it is a bit lewd for a woman to age, and that the menopause itself is somewhat ludicrous—enhances the embarrassment and shame, and, some believe, the flushes themselves. Although doctors no longer suggest that "it's all in your head," many think that the emotional turmoil the symptom causes ends up by making it worse.

Eventually the number of daily flushes and their intensity both start to diminish as the body becomes acclimated to the lower level of estrogen production. If your physician reassures you, however, that it will all be over in a year or so, he is just as likely to be wrong as right. According to a British study, one out of four women still has occasional hot flushes five years after her menopause, and for some they last nine or more.

Most women use terms like "a nuisance" or "annoying" to describe their experience with hot flushes, but for a few they are temporarily devastating, particularly because of the night sweats that interrupt sleep. Despite medical progress in other areas, one problem is still not knowing what to expect and for how long. Reports on the menopause are dotted with "maybe" and "doctors think it likely" because so little scientific research has been done, despite the fact that more than a million American women enter menopause each year.

The other symptom directly related to estrogen deprivation is a vaginal discharge and itching, sometimes leading to infection, and to vaginal discomfort during intercourse. The discomfort is caused by changes in the vagina produced by estrogen withdrawal—thinning, drying, loss of elasticity, slower lubrication at sexual arousal. (For a discussion of sex at menopause, see pp. 92–104.) These vaginal changes develop slowly; many women show no symptoms until a decade after the menopause, and others never develop them at all. Sex therapists hold that an active sex life protects a woman from postmenopausal vaginal discomfort.

Meanwhile other anatomical changes are occurring. A woman's uterus reaches its maximum size and weight in early adulthood, remains stable until the age of fifty, and then shrinks, weighing about fifty percent less when she reaches sixty-five. The luxuriance of her pubic hair slowly diminishes, but the change is seldom noticeable before her sixties. Her breasts may shrink and sag, losing fat and glandular tissue; some of this gradual change, however, is due to loss of tissue elasticity unrelated to the menopause. Surprisingly, women appear to be less concerned with droopy breasts than with other bodily changes. Many in their forties already notice a change and trace its start to childbirth. "There never was very much there to sag," says a forty-year-old mother of three, "and I couldn't care less."

Body configuration changes, with hips broadening and waist thickening, although it is unclear whether this is related to the menopause, particularly as the figure change often precedes it. Weight gain is apparently not dependent on menopause; the women studied for heart disease in Framingham, Mass., gained weight at this age whether they were menopausal or not. Many reseachers think that the hormone withdrawal alters the way the body metabolizes fat and some minerals, but no one has pinpointed exactly what happens.

Despite speculation about the profound effects, both physical and emotional, of hormonal change, there is still a belief, held by women as well as their doctors, that other symptoms associated with the menopause—palpitations, dizziness, headache, joint pain, irritability, weepiness, insomnia—are all in the head, and that they are experienced only by women who are neurotic, dependent, unsure of their own identity. Contemporary women are likely to say, "I'm going to have an easy menopause, because I've got my head together and I know where I'm at." Brave words, but they are based on an assumption that these symptoms can be willed in or out of existence, which is untrue of the hot flash, and guesswork about the others.

One woman, for example, who treated her menopause in a brisk, no-nonsense manner, couldn't understand why, as she sat at the breakfast table one morning, she unaccountably began to cry. "It's not like me," she sobbed, "but I just feel blue." It was a single episode, never repeated, by a person for whom violent mood swings are completely atypical. In her mid-fifties, she still remembers the incident and speculates about it. Was it the menopause, she wants to know, or a sad mood based on no conscious emotional concern, or neither of these? No one really knows; too many facets of the menopause are still a mystery.

But it is wise to remember that the doctors who now call the hot flash the only "real" symptom of early menopause used to denigrate it too. Several theories, none altogether satisfactory, have been suggested to explain this grab bag of other physical and emotional reactions, including:

• The symptoms occur right through adulthood, but women are conditioned to be alert to them at a time when they are anticipated—i.e., at the menopause. A headache at any other time, according to this theory, would be dismissed as just a headache, but now it receives extra significance as a "menopausal headache." The theory is bolstered by a survey reported in *Our Bodies, Ourselves* in which a group of women, aged twenty-five and upward, were asked to check off from a list of twenty-three symptoms (all popularly considered as menopausal) those that they had personally experienced at some time. Women aged twenty-five to forty checked more symptoms than those older, and women over sixty checked the fewest.

• Many menopausal complaints are actually related to the occurrence of hot flushes and night sweats. It is hardly surprising that a woman who is drenched by sweat during the night will complain of insomnia the next morning. Others feel irritable and bitchy over the loss of control, and the embarrassment that daytime flushes engender. One woman reports that she was upset by the irregular periods and severe cramps that developed during her mid-forties. Then the hot flushes started. "It could be very embarrassing when you're in company, and suddenly you're in this terrible sweat," she told the editors of *The Menopause Book*. "I was very disagreeable. I would complain bitterly and be very nasty."

• Other symptoms have a physiologic cause just as hot flushing does; they just haven't been discovered yet. When a menopausal woman tells her gynecologist that food tastes different or everything smells funny, he's likely to mutter under his breath about those nutty neurotic females. Yet it has recently been learned that the dryness of the vagina after the menopause may also occur in other mucous membranes. Thus smelling an unpleasant odor is a reaction to the drier nasal membranes; and a burning sensation in the mouth, affecting the taste of food, follows a similar reduction in the flow of saliva.

• Symptoms ascribed to the menopause may stem instead from other developments at midlife—a job crisis, a child who has left the nest or (even worse) has returned, divorce, widowhood, imminent retirement. Even a sophisticated doctor gets a physical event, the menopause, hopelessly entwined with social crises in the middle years, something he wouldn't be likely to do if his patient had pneumonia. "The menopause is a traumatic occurrence for a woman," one university specialist told me. "Her husband is busy at the office, the kids are growing away, and she's just sitting at home or belting a few at the country club." This comment also shows how a physician, no more scientific than the rest of us, generalizes from the experience of his own well-to-do patients, and comes up with a barely recognizable picture of the life of an average menopausal woman.

Until the answers are in, women and their doctors will just have to strike a nice balance between dismissing every ache and pain and mood swing with, "Forget it! It's just the menopause," and insisting rigidly that early menopause has *no* recognizable symptoms except for the hot flash. This in effect is what women do naturally: they listen to their bodies, wonder why, shrug and get on with their business.

Whatever the truth about these other symptoms, one myth has been thoroughly exploded: *clinical depression is not a product of the menopause.* Women do not suffer more mental breakdowns at this time; in fact, the early twenties is the peak period for depression and attempts at suicide. In a study on sex differences in depression, Drs. Myrna Weissman and Gerald Klerman confirm that women suffer from it more than men, that childbirth is a time of hazard, but "there is no evidence that women are at greater risk for depression during the menopausal period."

Less well publicized than the "horrors" of the menopause are the joys which follow it. Margaret Mead once coined the term "postmenopausal zest" (PMZ) to describe the surge of energy and well-being that she and others experienced. This may be due to the disappearance of the mild anemia that many women experienced with monthly bloodletting; or to the loss of the mood swings that for some characterize the menstrual cycle. "I feel like a teen-ager again," says one woman in her fifties. "I'm never tired." And a friend of mine, fifty-two, said, "I have more energy than when I was thirty-five. I believe in PMZ, but it has to do with a lot more than physiological change. It comes out of a new ego strength and a sense of independence."

Pills for the Menopause— Should You Use Them?

If this were being written only a few years ago, the following appraisals of estrogen replacement therapy (ERT) might be greeted with approval instead of cries of derision.

"There doesn't seem to be a sexy thing estrogen can't and won't do to keep you flirtatiously feminine." From a fashion magazine, 1973.

"Wrinkles recede . . . skin and hair get back their old consistency and sheen . . . [it gives] outstanding protection against heart attacks." From Dr. David Reuben's *Everything You Always Wanted to Know About Sex . . .* 1969.

"Long-term estrogen replacement is a necessity if women want to remain physically active after the menopause." From an article by Dr. Ivan Langley, Portland, Oregon, gynecologist, 1977.

Now, of course, the widely publicized reports that estrogen can cause cancer of the endometrium, the lining of the uterus, have caused ERT to become, for many, a dirty word. Paeans of praise like these helped to ensure its spectacular overuse during the 1960's and early 1970's. In 1975, the number of prescriptions written for Premarin, the most popular hormonal drug, soared high enough to maintain five million women on estrogen for the rest of their lives, although fewer than one and a half million reach the menopause in any single year. Eighty-five percent of the nation's gynecologists prescribed it, according to one estimate, as did internists and general practitioners, and many put their patients on high dosages for indefinite lengths of time. One doctor boasted that he gave estrogen to virtually all his menopausal patients because "most women suffer some symptoms whether they are aware of them or not." By now the number of estrogen users has receded but hardly disappeared; one report estimates that two out of every five women in their early fifties are taking or have taken the hormone drug.

Women approaching the menopause are confused about ERT. The idea of flirting with cancer gives them the horrors, but they still remember all the goodies that once glittered in the ERT package. Paula, who is forty-two, told me, "I think you're damned if you take it and damned if you don't. I don't like the idea of fooling around chemically with my body. But if estrogen would keep my skin young, I'd just run for it."

Alas! the final word is that it won't. The Food and Drug Administration says there is no indication that estrogens have any value in the treatment of nervousness or depression. "Neither have estrogens been shown to keep the skin soft or to keep women feeling young." If they are used for brief periods of time and in low doses, estrogens do have value, the FDA adds, in treating three problems of the menopause: hot flashes, thinning and drying of the vagina and osteoporosis. (See p. 198 for a report on this postmenopausal bone problem in women.) Dr. Alexander Schmidt, former commissioner of Food and Drugs, said, "Because these drugs can cause harm as well as good and because they are different from any other drugs in that they are given to otherwise healthy women undergoing the natural process of menopause, the FDA believes it essential that *women . . . decide for themselves if the risks are worth the benefits."*

If you are having hot flushes, should you take estrogens? Yes, as a short-time transitional aid, say cautious physicians, *if* your symptoms are severe enough to curtail normal living, if night sweats ruin your sleep, if daytime discomfort interferes with your job, school or other aspects of daily life—in short, if the symptoms are incapacitating. But if you take the hormones, you should observe the following precautions:

Before starting ERT, have a thorough physical examination, in which the breasts are carefully examined and a Pap smear taken. In addition, have an endometrial Pap test, a new screening procedure performed in the doctor's office, in which cells and fluid are aspirated from the uterus and examined under a microscope.

Repeat these tests every six months. At the same time evaluate with your doctor the need for continuing therapy.

The watchword should be: the smallest dose for the shortest possible time. Premarin comes in four strengths, distinguished by the color of the pill: 2.5 mg. (purple), 1.25 mg. (yellow), .625 mg. (red), .3 mg. (green). "I don't take much," one woman told me, "just the yellow pills, like everybody else." She is not aware that the red tablets, only half as strong, may control her symptoms adequately.

What women and their doctors find so seductive about estrogen is that it does the job of reducing hot flashes with spectacular speed, and also appears to provide an enhanced sense of well-being. "If you give enough estrogen, you can stop flushing completely," says Dr. Sidney Arje, vice-president of the American Cancer Society. "But that shouldn't be the goal."

Many women are disappointed when, after six months or a year on Premarin, they try to get along without it and find that hot flashes return promptly. This isn't surprising; by providing the estrogen that the ovaries are no longer producing, the pills postpone the time when the body will have to adjust on its own to the new status. Taking a small dose may help the adjustment, and time also helps. One woman stopped the drug "when I was waking up three or four times a night with hot flushes. That was nothing compared to what it had been before, which was every half hour, but I decided that what little discomfort I was having wasn't worth the risk."

The best way to wean oneself from the estrogen habit is not to do it cold turkey, but with the doctor's guidance to slowly diminish one's dependence. After several months on a daily maintenance dosage, try to take the pill every second day, or to cut it in half. Then lengthen the interval between pill days. The trick is to acclimate your body gradually to a lessened estrogen supply, even though some mildly annoying symptoms may accompany it.

To guide them in a selection of dosage, some doctors rely on tests of a woman's estrogen level, but many consider these tests inaccurate and unnecessary. The Pap smear will show the amount of estrogen present in vaginal cells, but not how much is circulating in the bloodstream. "The smear test gives a lot of false positives and negatives," says Dr. Edward Graber of The New York Hospital. "The blood test for estrogen is more accurate, but it's expensive, and the results are often ambiguous. I think the advice to have such a test every five years is nonsense. I believe in treating the patient, not the smear."

If you have high blood pressure, liver problems or breast cancer, you should not take estrogen at all. Any woman who once had serious complications, such as a blood clot, while on the Pill—or without it—should avoid estrogen at the time of menopause. If she has had a heart attack or stroke, or suffers from angina pectoris, she should use estrogens only cautiously and briefly when the need is extreme. A diabetic using postmenopausal estrogen should be periodically checked by her doctor for any changes in glucose tolerance. Better stay away from estrogens too if you are a DES mother—that is, if you were once given diethylstilbestrol, another form of estrogen used to prevent miscarriage. Hazards to the daughters of these women have been widely publicized, but there is also concern that the mothers who have used it may be more likely to develop breast cancer.

Cancer of the endometrium is considered the major hazard of postmenopausal estrogen replacement. The drug stimulates the buildup of tissue on the uterine wall, just as during the menstrual years, but without the balance of progesterone to cause a monthly shedding. Overgrowth of this tissue leads to changes in some women that could develop into cancer. Doctors advocate a regime of three weeks on estrogen and one week off, as a way to minimize the proliferation of uterine tissue.

Starting in 1975 a number of statistical studies have shown that endometrial cancer is more common among women who take or have taken estrogen. Latest figures indicate that a post-menopausal woman has about one chance in a thousand of developing this cancer in any year, but ten to thirty chances per thousand if she takes estrogen. The first months are not considered hazardous, but the risk rises the longer she takes the drug (particularly after five years) and the higher its dosage. Six months after she stops, the danger declines drastically. Latest figures from the National Cancer Institute show that the incidence of endometrial cancer has started to drop after a three-year rise, and officials relate the good news to a more cautious use of estrogen for the menopause.

One study also links estrogen with breast cancer, but this has not been confirmed. It suggests that estrogen users with benign breast disease are at greater risk for breast cancer. Other hazards are real, although less serious. A woman doubles her chances of developing gall bladder disease when she takes estrogen. Her fibroid tumors, which normally shrink in size with estrogen deprivation, may start to grow again. The drug can cause sore breasts and fluid retention in some women, probably making migraine headaches worse. "I gained weight and swelled up with water. My face looked puffy and my nose larger, and I just hated it," one woman says.

It was once believed that a plus for estrogen was its protective effect against heart disease, but this theory has now been thrown in the ash heap. (See pp. 128–29 for a fuller discussion of the puzzle of female sex hormones and heart disease.) According to the Framingham studies, the incidence of heart disease does rise at the time of menopause, but it rises twice as fast for a woman who takes estrogen. Dr. Robert Levy, director of the National Heart, Lung and Blood Institute, says, "When you give estrogens [to a patient], you're not helping her cardiovascular system."

One ticklish question is, What about the one woman in four who has had a hysterectomy? Many doctors feel that she is home free in taking estrogen because she has no uterus in which cancer can develop. All too often they appear careless about the strength of the hormone tablets they prescribe, and the length of time a patient uses it.

Among a small group of women, I found three who were still using estrogen, one for five years after her hysterectomy, one for six and the third for ten. Jane had a hysterectomy at the age of forty-eight, with only one ovary removed, leaving her sufficient natural estrogen to go through a normal menopause later. "When I started to have an occasional minor hot flash," she says, "the doctor put me on Premarin. He said it would make me feel better. Almost five years have passed, and if I ask him about it, he answers, 'Why stop? You have no uterus. How can you get cancer?'" Rosa has been on Premarin for ten years, ever since her ovaries were removed during a hysterectomy. "I got nervous about it recently and called the gynecologist. He said, 'Don't worry. But just to play it safe, why don't you cut down to a lower dosage?'" She had a few symptomless months on the smaller dose, and then determined to stop the drug altogether. At this point, at the age of fifty-six, she suffered the first hot flash of her lifetime. "I was miserable," she said. "I went right back on Premarin. I figured if the doctor wasn't going to worry, why should I?"

It is difficult for a woman who has had a hysterectomy to find firm, sensible guidance on ERT. Since you can't get endometrial cancer, and doctors differ on the other hazards, the best advice is, *be prudent*. If your ovaries were not removed, you are no more likely to suffer disabling symptoms from the menopause than any other woman. "Even when a patient has no uterus," says Dr. Graber, "I stick to the principle of the lowest dose for the shortest time."

A woman who has recently finished the menopause need not expect to develop the symptoms of atrophic vaginitis, the medical name for the estrogen-caused vaginal changes, for about five to ten years. In fact, she may never be aware of these changes, since the symptoms occur less commonly than hot flashes. Physicians frequently treat the condition by prescribing a topical estrogen cream applied to the vagina. It appears less hazardous than an estrogen pill that affects the whole body, but unfortunately the cream does not remain localized. It is absorbed into the bloodstream, making its safety over a pill only marginal. If your vaginal problem is lack of lubrication during sex, smear a bit of a hypoallergenic lubricant at the entrance and just inside the vagina. But don't use Vaseline or K-Y jelly; they may irritate sensitive tissues.

If you suffer from hot flashes but fear endometrial cancer, there are several alternatives to conventional ERT. The most controversial is the use of estrogen, supplemented by progesterone, in a way that mimics the natural flow of sex hormones during the reproductive years. A few gynecologists and a number of endocrinologists advocate this combination. "It is my belief that if you give low-dose estrogen replacement . . . cyclically combined with progesterone, it does not cause endometrial cancer, and may even help to prevent it," says a New York endocrinologist, Dr. Lila Nachtigall, in her book *The Lila Nachtigall Report* (with Joan Heilman). Dr. Nachtigall, groups in Texas, and at Duke University Medical School say that long-term followups of patients on the estrogen-progesterone treatment have uncovered few or no cases of cancer of the endometrium.

The rationale is that the progesterone counters the unopposed buildup of estrogen on the uterine wall, which is believed to be the source of the cancer hazard. Dr. Nachtigall prescribes estrogen alone for the first twenty-one days of a month and adds progesterone for the last seven. About three days later a simulated menstrual bleeding, usually light and lasting two to five days, follows. The patient cannot become pregnant, of course, because she no longer ovulates. Dr. Nachtigall says that eventually the uterine lining becomes nonfunctional, and the bogus menstrual periods end.

But why would a woman choose to keep on with the bother of menstruation? Juliet, fifty-five, vital, super-energetic, describes the terror she felt over an approaching menopause. "Until the menopause, my mother was a healthy peasant type like me. Then everything bad started to happen. She developed high blood pressure, had a coronary, became crippled by arthritis. I was convinced that the same thing would happen to me."

Juliet was turned down by two gynecologists when she asked for ERT. "I finally went to an endocrinologist who put me on a regime of estrogen and progesterone. All my friends thought I was crazy. I had a sort of menstrual period every month. I gained weight, and I was never really comfortable with it. After a year I had breakthrough bleeding in mid-cycle, and that was too much. I just stopped." Two years later Juliet has weathered a mild menopause; her health is good, and she is as energetic as ever.

Dr. Arje of the American Cancer Society comments: "A woman's uterus has gone through cycles all her adult life in preparation for pregnancy. Now it is at rest. I just don't think it's a good idea to start restimulating it, to extend its life span beyond normal. But if a woman does use estrogen, I think it's better to balance it with progesterone." Others are wary of the combination, pointing out that it is similar to that in the sequential birth-control pills, withdrawn from the market by the FDA several years ago because of reports of increased incidence of cancer of the uterus.

Some physicians believe that non-hormonal treatment for hot flashes, particularly the use of vitamin E, is useful; others call it a waste of money. One prominent gynecologist advises taking it along with a meal that has some fat in it. "It seems to be better absorbed if vitamin A is taken at the same time," this doctor says. "If it is going to work at all, a woman should notice some results in two or three weeks." But Dr. Graber of The New York Hospital says, "I've seen nothing to show that vitamin E helps hot flashes. It doesn't hurt. It just wastes your money."

Some physicians also recommended as helpful for hot flashes a prescription drug, a belladonna compound with sedative and antispasmodic effects. Convinced that emotional stress worsens the heat symptoms (although it does not cause them), many doctors advise the judicious use of tranquilizers for a short period of time. And for sleep problems, they suggest the traditional remedies—warm milk, a hot bath, herbal teas. In other words, be pragmatic. If it's not harmful and seems to lessen your symptoms, give it a try.

Without denying that there is a physical cause for menopausal symptoms, some feminists speculate that a woman's lowered social status at this time may make her discomfort worse. In several other cultures, a woman at menopause leaves the society of other women who are "unclean" every month, gaining higher status and greater respect. And in these cultures women do not report discomfort from the menopause. Perhaps, the feminists suggest, if aging was not considered so shameful for a woman, and if menopause was not a symbol for aging, there would be less demand for treating a natural process with dangerous drugs.

Instead of embarrassed whispering about the menopause, the feminists say, women should talk more openly to each other about the experience. A Seattle group, Women in Midstream, found that a majority of women they questioned were eager to talk with others. A sociologist, Pauline Bart, and a therapist, Marlyn Grossman, report that after one woman participated in a menopause consciousness-raising group, she perceived her hot flushes as almost pleasant sensations. Dr. Bart, who teaches at the University of Illinois, also wonders why there are no rites of passage for the menopause, as there are for a child's entrance into puberty: "There is no bar mitzvah for menopause."

Well, why not? Perhaps there should be a party for two—a woman and her mate—in which the occasion is celebrated with a ritual disposal of the tools of contraception, the diaphragm, the condom, foam. And this could be followed by tender lovemaking to reassure the woman that although she can no longer bear babies, her status as a loving sexual human being remains intact.

An Embarrassment of Urine

It starts before menopause, is exacerbated by the atrophy of genital organs that follows menopause; eventually it may require surgical repair. The symptoms are burning, itching, irritation, pain on urination, a feeling of urgency, and sometimes the involuntary release of a few drops of urine (or even a puddle) when one suddenly coughs, sneezes, laughs or exercises. Many women complain about these persistent and unpleasant problems of urinary function.

Rosa, fifty-six, has a chronic low-grade infection. "I have to urinate constantly, and there's often a burning sensation. I'm a bird-watcher, which means spending long hours waiting in the brush, and it really interferes with my hobby."

Eve, forty-seven, a kindergarten teacher, often feels a need to urinate. "In my class it's the teacher who runs all the time, not the kids."

Sarah, forty-five, suffers from stress incontinence. "In my thirties I used an IUD which gave me an endless series of bladder infections. Now my bladder is inefficient, overextended, and has started to prolapse [fall into the vagina]. I can't run, jump, play tennis without leaking. Jogging is out. It bothers me. I find it awkward, embarrassing, shaming."

The urinary problems of middle age have multiple causes, often related to the peculiarities of female anatomy, and to the effects of childbirth and menopause.

First, there's the urethra itself, the canal that carries urine from the bladder to outside; in a woman, it is only one and a half inches long and terminates in the urinary opening, close to the vaginal orifice, where it is subject to irritation from sexual intercourse, and infection from bacteria introduced into the vagina.

Men have a more practical arrangement: an eight-inch-long urethra that is protected by its position inside the penis.

Then there's the strain of childbearing, which can stretch muscles, loosen ligaments, weaken fibrous tissues that support the pelvic structure. Anne, for example, developed stress incontinence in her late thirties after delivering three babies, each weighing close to nine pounds. Infections that move from vagina to urethra may quicken around the time of menopause when the reduction of estrogen alters the pH of normal vaginal secretion, from acid, hostile to bacterial growth, to alkaline, an environment friendly to it.

Changes in the shape and texture of the vagina after menopause make it more sensitive to trauma from the impact of a thrusting penis. Brides sometimes develop a condition called *honeymoon cystitis*, a bladder inflammation related to the increased frequency of intercourse in early marriage. Some menopausal women get a similar condition, not because their sex life quickens, but because of the thinner, more sensitive tissues around the vagina. Remember to urinate directly after having sex. It may help.

Pelvic relaxation is the medical term for the displacement of the organs in the pelvic area, caused by frequent or traumatic childbirth years earlier, combined with weakening of the support structure and the uterine atrophy that follows menopause. There may be *uterine prolapse*, in which the shrunken uterus bulges into the vagina; *cystocele*, in which the prolapsed organ is the bladder; and *rectocele*, a herniation of the rectum.

Surgery is *not* always necessary. Some doctors prescribe estrogen or estrogen vaginal cream to restore the tissues. When cystocele or stress incontinence are mild, most recommend a do-it-yourself treatment called the Kegel exercise. The purpose of the exercise is to restore elasticity and tone to the muscles surrounding the vagina that help hold the pelvic structures in place. You will recognize these muscles if, as you urinate, you consciously try to stop the flow. The exercise itself consists simply of rhythmically contracting the muscles (as you might do to stop urinating), and then relaxing them, and repeating the procedure a dozen times or so on several different occasions during the day: when you're waiting in line at the supermarket or the subway, driving the car, at your office desk, for example. There is also a wonderful bonus: women find that if they use the Kegel exercise during intercourse, it will help initiate and later enhance the sensations of orgasm. And when you expect to have sex, try the exercise a few times in advance for a delightful anticipatory glow.

There are also ways to protect oneself from the urinary infections to which some women are prone in the menopausal years. Drink a lot of water, eight glasses daily or more. Try cranberry juice, a fruit drink which increases the acidity of the urinary tract. Wear panties with a cotton crotch; cotton allows the air to circulate. Because a full bladder is more easily irritated, a woman should urinate before having sex, and again right afterward, to wash out bacteria that may have been deposited from the penis.

If the Kegel exercise doesn't prevent prolapse, some doctors advise the use of a vaginal pessary, a doughnut-shaped rubber or plastic insert, larger than a diaphragm, which mechanically holds back the tissue from bulging into the vagina. If other methods fail, reparative surgery is usually advised. It involves a hysterectomy and shortening and repair of the sagging structures. Although ingenious techniques abound, surgery is not always permanently successful in treating stress incontinence or cystocele.

VI
Sex

Sexually, these are the golden years. Breasts may droop, chins double, skin flake, but a woman's body is more vibrant, responsive to caress, swifter to climax than when she was twenty. Although a male's sexual drive peaks in the late teens, a female is likely to discover her true sexual potential only in the late thirties and early forties, and then to maintain a peak of desire and fulfillment well into her sixties. For men, "the urgency is lost somewhere around middle age. For women the reverse is true," say Dr. Helen Singer Kaplan.

Experts speculate that the change is in a woman's head, not in her sex organs. "I'm my own person now," one woman says. "And the equality I feel includes equality in bed." Another describes herself as less inhibited. "I'm no longer tongue-tied. I can tell my husband what makes me feel good. We've learned to have more consideration for each other. Our techniques are better, and we know each other's bodies now, where to touch and to rub and to kiss."

Rebecca is forty, a former ballet dancer turned dancing teacher. A decade ago she and her husband were struggling with serious sexual problems, partly due to his fears of her career ambitions. For a time they even stopped having sex at all. Later the children were starting their teens. "My husband didn't feel comfortable having sex when they were awake, and often we couldn't outstay them. I think it was a vacation at Cape Cod, our first alone, that marked the change. We weren't tired, and our bodies were brown, and it seemed natural to be naked, to have sex day and night when it pleased us, to try new positions and new techniques. I used to worry because we didn't find time for sex more than once a week, but now, if the kids are gone, it could happen all day."

Only recently have women begun to realize that they remain sexual beings throughout life, and that lovemaking, no matter what the age, affirms the beauty of the body and its ability to provide pleasure, that it reinforces a sense of self, creates the intimacy that is the deepest communication of love. One older woman has described sex as "the ultimate closeness against the night."

But many miss out on the golden years. Never sexually awakened, some women think it's too late to start. Locked into sexual routine, others don't know how to break out. When the house is empty and they can have sex in the morning, the old Saturday-night habit remains too strong. Too rigid to seek new ways of pleasuring, they become bored with their own body and their partner's. Routine, unimaginative, sexual activity slowly dwindles away, almost before its loss is noticed.

A study of men and women, aged forty-six to seventy, made in the early 1970's at Duke University, seems to show at first glance that women lag in sexual interest and activity at every age. The research indicated that they lose sexual drive younger, have intercourse less often, and stop having sex altogether at an earlier age than the men. Among those fifty and younger, fourteen percent of the women (but none of the men) no longer had sex relations. Between fifty-one and fifty-five, the figure for women rose to twenty percent, and by sixty, it was forty-two percent. (An earlier Duke study reported that the average woman stopped sex relations at sixty, while men continued up to sixty-eight.)

Although these figures appear to bear out a traditional viewpoint that males enjoy sex and females only tolerate it, Dr. Eric Pfeiffer, the Duke psychiatrist who led the study, sharply disagrees. The dramatic difference in sexual behavior, he points out, is not due to loss of desire but largely to loss of opportunity. All but two percent of the men in the study were married, but among the women, one in four was either widowed, divorced or separated. Women more than men, Dr. Pfeiffer says, need a socially sanctioned sex partner in order to maintain sexual activity.

Asked why they had stopped having sex, more than one woman

in three said her husband had died; another twenty percent said the husband was too ill; eighteen percent explained that he had become impotent. "In a marriage it is generally the man who determines whether sexual relations continue or cease," Dr. Pfeiffer says. And when sexual relations stop, "the men blame themselves and the women blame their husbands."

The lesson for women approaching and entering middle age is of vital importance. For you, the time is *now*. Now or never you must shed the inhibitions, cast off the prohibitions against what is "nice" and what is "proper," and learn to use hands, body, lips as if they have just been discovered. Now is the time to experiment with what is pleasurable, and to ask your partner to help you. Not only is the reward immediate and joyful, but it is likely to be lifelong. You can enjoy sex into your eighties *unless* you allow your pleasure centers to atrophy through disuse. Use it or lose it is the name of the game.

For a woman confident of her own sexuality, the most important impediment—if one should develop—is likely to come from her husband. For when it comes to sex, the aging male is by far the weaker partner. Although the late middle years bring changes in the sexual capacities of both, they are far more significant in a man, and this situation is augmented by a lag in age averaging four years between husband and wife. A woman must be sensitive to these changes and learn simple techniques to counter them if she hopes to continue mutual sexual enjoyment into old age. But too few husbands and wives are aware of what to expect, and the family doctors they consult are seldom much wiser. In fact, physicians appear more likely than most to believe that fun in bed is the privilege of youth. When one woman of fifty asked her gynecologist for help with a sexual problem, he answered, "What do you two expect at your age?"

The number of men who are sexually impotent rises steadily with age, but there is absolutely no reason why it should. The problem arises from a confusion between impotence—the inability to get or maintain an erection—and the slower arousal time that is a normal accompaniment of male aging. In the teens the male penis engorges in seconds following the slightest sexual stimulus, perhaps only a glimpse of bare breast or buttock. But as the years pass, it takes minutes, and direct stimulation of the penis is often needed. "The erection may not be as large, straight and hard," write Dr. Robert Butler and Myrna Lewis in their book,

Sex After Sixty, "but it will usually be sturdy and reliable." That is, unless a man panics about his "waning" powers and suffers an incidence of impotence. (This is usually called secondary impotence to indicate later impairment in a man who was once normally potent.) For many men, fear snowballs following one or two impotence episodes, and so does the impotence, until humiliating failure becomes the norm, and a couple's sex life disappears. "The fallacy that secondary impotence is to be expected as the male ages is probably more fully entrenched in our culture than any other misapprehension," Dr. William Masters and Virginia Johnson write in their landmark book, *Human Sexual Response*. "*Secondary impotence is in no sense the inevitable result of the aging process.*"

In many such cases, although a husband's fear triggers the impotence, his wife suspects it's her fault and compounds it. For she half-believes society's myth that only a sex kitten is physically attractive to men, and finds her husband's avoidance of her in bed proof positive. "He used to get an erection just watching me undress," observes one wife. "Now I have to keep touching him to make it happen." And then comes the unspoken corollary: "He doesn't find my body sexy any more."

"This is a period when both partners can be terribly vulnerable," writes Dr. Helen Singer Kaplan in *The Menopause Book*. "It may be a difficult adjustment for a woman who has been accustomed to take the passive role in lovemaking and has relied on her mere physical presence as a stimulus for her partner. Now, when a man needs more direct tactile stimulation, it is important to realize that it is not because the woman is no longer attractive . . . but rather because the man is no longer an adolescent."

By a man's fifties, there are other changes that trigger a couple's concern. A young husband could reach climax and minutes later want to make love again; now hours, even a day, may pass before he is ready. And during lengthy love play, he may lose an erection and be unable to regain it. Although desiring intercourse, he may occasionally be satisfied without attaining climax. "Men in their late forties or older tell me that sex during the week just wipes them out," says a divorcee. "They're only ready over a weekend." But if a wife doesn't understand this, she may suspect that her husband is finding his orgasms in another woman's bed. (Sometimes, of course, she is right.)

Stress, fatigue and depression can lower sex drive profoundly in both men and women, but middle-aged men appear to be more adversely affected by the drugs they take or the illnesses they develop at this time. If you and your husband are looking forward to an evening of sex, *don't* precede it with a few drinks and a rich dinner topped off with a brandy or two. For as you slip into your slinky nightgown, your husband is likely to roll over and start to snore. Tolerance for alcohol diminishes with age, and the double martinis that were once an aphrodisiac are now more likely to work like saltpeter on a man. Shakespeare said that alcohol provokes the desire but takes away the performance, and it is an apt description of its effect on a middle-aged man.

Like alcohol, sedatives such as phenobarbital are depressants, likely to lower libido. But the mood-altering drugs—tranquilizers and antidepressants—may successfully blot out anxiety over performance for both men and women, and thus improve sex. Heavy doses of tranquilizers, however, can kill desire. Watch out particularly for the effect of medication prescribed for high blood pressure. Several of these drugs may cause impotence or ejaculation problems in a man; their effect on women is less clear. This is something to discuss with the doctor, who can usually juggle the drug regime to eliminate the problem.

Although many more women than men develop diabetes in the middle years, the disease affects his sexual ability much more profoundly than it does hers. In fact, erection difficulty is often the first tip-off to the development of diabetes in a male. Some evidence suggests that diabetes may also inhibit sexual arousal in a female, but it is inconclusive. (Research on female sexuality remains meager. Doctors explain that it is easier to document changes in male arousal since his sex organs are outside and visible. But it is also true that most researchers are male, more interested in the problems of their own sex.)

When a woman reports that marital sex has ended because of her husband's illness, the two most frequent reasons given are heart disease and prostate surgery. With better understanding and communication with his physician, neither excuse is necessary. Every man over forty risks a heart attack. And when one occurs, husband and wife may shun each other in bed, fearing that the physical exertion of sexual intercourse will cause a second coronary. I know a couple in their sixties who have not had sex for about fifteen years. He was forty-seven, she two years younger, when he had the first heart attack. After his recovery they tried only once to make love, but fear made him impotent, and by un-spoken agreement, they never tried again. They are friendly, but the lack of physical intimacy is obvious. They kiss perfunctorily; their hands never brush across the other's body; they appear physically dried up.

It is a pity, and it is unnecessary. Research studies show that sex and orgasm are usually only moderately exerting, about on a par with taking a brisk walk or climbing a flight or two of stairs. During intercourse, a man's heart rate climbs briefly, but only to about 117 beats per minute. And exercise training (see p. 112), prescribed for many cardiac patients, lowers the rate even fur-ther. The exertion of sex is no greater no matter what positions a couple assumes.

Many men believe that if they require prostate surgery, per-manent impotence will follow. This is not so. About one in every two men past the age of fifty experiences symptoms from an en-largement of the prostate, a walnut-size gland below the blad-der. Having a regular sex life is likely to reduce the chance for severe prostate overgrowth, but if the prostate becomes so en-larged that it interferes with urination or causes infection, sur-gery is usually advised. Despite the conventional wisdom, sta-tistics show that with any one of three surgical techniques (transurethral resection, retropubic or suprapubic procedures), a man has only once chance in ten of developing impotence. Only the radical operation performed for prostate cancer results in im-potence for a majority of patients.

If impotence should occur, the trouble is usually not with the knife but the head—the man's, his wife's and the doctor's. Many doctors still think that it is unimportant to preserve sexual func-tion in a man past sixty. For all three, impotence may become a self-fulfilling prophecy. But if the couple is reassured by the sur-geon *before* the operation, and if the wife shows her confidence in his continued potency, then many more years of sexual pleas-ure may lie ahead.

Although physical changes occur in a woman's sex organs after the menopause, they are no insuperable barrier to her sexual en-joyment into old age. By late middle age many men are unable to achieve a second orgasm within a day, but a woman may con-tinue to have multiple orgasms until she is ninety. "Women may not always have the desire," says Dr. Helen Singer Kaplan, "but they have the ability."

In a young woman, vaginal lubrication occurs within seconds of sexual arousal, but after the menopause it may take minutes —perhaps as many as five—of sex play or direct stimulation before she becomes moist enough for comfortable penetration. This change is parallel to the slowing of an erection in a man.

Within a decade after the menopause, loss of estrogen alters the vagina, making its walls thinner, less elastic, more sensitive to irritation from a thrusting penis. The best treatment for this development is not medication, but sex. Regular intercourse once or twice a week helps preserve the size and shape of the vaginal space, and slow the deterioration in lubricating ability. There is even some evidence that regular sex may stimulate production of estrogen. For a woman without a sex partner, masturbation is a substitute that helps preserve the muscle tone and lubricating ability of the vagina.

Usually only after she has reached her sixties may a woman notice some mild changes in orgasm. It may be shorter with fewer contractions, but no less pleasurable. Occasionally it may produce a brief, painful spasm within the uterus. In some cases a woman's clitoris may shrink in size, but not in sensitivity.

Menopause is no physical barrier to sex enjoyment, but for some women it remains an emotional barrier. If she equates sexuality with fertility, she may unconsciously think that it's not quite nice to have fun in bed when the possibility of making a baby is nil. And the myth still persists that sexual desire plummets with the loss of estrogen. Natalie, forty, confessed her confusion on this point. "Some women tell me that after the menopause it's Old Ladiesville all the way. You become less feminine and you don't care about having sex. Maybe that's an old wives' tale. I hope so, because we're still just as active as ever."

It *is* an old wives' tale. In fact, the opposite may even be true. Estrogen is not a hormonal aphrodisiac, but androgen, the male sex hormone which women secrete in small quantities, is. Many women enjoy sex the most just before or during the menstrual period when production of female hormones is at a low ebb. Some sex therapists hold that the same phenomenon occurs at the menopause, when the teeter-totter balance between estrogen and androgen production changes, with a woman producing the same amount of androgen but far less estrogen.

For many women sexual pleasure increases as she approaches and enters menopause. For one thing, she need no longer fear an unwanted pregnancy. For another, she and her husband are no longer inhibited by the nearby presence of their teen-age youngsters. And for a third, the physical changes occurring in her partner make mutual enjoyment easier. "When we were first married," says one wife, "he was too much for me. He wanted sex every night, and frankly, I didn't. But now he's slowed down a little and I've speeded up a bit, and we're just a much better match for each other." Another husband peaked too rapidly, leaving his wife unsatisfied. But now with his slower arousal, he is able to delay his own ejaculation until she too reaches sexual climax.

It sounds idyllic, but it doesn't always work that way. Entering middle age does not automatically confer on a woman the sexual joys she may have missed during the first twenty years of her marriage. Most women now in middle age grew up before the sexual revolution proclaimed that the female too has a libido that needs to be satisfied. Some are still orgasmic innocents, others too inhibited to try techniques like oral sex, once condemned as perverse and now accepted as perfectly normal. A woman may enjoy sex until her nineties *if* she wants to. But a substantial minority simply doesn't care enough to work at it. A few years ago Marjorie Fiske Lowenthal and Dr. David Chiriboga of the University of California Medical School at San Francisco made an intensive study of fifty-four men and women whose youngest child was about to leave home (the average age of the women was forty-eight, and of their husbands, fifty-one). One woman told the interviewers that she and her husband no longer had sex relations. "I'm happy about it. I am not a sexy person and I never have been."

Others are aware of what they have missed and wish wistfully to change before it is too late. Masters and Johnson wrote in 1970: "It appears that women in the middle years . . . are more responsive and more orgasmic than younger women, but find it increasingly difficult to find adequate satisfaction in marital intercourse."

Where does the trouble come from? A statement by Dr. William Goode, a Stanford University sociologist, is worth repeating: *"The most important sex organ is the human mind."* These are some of the myths and half-truths in a woman's mind that may interfere with her sexual satisfaction:

The myth of the vaginal orgasm. Sigmund Freud claimed that an orgasm produced by stimulation of the clitoris was "immature" compared to one resulting from vaginal stimulation during intercourse. Sex therapists believe that this is bunk.

The clitoris is a small mound of tissue in front of the vagina, half-concealed by the vulva, that is exquisitely sensitive to touch. The vagina is sensitive only near its entrance. Although together they may produce the sensations leading to orgasm, it is the clitoris that is the crucial organ. Surveys have shown that one-third to two-thirds of all women need direct stimulation of the clitoris to achieve climax. Intercourse alone is seldom enough; most require the use of finger, tongue or vibrator to reach orgasm.

But some women, and many of their husbands, do not even know where the clitoris is. As part of her emerging autonomy during the middle years, a woman should explore her own body to discover those places that give the most joy, and then communicate this knowledge to her sex partner. A responsive woman can reach climax within eight minutes during coitus, but it takes her only two minutes with masturbation. The difference, says Dr. Harold Lief, psychiatrist and sex counselor at the University of Pennsylvania, is psychological, not physiological. Alone, she has no anxiety about her husband's satisfaction, and can learn how best to achieve pleasure for herself. Sex therapists advise a woman to masturbate in order to explore her own path to orgasm. If you're still hung up from your own mother's warnings about masturbation, you should realize that it's far from uncommon among women. Masters and Johnson report an increased rate among those past fifty, and another survey indicates that one in four women continues to masturbate after her seventieth birthday.

When the muscles supporting the vagina have been damaged by childbirth or have atrophied through disuse, orgasm may be weak or nonexistent. Sex therapists now advise women who have difficulty achieving climax to practice exercising these muscles to improve tone and heighten sensation. Practice the Kegel exercise (see p. 90)—tightening, then letting the vaginal muscles go lax—several times a day for about a hundred contractions in all. Try consciously to contract the muscles when you are close to orgasm; many women find they do this without thinking about it. (After bearing several children, some women worry that their vaginas are too stretched to provide much friction to the male penis. Although this is rarely true, if the Kegel exercise is performed during intercourse, it also heightens sensation for the partner.)

The myth of the mandatory orgasm. Many couples believe that to be successful, sex means intercourse, and intercourse means the achievement of orgasm. And middle-aged husbands in particular, trying to catch up with the sexual revolution, doggedly pursue a wife's orgasm as if it were a required masculine duty. In *Worlds of Pain*, a study of working-class couples, Dr. Lillian Breslow Rubin, a San Francisco sociologist, quotes the complaint of a thirty-five-year-old wife: "It's not enough if I just let him have [sex] because if I don't have a climax, he's not happy. I get so tired of everybody wanting something from me all the time. I sometimes think I hate sex."

Orgasm need not be a required goal for every sexual encounter. Wives have always known this, and now husbands, with their previously urgent need for ejaculation on the wane, are learning it too. "We used to rise at seven, but now we set the alarm for six-thirty to allow us plenty of time for snuggling," a woman of forty-two with a husband twenty years older told me. "Sometimes it leads to sex and orgasm for one or both of us, but if it doesn't, neither of us cares."

Freed of the children's constraining presence, now is the time for couples to throw out the sexual rule book, to have sex in the morning if they're too tired at night, to shower together and stretch out in the nude, to touch and caress without any preconceived notion of what will happen next. Sex is for fun, and other paths to pleasure beside intercourse should be investigated—fingers to touch, hands to caress, tongues to explore, a vibrator, an erotic book or picture, sexual fantasy.

The myth of sexual service. In *Worlds of Pain*, Dr. Rubin describes the sense of duty that many working-class women bring to sex. "I don't use excuses like headaches," one wife said. "If my husband wants me, I'm his wife and . . . it's my responsibility to give it to him when he needs it."

According to Dr. Helen Kaplan, a middle-class woman, sophisticated enough to seek sex therapy, does not think very differently. "When I see his erection, I feel I must take care of it at once," one patient told Dr. Kaplan. And another, slowly becoming aroused herself, thought, "That's enough. He must be getting tired. We should go ahead now and finish it off."

Taught from childhood that sexual pleasure is a man's due, many women still find it impossible to ask or take for themselves. But to reach climax she must concentrate on her own body instead of being preoccupied with his. In middle age, often for the first time, many women learn that selfishness is not a dirty word, but a major factor in the increased sexual joy that follows.

The myth of the passive wife. The male initiates sex. The female responds. Even a group of college students, questioned recently, admitted to holding this viewpoint. They—and their mothers—cannot shake the belief that the male ego will be dangerously bruised if the female attempts to take the initiative. Female aggressiveness is widely described as the villain behind the current rise in male impotence. Many sex therapists believe this is nonsense. "More impotence is relieved by sexual openness," says Dr. Kaplan, "than is caused by it."

Talking honestly about their needs and fears is one of the best antidotes to the sexual boredom that strikes many couples at middle age. For many women boredom masks timidity, which in turn masks anxiety. Sex therapists call the phenomenon "performance anxiety" and "spectatoring." When a woman is going through the motions of love play, says Dr. Harold Lief, she has churning inner thoughts: "Will I have an orgasm? Will I take too long? Won't he become impatient?" And then a mounting pressure to perform: "I *must* come this time. I *can't* fail him again." Meanwhile her husband, tense over the agonizing slowness of his own erection, is silently suffering his own performance anxiety. No wonder their sexual encounter turns out perfunctory and dull. But if each admits to anxiety, talks about it openly to the other, then it shrinks in size, and though the problem may not be instantly cured, it is likely to be ameliorated.

Because of performance anxiety, some women even shrink at the touch of a husband's hand, recognizing it as a kind of sexual sign language. "My first husband never touched me unless he wanted to have intercourse," a divorcee, recently remarried, told me. "But John and I touch all the time. We know it means tenderness, not a call for sexual action." Honest communication can lead to understanding that tenderness has its own values, and that love between long-married persons does not rise or fall on whether a single orgasm is won or lost, or even attempted.

Even after twenty years together, it is difficult for many couples to talk openly about sex, but the problem is compounded for the divorced or widowed. "It still doesn't come easily for me to tell a man what I need," says an interior designer, divorced for fourteen years. "It's hard for a woman to have good sex in a new relationship. I just can't start off hot."

Often the problem is worsened by a lack of certainty about one's continued attractiveness in a society that accepts a John Wayne but not a Bette Davis as a sex object. Susan Sontag writes: "The time at which [women] start being disqualified as sexually attractive persons is just when they have grown up sexually. The double standard about aging cheats women of those years, between thirty-five and fifty, likely to be the best of their sexual life."

Yet some men, with their own performance uncertainties, welcome the unique qualities of an older woman—warmth, experience, compassion. A friend of mine, fifty-two and twice widowed, says, "The men I know want an evening of lovemaking that will include gestures of affection without the demand to perform like a seventeen-year-old. And with a mature woman they end up performing far better than they ever expected."

Other newly divorced women, though, relish the new freedom to be themselves, and that may include a free and adventurous sex life. One recently divorced woman said, "I know I'll probably settle in at some point, but for now, I'm loving being popular with men, a sort of forty-five-year-old prom queen. It's exciting and flattering, and since I'm careful not to have sex with any men I don't truly care about, it's also rewarding on a deeply emotional level. It's as if I have a lot of beloved friends, some of whom are lovers."

Yet for many divorcees and widows the thought of starting a new sex life contains an element of cultural shock. "We enter the dating world with a set of standards left over from 1950 on how to deal with sex," a divorced sociologist in her late forties told me. "For us the new freedom is accompanied by the old anxiety." Many find the casual sexual encounter bruising to a sense of self-worth. In Baltimore I met an unusually attractive woman, with vivid coloring and curly white hair, who had been abruptly abandoned a year ago by a husband of twenty-five years. "It's still difficult for me to think of uncommitted sex," she said. "If it's caring and sharing it's fine, but sex alone doesn't do anything for you. You can get up in the morning and not like yourself."

Sex therapists believe that the newly single woman shouldn't automatically veto her unique opportunity to be adventuresome.

But New York psychiatrist Natalie Shainess warns, "If you can enjoy the encounter for what it is worth . . . then go ahead. But if you believe that sex is . . . meaningless unless it occurs within the context of a committed relationship, you must weigh the emotional consequences to your own sense of self-esteem."

Some years ago an older friend who had enjoyed sex and orgasm in her younger years told me that although she and her husband were still healthy when they hit the sixties, their sex life had ended. "I'm not sorry," she said. "I think it's a vastly overrated activity." I've thought of this comment occasionally and wondered whether I would agree when I reached her age. Well, here I am, and I am certain that she is wrong.

An aging marriage has its special problems. Husband and wife tire more easily, flare into irritability more often, become self-centered, perhaps a bit depressed over the backaches and the arthritic fingers that forecast physical decline. Often sex is less frequent, the goodnight kiss more perfunctory, and the affectionate touch or caress half-forgotten.

But occasionally sex is glorious for both, and when this happens, it is far more glorious than in the days when mutual joy came so easily. It renews life and reaffirms the body's ability to come wildly alive. It reinforces intimacy, sets one to touching and nuzzling all over again. It is self-assertion and a surge of confidence that one can still give and receive the great gift that man and woman hold for each other. If there were ever a fountain of youth, this is it.

Dr. Leon Zussman, a New York sex counselor, offers this reminder: "The wish for touching, caressing and sexual contact exists until we die." It is important to bear in mind, especially for those who in the middle years may be inadvertently drifting into a sex life that is routine and perfunctory. For by your inaction, you may be allowing to dry up by default, and perhaps for always, the physical expression of love through which women and men communicate.

Venereal Disease

It is almost impossible for you to get a venereal disease if you have sexual relations with only one partner and both of you remain faithful to the other. But if you *or* your husband has an affair, if you are divorced or widowed, and have a nonmonogamous relationship, then you risk developing gonorrhea or syphilis.

In these days of easier sex mores, it is no longer true (if it ever was) that "nice" women don't catch VD. Constance, who at fifty-six has been divorced for fourteen years, takes the hazard seriously. She describes herself as quite conventional, not promiscuous, but she does have sex occasionally, and when she does, she worries. "Men don't want to wear condoms any more," she says, "so you can't gain protection that way. If I have a date with a man, and he tells me he's been to a party where everyone has intercourse with everyone else, I'm particularly wary. At every visit to a gynecologist I ask him to check me for syphilis and gonorrhea too."

And when I asked Paula, who is forty-four, with a husband and three young children, about being unfaithful, her answer was only half-joking: "The idea intrigues me, but not the reality. It would be just my luck to pick a lawyer with the clap, and how would I ever explain *that!*"

Gonorrhea, almost thirty times as prevalent as syphilis, is now the most frequent communicable disease in the United States, except for the common cold. Its incidence appears to be increasing among women. When the Public Health Service made random screening tests in 1977 among symptomless women in the offices of private physicians, in cancer detection clinics and family planning centers, one in twenty turned up positive. Most VD occurs in young women, who have more sex partners, but only the celibate avoid playing, at some time or other, the game of venereal roulette. A woman is estimated to have about a forty to fifty percent chance of catching gonorrhea following a single exposure to it if no precautions are taken. If she is on the Pill, the likelihood of infection *doubles;* it makes the vaginal environment more receptive to the gonococcus.

In fact, the Pill and other modern contraceptive methods are considered responsible in part for the recent surge in gonorrhea. Men have stopped wearing condoms to protect their partners from pregnancy, and foreclosed the condom's other role—prevention of VD infection.

What a woman really wants to know about VD is how to avoid getting it in the first place. In a brilliant two-part article that appeared in 1973 in the magazine *Viva,* science writer Edward Brecher gives practical advice on just this point. His thesis is that most doctors and health agencies try to act as moral policemen over a woman's sex life. Although they will prescribe antibiotics to cure venereal disease, they won't tell a woman how to prevent it. This makes her far more vulnerable to VD than a man; early symptoms usually send him running to the doctor's office for treatment, but in four out of five women there are no early symptoms, or they are so slight as to go unnoticed.

These are some of Brecher's suggestions for avoiding VD:

Use one of the contraceptive creams, jellies or foams sold over the drugstore counter to prevent pregnancy. Many of the jellies smeared on the rim of a diaphragm fall in this category. Brecher says, "The chemicals used in some (not all) of these products simultaneously kill the spirochetes that cause syphilis and the gonococci which cause gonorrhea."

Urinate directly after having intercourse, then wash your genitals well with soap and water.

Persuade your partner to wear a condom throughout intercourse, not merely just before ejaculation.

Take a lesson from an intelligent prostitute: before a customer's penis enters her vagina, she carefully examines it, then washes it thoroughly in soapy water. It's a bit more subtle if you suggest that you and your partner take a bath together. (A yellowish, pus-like discharge from the penis is the tip-off to early gonorrhea in a male. A small sore called a chancre on the penis or the lip may signal syphilis.)

If you have reason to suspect exposure, ask your doctor or a clinic promptly for a "morning after" VD pill—a penicillin or tetracycline tablet strong enough to ward off infection, if it is taken within eight hours of contact.

If a woman develops symptoms of gonorrhea at all, they are likely to appear in three days to three weeks following exposure, and to include one or more of the following: frequent painful urination, a burning sensation in the genital area, vaginal discharge. After the menopause, vaginal and vulvar swelling and pain are more likely. If these symptoms are missed or don't appear, the infection may travel upward to the uterus, tubes and abdominal cavity, causing serious problems such as sterility, urinary tract damage, or arthritis. To diagnose gonorrhea, a physician must make a culture of infected material, a procedure that takes up to two days. The disease is cured by penicillin or tetracycline.

Early syphilis is also hard to spot in a woman, although men easily recognize the first symptom, the small sore at the point of contact. This appears two to three weeks after exposure on a man's penis or his lip, but in a woman it is hidden inside the vulva or vagina, and because it is seldom painful, is easily missed before it heals. Syphilis is diagnosed by a blood test and cured by penicillin. Untreated, it is a dangerous disease, causing a skin rash that does not itch, sore throat, low-grade fever, falling hair about two months after exposure. It continues to inflict silent damage to organs throughout the body, without showing further symptoms for another eight to ten years.

One last word of caution: Forget the old myth "I caught it from a toilet seat," but do be careful about being kissed on the mouth or body by a person who has a sore on the lip. It could be a cold sore, transmissible to genital areas by direct contact, causing genital herpes, a viral infection that is almost impossible to cure completely. And then, of course, it could be a syphilitic chancre.

VII

Keeping Physically Fit

Despite the exercise mania that grips Americans of all ages, the pragmatic question for many women still is—What's in it for me? And if she's in her middle years, relieved of the burden of chasing small children around, her flip answer is likely to be: Not very much. Joan, thirty-nine and plump, has recently deposited her youngest in school all day, and says, "I like to sit. It's wonderful to be alone in a quiet house—reading."

It may be wonderful for Joan today, but it won't be tomorrow. For if she wants her energy level to remain high, her body firm and flexible, she's missing the nearest thing around to an anti-aging pill. The time to start regular exercise is *now*. After the age of thirty-five joints begin to stiffen, bones weaken, muscles to become flabby and fat to sag. "Most people don't wear out. They rust out," write Dr. Robert Butler and Myrna Lewis. This development can be postponed for many years with the right kind of exercise performed in the right way in the right amounts.

Dr. Mary Catherine Tyson, an internist, writes: "We are designed to *need* exercise . . . [It] is of vital importance to women as a means of delaying or even preventing some aspects of aging of the body. It improves the circulation of the blood and the tone of all the muscles . . . An under-exercised older woman ages more rapidly. Her bones . . . become fragile . . . Her stature decreases . . . her flabby muscles cannot maintain good posture

. . . There is no reason why this should happen, for it is the inevitable consequence not of age but of inactivity."

Particularly among women, the forties are a danger zone for a letdown in physical activity. This is the time when the number who don't even exercise once a week jumps to over fifty percent, when two-thirds of the joggers and bicycle riders give up, as do half the swimmers. Although at least one out of three women continues to walk for exercise, the walking often slows to a stroll, only a sham for vigorous action.

Women exercise less than men, and Canadian studies show that they are less fit. Many don't even see why a female needs to be active. When two Canadian physical education professors wanted to test adults for physical fitness a few years ago, they telephoned a list of names they had picked at random from the telephone book. If a woman answered, she often declined to participate. "Why bother about me?" was a common reply. "But I sure wish you'd test my husband."

A sizable minority of women over thirty-five appear to have been stung by the exercise bug recently. Among those I interviewed, about a third were active in sports—tennis particularly, but also jogging, swimming, jumping rope, yoga, dance—and most had started within the year. Carol, forty-six, a second-grade teacher, says, "I've been pretty upset about the flab that's developing on my thighs, buttocks and arms. When my kids were little I didn't have time, but now with middle age creeping up, I know it's important to condition my body. I've started to play tennis three times a week, even though it means being on the court at 7:45 A.M." Paula, forty-two, another new tennis player, says, "I move well, and I want to keep on moving well in my fifties. I'm in better shape now than I used to be."

The reasons most give for initiating physical activity are to feel young and healthy ("It's not to fight aging, but to make where you are right now so much better"); to avoid the appearance of sagging flesh ("I don't dig an old person's body with the skin hanging loose"); to help an aching back ("When I exercise, the kinks seem to smooth out"); and just to have fun.

But for two out of three, these reasons don't seem compelling enough. To their persistent question—What's in it for me?—these significant answers were given at an international conference in Washington, D.C., convened in 1978 by the National Institute on Aging:

Adequate exercise may postpone a decline in aerobic capacity by as much as twenty years. Aerobic capacity is what you haven't got much of when you huff and puff to exhaustion in running to catch a bus or climbing a few flights of stairs. Technically, it is the ability of your heart to beat faster, lungs to expand, and blood vessels to swell in order to carry needed oxygen swiftly to the working cells of the body. Regular exercise challenges and works out these vital organs, increasing the ability to process oxygen by ten to fifteen percent; without it, they loss efficiency and start to atrophy from disuse as early as the age of twenty.

A change in body composition, in which lean body mass—muscle, bone and other tissues—is lost, and fat is gained, normally starts about the age of thirty. Regular exercise delays this change. Some researchers chalk up an additional benefit: they believe that a slowing in the rate of metabolism, long assumed to be the cause of middle-age weight gain, need not occur if the youthful relationship between lean body mass and fat remains stable.

Regular exercise teaches the body to perform more work at less cost to the heart. It may decrease the risk of heart attacks, and if they do occur, may lower the likelihood that they will be fatal. (Studies of Harvard alumni and California longshoremen were cited to prove a decrease in the number of coronary attacks, but some cardiologists remain skeptical. The American Heart Association says cautiously that it is "prudent" to exercise.)

Exercise is better than a tranquilizer for jangled nerves and depressed moods. The late Dr. Paul Dudley White called it "the best tranquilizer ever made."

Other research studies have shown that exercise can lower high blood pressure, protect bones from thinning, decrease fatigue, battle insomnia, curb constipation. "People who are in good physical condition even enjoy sex more," says Dr. Jesse Steinfeld, former Surgeon General of the U.S. Public Health Service. "If that isn't a motivating factor, I don't know what is."

Don't count on exercise alone, however, to drop off the excess pounds or make flab disappear from a favored target area. You can't lose weight without cutting down caloric intake, but when dieting is combined with more activity, the pounds will be shed faster. Dr. Lenore Zohman, who heads the Cardiopulmonary Rehabilitation program at Montefiore Medical Center in New York, says that in order to burn off the calories from a single martini, one would have to jog for fourteen minutes straight. She adds, however, that a woman who doesn't eat more than she formerly did, by a single calorie, *and* starts to bicycle an hour a day at the speed of eight miles an hour, is likely to lose about a pound every ten days. Those who scoff at exercise insist that it increases the appetite, but this has not been shown to be true.

One woman told me that she worked out with dumbbells to get rid of fat from her upper arms and to keep her breasts firm. Unfortunately, it's not really possible to set your dieting sights on a particular limb. A gym that advertises its machines will melt inches off your hips simply isn't telling the truth. According to Dr. James Hodgson of Pennsylvania State University, "Whatever mechanisms are involved in good weight-reducing, exercise seems to take weight off the whole body." And Dr. Willibald Nagler, physical medicine specialist at The New York Hospital, adds, "There is no evidence that exercises for a sagging breast do any good at all." This is apparently because breast firmness comes from supple, elastic tissue, not muscle. If sag is a problem, stand straight and tall. It helps.

Exercise, however, will change jiggly fat into firm muscle, and by doing so, develop a trimmer body. Traditionally, females have been discouraged from heavy exercise for fear they would turn feminine curves into masculine-looking, muscular bulges, but this isn't so either. What makes muscles bulge is testosterone, the male sex hormone. Even professional women athletes never develop the rippling musculature of the iron pumper.

Where most women go wrong is not in too strenuous exertion, but in a program that is too mild, too brief and too infrequent to do much good. According to a Stanford University study, only one woman in twenty maintains an adequate exercise level. I have a friend who devotes ten minutes of an occasional morning to jogging easily from room to room in her house. Another enjoys a weekly calisthenics group "because it doesn't work up a sweat." Others join bowling groups, in which they sit and chat ten minutes for every minute of exercise, use a cart when they golf, or practice isometric exercises without leaving the office desk.

Although these women aren't wasting their time, their activities will not retard the aging of heart and lungs, nor increase aerobic capacity. What is needed is activity that is rhythmic, repetitive, and involves motion of the entire body, that makes the heart beat faster, breathing quicken, and works up a sweat. This is called cardiovascular exercise, and includes brisk walking, jogging, skating, cross-country skiing, bicycling, swimming, jumping rope, performed at least three times weekly for about half an hour. Sports like tennis and badminton are not quite as useful because they alternate spurts of activity with waiting periods. Golf and downhill skiing require too little sustained exertion to make the heart pump hard. Water skiing is an isometric exercise that strengthens some muscle groups without exerting the entire body. Aerobic dancing, a new program that some Y's offer, is excellent; so are folk- and square-dancing; interpretive dancing is less effective.

In order for your exercise to have an aerobic effect, it must quicken the rate at which your heart beats, and sustain the accelerated level for about twenty minutes. The way to find out if this is happening is to count your pulse (it usually beats at the same rate as your heart does) during vigorous exercise. Walk a mile at a pace that makes you sweat a bit but is not uncomfortable. Then stop, and immediately feel for your pulse by resting two middle fingers on the radial artery of the wrist or the carotid artery in the neck, lying about an inch below the curve of the jawbone. Count the beats for fifteen seconds, then multiply by four. A resting pulse beats between sixty and eighty times a minute; during exercise, it should be pushed well above a hundred; how high depends on your age and physical condition.

Each of us has a point, and it varies from person to person, when we cannot push ourselves physically any further, when the heart won't beat any faster, or the lungs and blood vessels deliver more oxygen to the tissues. To condition the body but not overtax it, exercise should be sustained at seventy to eighty-five percent of that point. This is your individual target zone. Assuming you're in normal good health, there's a formula for figuring out your target zone that takes into account the heart's decreasing capacity with age for maximum exertion. Starting with the figure 220, subtract your age in years, and then multiply by seventy to eighty-five percent. If you're forty, the target zone for your exercise is 120 to 150 pulse beats per minute; if you're fifty, 115 to 140 beats. If your pulse beat doesn't get that high during exercise, you're not achieving a conditioning effect; if it soars higher, you're overdoing it.

Suppose, for example, you've just finished that brisk, mile-long walk, counted your pulse and found that you've reached but not exceeded your target zone. The walk took twenty minutes—a rate of three miles an hour—adequate for an exercise novice. But as you keep on walking three times weekly, you're soon likely to find that the three-mile-an-hour pace no longer nudges your pulse up high enough. It's time to try walking a mile and a half, and then to increase the pace to four miles an hour. If that's not sufficient stimulus, you might start jogging—a minute's walk, a minute's jog until you're comfortable with the faster pace. The point is that this exercise is dynamic. As you get in better condition, you can do more with less exertion to the heart. Even your resting pulse rate will decrease. One woman slowed hers down from eighty-two to fifty-seven beats a minute after several months of jogging.

Linda, thirty-five, a Connecticut housewife, told me of her dramatic change in aerobic capacity after she joined an aerobic dancing class. On the first day, the group exercised moderately for about ten minutes and then stopped to count their pulses. "Although I didn't feel particularly winded, mine had soared far too high—over two hundred beats a minute." She was told to stop and rest, and then to resume at a slower pace. There's nothing wrong with Linda's heart, but she was twenty pounds overweight and hadn't exerted herself physically in years. "I'm lazy," she says. "I sit on my behind a lot. I move only when there's a really good reason." But after several more sessions, Linda found that she could perform as vigorously as the others without raising her heart rate over a target zone of 130 to 160 beats per minute. In fact, no matter how frenzied the dance, her pulse rarely rose over 140 beats.

If you, like Linda, are starting to exercise for the first time in years, these are a few precautions to observe:

Vigorous exercise should neither start abruptly, as if you were out to win a hundred-yard dash, nor be stopped suddenly by lying down exhausted on the gym floor. First warm up with five to ten minutes of gradually increasing intensity, and after twenty minutes of vigorous exertion, slow your jog to a walk, your walk to a stroll, as you cool down. Cardiologists believe that snow-shovelers drop dead not because they have bad hearts, but because they're out of condition and begin at top speed to pile heavy loads of wet snow onto the shovel.

Wait until half an hour after a light meal, ninety minutes after a heavy dinner before engaging in vigorous activity. Watch the thermometer: swimming is the only sport to try when humidity is high and temperature soars into the nineties. Don't go in the steam room or sauna or even take a hot shower directly after exercising. It's better to wait fifteen minutes before having a tepid shower.

If you experience chest pain, abnormal heart rhythm or sudden dizziness during your exertion, it's wise to quit and to consult your doctor. Your heart rate should slow down to normal within fifteen minutes after you've finished exercising. If it doesn't, if you still feel fatigued hours later, or if you sleep poorly that night, you're probably overtaxing yourself, and should moderate the program.

Some physicians advise every person over thirty-five to have a stress test before embarking on an exercise program; others consider this to be exaggerated caution. A stress test is a way of monitoring in the doctor's office what happens to your heart and lungs and blood pressure during vigorous exercise. While you pedal a stationary bicycle or walk a motor-driven treadmill at an accelerating speed, your heart rate, electrocardiogram and blood pressure are being recorded. The results allow the physician to prescribe an individual program—cautioning a sixty-year-old overweight woman, for example, to keep her pulse rate at one hundred or lower.

Stress tests were designed for men, particularly for the one in ten who develops silent heart disease after thirty-five. Whether they are also necessary for healthy women is really not known. Although death from heart disease rises sharply among both sexes after thirty-five, males die of heart attacks during the next two decades more than four times as often as females do (see p. 129).

Moreover, a recent report suggests that stress tests designed for men give too many false positives when they are used for women; the results appear to show the women have heart disease when they don't. One reason for this, according to Dr. L. Thomas Sheffield, University of Alabama Medical School cardiologist, is that women start out with a lower exercise capacity than men. Adding to the confusion, Dr. Sheffield's recent study of women suggest that as women grow older, they don't lose their exercise capacity as quickly as men do. Thus, a stress test, if you get one, may be of doubtful accuracy. "In the past, cardiology research has neglected women somewhat," Dr. Sheffield admitted, in a classic understatement.

Nevertheless, if you are starting cardiovascular exercise after many years on the sidelines and are more than twenty pounds overweight, if you smoke heavily, have high blood pressure or diabetes, or if a close blood relative developed heart disease before the age of sixty, you should confer with your doctor about having a stress test first. For those in average health, cardiologist Dr. Marvin Moser suggests, "If you're in the forties, have no special risk factors, and want to start jogging, I'd advise only the precaution of an ordinary resting electrocardiogram."

Suppose you're convinced about exercise but are desperate to find the time. One solution is to weave some of your exertion into the day's routine. On your way to work, get off a few bus stops early and walk or jog the rest of the way. Climb the stairs to your office instead of taking the elevator. (Five minutes of climbing stairs uses as much energy as ten minutes of skiing.) At home you can become a mad housewife, dashing through the chores at double speed, like a movie run too fast. You'll expend twice as much energy by scrubbing the kitchen floor on hands and knees as by using a mop. Whisk the vacuum cleaner around like a maniac, sweep the floors at a jog, wash the windows—if you keep this up for twenty minutes or so, your heart will get adequate conditioning. For the winter months, keep a rowing machine or a stationary bicycle (preferably one with a tension wheel to regulate the work load) in the house, and give yourself a workout while you watch TV.

If you're pressed for time, skipping rope for ten minutes provides a conditioning effect equivalent to thirty minutes of jogging. Some women find rope-jumping too bouncy—"it makes me feel as if my insides are being pulverized," one says—but a gynecologist assured me that unless ligaments are already weakened by childbirth, it does no harm. A woman should wear a bra to keep her breasts from jiggling free when she jumps—and also when she jogs or plays tennis.

Natalie, an athletic forty, started jumping rope last fall when her tennis schedule slowed down for the winter. A bookkeeper, she says, "I jump rope when I expect to be sitting all day. Otherwise I'd be roaming the house like a tiger at two in the morning." Using a rope with a counter, she jumps before breakfast. "I start off slowly with twenty-five jumps, relax for a minute or two, then aim for about three hundred in all." She also jogs, plays singles on the town's tennis team (although she was a novice five years ago) and skis. "I have a lot of energy to burn, that's for sure," she says.

For every Natalie, there are probably two other women who couldn't care less about burning energy. "I tried a weekly exercise class a few years ago," says Marjorie, forty-nine, "and every time was agony. I never became one bit more supple. So I said to myself, What kind of a masochist are you? and I haven't budged since."

There are certain women for whom exercise will always be a form of masochism, but most just haven't hit on a kind they enjoy. "The most potent motivational force is the pleasure principle," says Dr. Zohman. She suggests that a woman look back to childhood for the activity that was most fun then. Some need the stimulus of a group; they should look into the programs at their local Y, where cardiovascular exercise is usually stressed. Loners may prefer an early-morning nature hike. My sister merely walks the dog before breakfast every day, but at a pace that leaves them both panting.

If a yoga or exercise class, or early-morning calisthenics to the radio has always been your bag, don't jump to the conclusion that you've been wasting your time. Yoga relaxes tension, keeps the joints limber and teaches proper breathing. Calisthenics strengthen back and abdominal muscles, warding off the back trouble to which you're becoming more susceptible with the years. These are not a substitute for the kind of exercise that conditions heart and lungs, but they are certainly an adjunct.

Some exercises should be avoided, however. One of these is the push-up, a muscle-strengthener for the professional athlete, but of little value and some potential harm to you. Sit-ups are basic to strengthening flabby stomach muscles, but you should perform them with the knees bent, not touching the floor, and the back curled forward, not rigidly straight. As muscle elasticity declines after the mid-thirties, stretching and bending exercises become even more important for the tennis player, jogger or skier.

The most important component, however, is enjoyment. Linda who used to deride unnecessary motion, has become totally involved with aerobic dancing. "I float around on a high for hours afterward," she says. "I've always been a person with two left feet, but when the music starts, I just can't sit still."

VIII
Health in the Middle Years

You're forty years old and feeling great. A decade ago when your children were small, you used to sneak a nap in the afternoon. That's impossible now with your nine-to-five job, and besides, you no longer get sleepy. You seem to have more energy than ever, and you seldom need to call the doctor. But forty is an important birthday, life's midpoint for a woman. Although you feel supervigorous, how do you keep on feeling that way?

Perhaps it's time to stop and think about what you want and expect from your body in the next twenty years. You want to extend the period of maximal physical energy; you want a mind as sharp as ever, and continued capacity for joy and intimacy. Good health is basic, but how to achieve it? Do cancer, heart disease, crippling arthritis lie around the corner? Should you start now to have checkups twice a year, more Pap smears, frequent visits to a cancer-detection clinic?

When I asked a distinguished physician what a woman should do to safeguard her health during life's second half, he thought a minute, then said, "Tell her to wear a seat belt." He wasn't really joking. What he was attempting to encapsulate was the essence of a new medical philosophy called behavioral medicine. It holds that your health is not in your doctor's hands, but in your own. The life style that you practice, not the medications that you take, is the essential determinant of your future well-being.

Three out of every four deaths in the United States are caused by circulatory disease—heart ailments and stroke—by cancer, and by accidents. Medicine has no cure for any of these, but perhaps you do. The other driver may be a nut, but if *you* drive carefully and buckle up the seat belt, you'll increase *your* chances of surviving a potentially fatal accident. What you eat, how you handle stress, whether you smoke, if you exercise or are sedentary—these choices in daily living may determine whether you avoid circulatory disease and cancer, or succumb to them prematurely.

If doctors found a cure for cancer tomorrow, it would only add about two years to the nation's life expectancy. But if we all avoided obesity, the increment would be four to five years. Smokers who don't kick the habit by the age of forty are twice as likely to die prematurely as nonsmokers. A stressful life style increases the likelihood of developing high blood pressure and ulcers, both now more prevalent among women than they have ever been.

But some people adopt a fatalistic attitude, pointing to their heredity as the potential kiss of death—"There's breast cancer in my family"; My mother died of diabetes." Heredity *is* important in assessing one's potential longevity. But once you recognize it, you can do something about it. You *are* at added risk if high blood cholesterol or rectal polyps are common in your family, if a close relative succumbed *early* to cancer or heart disease, or is chronically ill with arthritis or emphysema. But just being alert to the risk decreases it—avoiding overweight if your mother had high blood pressure or diabetes, doing breast self-examination faithfully if she or an aunt had breast cancer.

One woman told me of the awesome longevity that lay in her future. Both her parents survived almost to ninety, as did several aunts and uncles. "The lesson for me," she said, "is not so much *whether* I make it, but *how* I make it. For it's the quality of life I care about. I want to avoid chronic diseases like arthritis as well as the cancers and coronaries." This is as true for most of you as it is for her. Women are living longer than ever, and the gap between them and their men is widening. In 1900 a woman of forty-five could expect to live to seventy, only a year longer than a man the same age. Now she can look forward to six more years than he can. Her life expectancy is eighty, and his is short of seventy-four.

Dire predictions that the age differential will narrow as women assume men's tension-filled jobs have not become reality. But women are smoking more and drinking more, and results are already showing up in the incidence of lung cancer, emphysema, ulcers. Among women aged thirty-five to forty-five, more than one in three is now a cigarette-smoker—catching up rapidly with men of the same age. And in 1975 for the first time *more* lung cancer was reported among Connecticut women aged thirty-five to forty-five than for men the same age. The comment of one shocked statistician—"You've come a long way, baby!"

It's not necessary to belabor the bad news for those who smoke: they risk having lungs that age prematurely, a two to three times greater chance of dying from a heart attack, a twenty-four-fold increase in death from lung cancer, nineteen times the likelihood of developing emphysema, the chronic lung disease that makes breathing difficult and eventually kills. But if you quit right now, your odds for living longer and better will slowly improve. In fifteen years the odds will be almost the same as for someone who has never smoked.

Careful attention to nutrition and exercise do not produce such easily recognized changes, but it is now widely accepted that regular exercise improves the quality and probably also the length of one's life span. As for what you eat, practically everything has been damned, despite an unfortunate lack of hard facts. The latest speculation is that diet plays a role in the development of cancer, as well as affecting circulatory disorders. No ideal diet has been developed, but these points are accepted by most nutritionists: Don't eat more than you expend in energy; put an extra stress on foods low in fats; include plenty of fiber in daily meals.

A 1975 article in the *New England Journal of Medicine* had this to say about life style and health: "It is generally assumed that people would rather be well than sick . . . But many people really don't behave that way. It is a crime to commit suicide quickly. However, to kill oneself slowly by means of an unhealthy life style is readily condoned and even encouraged."

When to See the Doctor and Why

Preventive medicine is now in style, but it has a new twist. It is no longer medically fashionable to regard the body as a machine, with the physician as the mechanic to whom one brings in the engine for a checkup once a year or every ten thousand miles. Doctors are now being advised to assess the whole person, not a single clogged nut or bolt, and to help her understand the risks and benefits inherent in her life style, and thus make intelligent trade-offs.

Medical statisticians, finally taking a jaundiced look at that sacred cow of preventive medicine—the annual checkup—are coming up with some surprising answers. They are looking critically at the checkup's traditional components—urinalysis, Pap smear, blood-pressure reading, electrocardiogram, blood cholesterol—and assessing whether they are necessary, and how often, and for whom? If you've always insisted that you, your husband and children have a complete physical every year, innovative doctors will tell you that it's time for a change.

One physician, after studying the results of the annual physical in terms of prevention of sickness and death, described it as "virtually always an annual fiasco." Recently both the Mayo Clinic and the Kaiser-Permanente medical group stopped advising their patients to get one. Both groups now recommend that normally healthy people follow a schedule that includes three complete checkups during the decade of the thirties, four during the forties, five in the fifties and annual exams starting only in the sixties. The Lifetime Health Monitoring Program, developed by two doctors—Lester Breslow of UCLA and Anne Somers of Rutgers—suggests even fewer complete exams—every five years between thirty and sixty, but augmented for those aged forty to sixty by a few selected tests given at two-and-a-half-year intervals. After fifty, Drs. Breslow and Somers advise annual checks on overweight, high blood pressure and certain cancers.

A thorough physical should take about an hour, and give priority to history-taking, which gathers information about a patient's heredity, past illnesses, present symptoms and general well-being, including sleep, diet, sex and emotional behavior. Studies show that more than half of all internal illness is picked up by the history, twenty percent by the physical exam and another twenty percent by lab tests.

The inexpensive tests performed in the doctor's office—urinalysis, blood count, blood pressure—are now considered the most valuable. These tests should be made routinely and at least every year or two for women under fifty. Others should be used more sparingly, including:

Electrocardiogram. Many women start in their forties to have an annual EKG. But Dr. Stephen Scheidt, cardiologist at The New York Hospital—Cornell Medical Center, doesn't feel this is necessary. "Why should you test annually for a rare disease?" He believes that a healthy woman should get a baseline electrocardiogram, to compare with later tests, between her mid-thirties and mid-forties. "If it's normal, I don't think it needs to be repeated until after fifty, unless symptoms occur." But starting in the fifties, a woman should have an EKG as frequently as a man, says Dr. Scheidt. "Men should start having stress tests after forty," he says. "I'd just draw the line ten to fifteen years higher for a woman."

Automated lab tests. Tests for blood fats (cholesterol) and blood sugar (diabetes) are the two most important automated lab tests. Dr. Scheidt suggests a cholesterol test during a woman's twenties; if the result is normal, it should be repeated —at five-year intervals only—until the menopause. Dr. Marvin Moser advises checks on cholesterol and blood sugar every few years, starting at age forty-five.

Chest X-ray. Perhaps you are getting one annually, but doctors have found that there's little payoff. Among ten thousand symptomless persons who had chest X-rays in their thirties, only three abnormalities were found. If you smoke, you're certainly concerned about lung cancer. The sad news is that a chest X-ray rarely uncovers the disease early enough to save a life. "The yearly chest X-ray is better than nothing in a healthy smoker— but not much," says the *Harvard Medical School Health Letter.*

Gastrointestinal studies. Many doctors believe that a rectal exam should be a routine part of a physical in a patient older than forty. It checks the lowest segment of the intestinal tract for colorectal cancer, which ranks third among malignancies as a cause of death for women aged thirty-five to fifty-four, and second between fifty-five and seventy-four. (Nine out of ten cases are diagnosed after the age of fifty-two.) Because an important symptom is rectal bleeding, another useful screening device is a specially prepared kit, which the patient completes and then mails to her doctor, that tests for blood in the stool. A sigmoidoscopy (examination of the lower colon by means of a lighted tube) is advised only if blood is found or there are other suspicious symptoms. Barium X-rays of the gastrointestinal tract are *not* considered routine; they should be done only when symptoms warrant.

Other tests. Most doctors advocate a test for glaucoma (see p. 205) every two years after age forty, and for venereal disease in a woman who has more than a single sex partner.

A comparable critical look at the gynecological checkup has apparently not been made by skeptical researchers. Most gynecologists advocate an annual exam, and some think it should be increased to two a year following the menopause. Practically all advise a once-yearly Pap smear, but some doubting Thomases are also being heard.

When a woman has several consecutive negative Pap smears, chances are slight that she will develop cervical cancer during the next few years. A Canadian health task force, for example, suggests that every woman over eighteen who is not a virgin should have two Pap smears one year apart. Further tests should be made every three years until she is thirty-five, and then every five years until she is sixty, at which point if all are negative, she may stop. But high-risk women should keep having an annual Pap. One rationale for this surprising advice is that the incidence of cervical cancer, the disease the Pap uncovers, increases only up to the age of fifty. Another point: there is evidence indicating that when a woman's first two Pap smears are negative, there is only a slight chance that she will ever have a positive one. You may want to discuss the new Canadian schedule with your own physician. It certainly isn't wise to stop the annual habit of the Pap test on your own initiative.

A proper gynecological exam should include these features: examination of the breast, abdomen and external genitalia; pelvic examination in which the vagina, cervix, uterus, ovaries and pelvic support muscles are checked through the inserted speculum or by an examining finger; rectal exam which checks the anus and the rectum, as well as any abnormality of the cervix and uterus.

Macho Doctors and Timid Patients

If the annual physical is going out of style, if the multiphasic lab tests have turned out to give too much useless information and too little that's pertinent, then we're back to the beginning—the relationship between each patient and her doctor. If this is one of mutual respect and trust, then a woman should see her doctor whenever she develops a worrisome symptom, and he will investigate, viewing her as a person in pain and not merely as a female who complains.

But a good deal of fence-mending is necessary before most doctors respect their female patients, and before women trust their male doctors. Why does this uneasy relationship exist? One reason is that a women goes to the doctor more often than a man, and she is less reticent in talking about pain, fear and discomfort. But more than eight in every ten physicians are male, and they identify more comfortably with the *macho* credo—strong men accept pain stoically. Hence the widespread prejudice that women complain more, and their complaints mean less. I ran across this kind of bias recently when I talked to an orthopedist about back pain. "A pinched nerve is the most common complaint of the middle-aged female," he told me. "Men, of course, get it equally often, but they tolerate it better."

Middle-aged women, and particularly the elderly, are the most frequent victims of physician stereotyping. Many doctors stubbornly hold to these generalizations about them:

A woman's real problem is not-enough-to-do-itis. A friend of mine, whose husband had just died after an exhausting siege with cancer, who was a full-time teacher and who cared singlehandedly for a large house, told her doctor that she felt draggy, overtired. "The trouble is that you're bored," was his instant diagnosis. More amused than angry, my friend commented later, "I think he must have been diagnosing his own wife."

Jumpy nerves are the root of her complaints. "Whenever I have a symptom, my doctor blames it on anxiety," one woman says. "My last anxiety turned out to be gallstones. Before that it was uterine polyps."

Females are neurotic. Recovering from a heart attack, a woman in her forties recalls, "Despite ten days of pain and abnormal ECG readings, the doctor kept trying to convince me and my family that it was all in my head."

Most women are hypochondriacs. Among themselves, doctors describe a hypochondriac as "a crock," and later, "an old crock." One physician, who asked me not to use his name, said, "Our hospital did a follow-up on a group of women who had all been labeled neurotic crocks. The results shook us up. Within five years, one out of two of these 'hypochondriacs' was dead."

Her time is valueless. A medical magazine, offering practical advice on how a doctor should plan his office hours, wrote recently, "A receptionist can schedule for the first hour patients who are least likely to mind waiting. That means people with time to spare—the elderly, or housewives with grown children."

She is too emotionally fragile to be leveled with. One woman asked her doctor about the side effects of a drug he had prescribed, and was told, "You don't want to know."

But women are not blameless either. Too often we are over-awed, embarrassed, tongue-tied, subservient to our male doctors, and thus contribute to the arrogant treatment we get. In California, the American Friends Service Committee sponsored a conference on health in the middle years. "Even now I have to have my list of questions for the doctor," said one participant, "or I get overawed and forget what I was going to ask." And a nurse mentioned a woman patient who spoke cogently about her painful symptoms until the doctor arrived. "How are you?" he asked. And she answered, "Well, I'm okay, I guess," and lapsed into silence.

Canny consumers in other areas, women still accept what they've bought from a doctor—a prescription, a series of shots, even an operation—without really examining the merchandise. Then they get angry at themselves for being taken. "I asked the doctor what my medication was for," says one woman, "and he answered, 'It's good for you.' I was furious, but like a dope, I made another appointment."

The upshot is that your ego is bruised, and so is your health. "Effective medicine is impossible without the physician's seeing past the stereotypes," Dr. Robert Butler declared recently. Because of stereotyping, some women end up with the wrong treatment. When physicians view their female patients as "anxious," it's hardly surprising that three out of four tranquilizer prescriptions are written for women. Others miss out on the right treatment. Although it is known that menstrual cramps can be cured by suppressing ovulation, many physicians still stick to the view of a 1972 gynecology textbook, "[Menstrual] pain is always secondary to an emotional problem."

What should a woman do? Be more assertive, says Dr. Barbara Brockway, of the University of Wisconsin. The physician has information you need, she says, in order to make an informed decision about your body. "It is a patient's right as a consumer to get that information and the physician's responsibility to give it." If you are too timid to assert yourself, and thus fail through ignorance to make a decision in your own best interest, it is not the doctor who will suffer, but you.

A woman who is overimpressed with medical omniscience fails to realize that it is *she* who is the expert about her own body; she knows when a pain is different enough to excite concern, when she really feels *sick*. The doctor's knowledge is secondary, and because he also has dozens of other patients to consider, it's often fragmentary. He doesn't know best. Given the facts, you do.

Many women are reluctant to confront their physician for fear of exciting his anger, or, even worse, his contempt. A woman I know has been on heavy cortisone medication for four years to treat a rare muscle disorder. She is aware of the medication's hazards, but when her friends ask her to consult a second physician, she balks. "My doctor is so sweet, and he's getting old," she says. "How can I hurt his feelings?" *His* feelings, indeed, when it's her life that's endangered!

Other women have told me that the best development of the middle years is a new-found ability to know what they want and to ask for it without embarrassment or guilt. Now that you can stand up to your husband, your boss, even your children, because in your own head you feel competent and equal, it's time to stand up to your doctor, too. And if he persists in thinking of you in stereotyped terms, if he refuses to level with you about your own body, then it's time to bid him goodbye and take yourself off to another doctor.

IX
The Woman's Heart

The axiom that we are as old as our arteries—and as healthy—is one bit of folk medicine that is probably true. If a guess-your-age expert had X-ray eyes, and could look at the arteries of a random group of women, he'd be far off their chronological age, picking, perhaps, a fifty-year-old as thirty-five, or a forty-year-old as fifty-five. For although the process of arteriosclerosis (thickening and stiffening of the arteries) is an aspect of aging, just like wrinkles or gray hair, heredity tempered by life style affects the rate of its development drastically.

There is a particular kind of arteriosclerosis that may be highly lethal—often at quite young ages—called atherosclerosis. It is the villain behind the occurrence of coronary heart disease, number-one killer of women after the age of fifty-five, and stroke, which ranks number three after thirty-five. Atherosclerosis is the process that causes the inner lining of a major artery to thicken as deposits of fatty plaque are laid down, somewhat like rust coating the inside of a pipe. These deposits clog, and may eventually block the large arteries, leading to a heart attack, if a coronary artery is affected; or a stroke, in the case of a cerebral artery.

As a woman, you are at no great risk now of coronary heart disease, though your middle-aged husband is. For both of you, stroke becomes an increasing hazard after the age of forty-five. Now is the time to understand these dangers and to guard against them. It would have been better to start in childhood to protect your arteries, but in middle age it is crucial.

Coronary Heart Disease

Doctors now know a great deal about this disease that causes early death from heart attack. They know that part of the heart muscle dies from starvation when a coronary artery, hopelessly clogged with fatty deposits, can no longer supply it with blood. They know that two medical conditions—high blood pressure and high blood cholesterol—plus one habit, smoking, help set the stage for coronary artery disease. These are called the risk factors. But they have not discovered the magic ingredient, whatever it may be, that protects most women from suffering a heart attack in middle age.

It's like a jigsaw puzzle with a couple of pieces that look right but stubbornly refuse to fit. Consider this constellation of facts:

The statistics. By the age of sixty, every fifth American man has already suffered a heart attack, but only every seventeenth woman has. Decade by decade, it develops this way: during early middle age (thirty-five to forty-four), 64 out of every hundred thousand white males die of a heart attack, 12 in every hundred thousand women. In the following decade (forty-five to fifty-four), the figure rises to 276 deaths in a hundred thousand for a man, 58 for a woman; between fifty-five and sixty-four, to 752 for a man, 227 for a woman. Although it is widely stated that the heart attack rate equalizes in old age, the figures for the decade from sixty-five to seventy-four are 1,700 for a man, 731 for a woman.

The arteries. A recent report from the National Heart, Lung and Blood Institute says that even though they experience no symptoms, *most* men and *many* women are likely to have moderately advanced coronary atherosclerosis after the age of fifty. There is evidence that for men, the disease process starts in youth. Autopsies of twenty-two-year-olds killed in the Korean War showed some signs of atherosclerosis in more than three out of four cases. Are young women any different? No research has been attempted to find out the natural history of this major killer in females.

The risk factors. If high blood pressure (hypertension), high blood cholesterol level and smoking were rare among women in middle age, it would explain the huge gap between the sexes in heart attack rate. But they are not. Although younger men have more hypertension, women start to catch up by the late forties; after fifty-five, more women than men have high blood pressure. Women past forty-five also have higher cholesterol rates. Fewer women smoke, but the gap is narrowing steadily. Recently some cardiologists have reported their "impression" that heart attacks are rising among women under forty-five; they suggest this is due to a rise in smoking. However, statistics on heart deaths show no change in the gap between the sexes.

Probable risk factors. Other factors are suspected as risky, but they also fail to explain why women have fewer heart attacks. Among them are diabetes, which more women than men develop at middle age; obesity—there are more fat women; lack of exercise—women lag on this count. Stress is also a risk factor, but it's hard to define. The conventional wisdom states that men, who must hustle to make a living for their womenfolk, are under greater stress. But if this ever were true, it hardly holds today when one woman out of every two holds down a job, raises a family and manages a household—a stressful existence indeed.

Heredity. One woman, only forty-seven when she had a heart attack, believes heredity is the cause. "My father died at forty-five of heart disease." It appears to make sense, but does it really? Heredity is certainly a highly important influence on heart disease, but the exact genetic relationship is not clear. If a close relative (parent, sibling) had a heart attack at a young age, say the experts, then you are at extra risk. But if every woman whose father or brother suffered early coronary disease followed suit, then women would have this lethal illness just as frequently as men.

Until recently a simple explanation for the female protection from heart disease was estrogen, the hormone women secrete up until the menopause. But researchers are now rejecting this theory because most of the evidence just doesn't fit it.

Estrogen does not protect black women, although they manufacture it no less than whites. They have far higher rates of heart disease than white women, starting earlier in life. Perhaps it is significant that more blacks are obese, have high blood pressure and live under severe economic and social stress.

National statistics don't match the estrogen theory. If estrogen protects women before the menopause, then its diminution in the forties and fifties should be marked by a steep rise in heart attacks, approaching the figures for male. Instead, over a thirty-year span, starting with an extreme low at thirty-five, the incidence of fatal heart attacks rises steadily among women, quadrupling each decade, but slowing down slightly after sixty-five. What the statistics *do* appear to show, at least in fatal heart attacks, is that women lag by a decade or two behind men. They have fewer heart-attack deaths at fifty-five, for example, than men do at forty-five. Although the lines converge in old age, women never quite catch up, even at the age of seventy-five.

When the estrogen theory was fashionable, medical researchers suggested that administering it to men with coronary heart disease might protect them from suffering a second heart attack. This was done in many centers, and the results were so discouraging—heart deaths went up, not down—that the project was halted abruptly. One of the curious properties of estrogen is that it lowers blood cholesterol and raises blood pressure, apparently reducing one risk and enhancing another.

All of this appears convincing evidence that estrogen is *not* the mysterious X that protects women from heart disease. Now still another piece that doesn't fit has been added to the jigsaw puzzle. The Framingham heart-disease researchers have recently analyzed the records of the women they have been studying since 1948, all of whom have now passed the menopause. They found that in this group at least, heart disease did jog upward after the menopause. More significantly, it changed in character from a milder form (angina pectoris) to the more serious, sometimes fatal, heart attacks. The Framingham group, whose study involves a relatively small number of women, suggest that a much more complex change in hormonal status is involved than the loss of estrogen alone. For the study also shows that, far from protecting women, the taking of estrogen pills after the menopause is accompanied by a doubling of the rate of coronary heart disease.

Dr. Stephen Scheidt sums up the muddled estrogen theory this way: "I believe that there is real protection from cardiovascular disease for the female sex during the menstrual years. It is not based on estrogen or on any other known hormone. I don't know where this protection comes from. The full differences between men and women have not been explored, and should be."

Other cardiologists agree that research into the remarkable protection enjoyed by women before the menopause has been seriously neglected. Dr. William Kannel, who has recently retired as medical director of the Framingham study, said a few years ago, "I think the American Heart Association and other groups have not given sufficient emphasis to the problems of women and heart disease. The tendency has been to focus attention on men, who are more vulnerable, neglecting women by inference." If more attention were paid to why women are immune, at least until late middle age, then both sexes might benefit. A recent report from the Framingham group concluded, "Somewhere in this tantalizing mystery may lie a lesson of profound importance in understanding the genesis and course of this disease, perhaps in men as well as women."

Right now federal researchers are feeling vastly pleased with their efforts against the heart disease epidemic that kills many men—and some women—in their productive prime. Between 1970 and 1975 deaths from cardiovascular disease decreased by fourteen percent, and are still heading downward. Most believe that the reason is increased attention by doctors and patients to the risk factors. People are changing their life styles, exercising more and eating fewer heavy, fatty meals. They are having their blood pressure checked, and taking their medication when it is recommended.

Because some women do die of heart attacks in middle age, because sensible living now helps to protect one's health later and because heart disease is the leading killer of women at fifty-five and older, these admonitions are important to follow:

If you should develop severe chest pains, get to a hospital emergency room immediately. The cause could be indigestion, muscle strain or even hiatus hernia (a common condition after fifty in which the esophagus protrudes into the diaphragm); but it could also be a heart attack. Don't temporize. More than half of all cardiac deaths occur before the victim gets to a hospital; often he or she has just delayed too long.

If you smoke, stop. Heavy smokers have about a threefold increased risk of heart attack, and the risk is even higher for women younger than fifty-five. Whether the low-tar, low-nicotine brands decrease the risk is still a matter of controversy; some studies suggest that their effect is definite, but slight.

Even if your blood pressure has always been normal, have it

checked yearly. Don't overeat and particularly avoid large heavy meals. Exercise at least three times a week at a sport that works up a sweat and leaves you panting (see Chapter VII).

The evidence is only suggestive that a highly competitive person who tries to crowd eighty active minutes into every hour is at extra risk for a heart attack. Physicians agree, however, that reducing stress is good for your health. The woman mentioned earlier who suffered a coronary at forty-seven is the kind of person who relishes the challenge of tackling more work than any sensible person could possibly accomplish. We all know women like that, and most do not develop early heart disease. It is significant that this woman also had high blood pressure and smoked two packs of cigarettes a day. When risk is piled upon risk in heart disease, the danger multiplies geometrically, becoming more than the sum of its components. In her case, factor X, which protects women from heart attacks, was apparently ambushed by the presence of too many overwhelming pressures.

If you are still taking the Pill, change to another contraceptive at forty or earlier. At this age use of the Pill tends to raise your risk of a heart attack (see p. 52).

If there is heart disease in your family, particularly on the female side, don't bow to what you think is inevitable, but pay extra attention to controlling the other risk factors.

Factor X is a bonus that women have. Don't negate it by living a coronary-prone life style.

High Blood Pressure

Some pundit said that half the people in the United States with high blood pressure (hypertension) don't know that they have it. Among those who know it, half are not receiving treatment. And of those getting treatment, it is inadequate for half.

How could this happen? It's easy and it could be happening to you. Take this series of scenarios. You go to the doctor and neither of you notices that he has failed to check your blood pressure. This happens typically in six out of every ten doctor visits. And even among patients over forty-four, the years when hypertension becomes prevalent, it occurs almost half the time.

Often the doctor measures your blood pressure but doesn't bother to tell you whether or not it's normal. This occurs one out of three times. And three out of four times he will probably fail to tell you the exact numerical reading. Or he says, "Your pressure is a little high," and writes a prescription but doesn't follow up on whether the medication is effective or not. Or you stop the medication because it makes you feel ill, or forget to renew the prescription. A business executive, usually medically canny, told me her private formula for taking her blood pressure pills. "I always take them on weekdays because I'm tense and overworked. But on weekends or during a vacation, I'm relaxed as a kitten, so I just don't bother." But the *tension* part of hypertension refers to your blood vessels and not to your emotional state. Making a similar error, some people substitute tranquilizers —which do not help—for their prescribed blood pressure medication.

Why is it so important to watch your blood pressure? Because hypertension is a potential killer, the precursor not only of coronary heart disease, but of stroke and serious kidney disease. High blood pressure is most likely to develop in the middle years. Black women are at the heaviest risk. By the forties, they have more hypertension than black men or whites of either sex, and over half are afflicted by the age of fifty-five. Hypertension is a common disease. Before thirty-five, fewer than one woman in twenty have it, but after fifty-five the figure rises to more than one in three.

Although doctors often don't tell you what your blood pressure is, they should. In 1977 a report of the Joint National Committee on Detection, Evaluation, and Treatment of High Blood Pressure said: "At the time of blood pressure measurement, each subject should be informed of the numerical value of his blood pressure in writing."

But suppose your physician puts a blood pressure cuff on your arm, pumps it up, looks and listens, and then says, "Your blood pressure is 120 over 80." Would you know whether to frown or chortle with joy? You should chortle, because a reading of 120/80 is normal. (Keep smiling if it is lower—110/65, for example. In general, the lower the pressure, the smaller the chance of serious artery disease.)

The first number is the systolic or pumping pressure. It means that when the heart contracts, squeezing blood out into the arteries, pressure in the arteries rises to 120 millimeters of mercury. The lower number is the diastolic or resting pressure; as the heart relaxes, pressure in the arteries falls to eighty millimeters of mercury. Doctors used to worry mainly over a high diastolic reading. And their patients, familiar with the erroneous old wives' tale that blood pressure should be one hundred plus your age, were concerned with the systolic. It is now believed that both are significant. Among women, particularly as they grow older, systolic pressure may be a more accurate indicator of the development of heart disease.

Here is how to interpret the blood pressure findings that the doctor may report. Most of this advice comes from the 1977 report of the Joint National Committee on Detection, Evaluation, and Treatment of High Blood Pressure.

Among adults, a blood pressure reading between 120/80 and 140/90 is considered within normal range, but, of course, you don't need to worry if it's lower.

For those younger than fifty, a range between 140/90 and 160/95 should be rechecked every two to three months. Over fifty, it should be checked in six to nine months. (When people are nervous, their blood pressure may shoot up, and a second or third reading may be necessary to determine what it really is.)

At any age a blood pressure reading of 160/95 or higher warrants a second check in a month. A diastolic pressure over 90 but under 105 is considered borderline, and the doctor should decide on an individual basis whether to prescribe medication or advise other measures like weight reduction first.

Those whose diastolic pressure is 105 or higher should be treated promptly with medication.

What makes the diagnosis of high blood pressure so ticklish is that the patient is usually quite unaware she has it because she feels no discomfort. Headache and dizziness are widely regarded as high blood pressure symptoms, but they rarely are. This is a disease that does silent damage.

Blood pressure measures the force exerted by the bloodstream against the walls of the arteries. When extra force is needed to pump the blood through the body, the heart must work harder, and eventually the heart muscle enlarges (like the leg muscle of a jogger), and no longer pumps efficiently. In addition, fatty deposits (plaque) accumulate more rapidly on artery walls, making the passage of blood increasingly difficult. But when the blood pressure is reduced, the heart often returns to normal size, and the deposition of plaque slows down.

If you are obese, twenty or more pounds overweight, losing weight may be the first step your doctor advises to lower your blood pressure. A hefty weight gain in the twenties and thirties may make you particularly susceptible to hypertension; there appears to be a stronger correlation in women than men between overweight and hypertension. Although other measures are usually needed, a recent study in Israel has shown for the first time that some people can bring their blood pressure back to normal merely by losing weight.

For those who have a tendency to high blood pressure, salt should be a dirty word. Many of us have developed the habit of consuming four or more teaspoonfuls a day, although we don't need more than half a teaspoon. In addition to salt used in cooking or added at the table, snack foods—potato chips, pretzels, pickles, bacon, luncheon meats—are particularly high in salt. If your blood pressure is normal or low, like that of your parents before you, you have no reason to limit the salt you eat. But if there is high blood pressure in your family, high salt intake may help trigger a blood pressure rise. The child of hypertensive parents who eats a normal American salty diet, will show a slightly elevated blood pressure by the age of two.

The danger with salt is that it increases the amount of fluid circulating in the bloodstream, and thus gives the heart more pumping to do. A diuretic (water pill) reduces both salt and fluid, and is often the first drug prescribed for those who need medication for hypertension. Other drugs that may be added affect the nerve impulses that seem to be related to the increase in pressure, or lower the force with which the heart propels blood into the arteries. Some of these may have unpleasant side effects, which your doctor should mention *before* you start the medication. A woman with hypertension must expect to swallow her pills for the rest of her life, which will probably last longer because of the medication.

Relaxation techniques—transcendental meditation, biofeedback and others—have recently become popular as a way to reduce the stress that may be a cause of hypertension. If they happen to work—that is, if they lower the blood pressure and keep it down (and they often don't)—then they're a fine idea for you.

Although the popular notion is that hypertension is a disease of high-powered supertense individuals who would recover if only they learned to slow down, it is apparently not that simple. All kinds of people get hypertension, secretaries as well as Madison Avenue types. If a stressful life style is a cause, the explanation may lie not in how much stress we encounter, but in how we deal with it. Learning to relax is healthy, even though it may not cure your high blood pressure.

Because it's better to prevent than to treat high blood pressure, you should be aware of hints of its impending development. That isn't easy because, in nine out of ten cases, the cause is unknown. But you are likely to have a tendency toward hypertension if it is present in your immediate family; if your blood pressure was on the high side of normal during adolescence or young adulthood; if an occasional reading spikes high but later returns to normal.

Although blood pressure among Americans rises with age, doctors no longer consider this a normal development, and certainly not a healthy one. About thirty percent show no elevation as they get older. If your blood pressure was on the low side of normal in early adulthood, it is not likely to soar later. And if you reach the age of fifty with a pressure of 120/80 or lower, you are probably home free from the danger of developing hypertension.

High Blood Cholesterol

Most of us have trouble understanding the blood pressure figures, but we're even fuzzier when it comes to cholesterol level. When you have a complete checkup, the doctor or his nurse usually draws blood from a vein and sends it to a laboratory for analysis. Among the factors measured is the serum, or blood cholesterol. But there appears to be a conspiracy of indifference against telling a patient what the lab report says.

About ten days after her checkup, a woman I know telephoned the doctor to ask about the cholesterol report. She relayed her request to a secretary, and after a pause, the answer came back, "It's normal." She explained that she would like to know the exact figure. Another pause, then, "The doctor says not to worry. It's perfectly normal."

It *is* true that the figures are hard to interpret, and recent developments have made them even harder. A serum cholesterol count measures the amount of this fatty substance circulating in the bloodstream. This is significant, because, as we have noted, cholesterol is the major component of the fatty plaque that builds up on arterial walls in atherosclerosis. Hypertension is usually considered the most serious risk factor for the development of heart disease and strokes, with high blood cholesterol a close second.

But to gauge your own status, you have to know what a normal blood cholesterol level is, and this is far from clear. After the age of forty-five the average level for both men and women is about 230 milligrams per one hundred cubic centimeters of blood, with the level in women continuing to rise (possibly related to the menopause) and that in men dropping slightly after sixty-five. But "average" is not ideal, and when your doctor says your blood cholesterol is normal, he probably only means that it is average. Three-quarters of the heart attacks reported in the Framingham study occurred within the "normal" range, and the typical Framingham heart attack victim had a cholesterol level of 244, not much higher. You would be better off with a cholesterol close to 200 or even below. According to the Framingham physicians, the likelihood of a heart attack for a person with a level below 150 is practically nil.

Medical dogma used to hold firmly that eating less saturated fat in order to lower blood cholesterol would protect against heart attacks. Now this view is being widely questioned. The human body manufactures cholesterol, and also takes it in from the daily diet, particularly from eggs, meat, butter. The cholesterol we eat accounts for only ten to twenty percent of the body's supply. Changing the diet will reduce the level somewhat, and medication will reduce it even more. But will this cut down the incidence of heart attacks? Doctors used to be certain that it would; now many are wavering. A controversial 1977 article by Dr. George Mann in the prestigious *New England Journal of Medicine* said flatly, "No diet therapy has been shown effective for the prevention or treatment of coronary heart disease."

Right now patients are getting different signals from their doctors, depending on each physician's degree of faith in the diet gospel. In a column addressed to patients, the newspaper *Medical Tribune* said last year that reducing cholesterol *may* be helpful, mainly because it helps to cut down calories. It also reported that at an American College of Physicians meeting one group of doctors agreed that it doesn't matter how much fat people eat after the age of fifty or fifty-five, because the significant time to reduce dietary fats is in childhood or youth.

Some cardiologists now hold that it is not the fat you eat, but the way your body handles it that counts, and that this may be inherited. There is some evidence that women metabolize the cholesterol they eat better than men do. The thrust of current advice appears to be: eat *prudently*. *Drastic* changes are seldom necessary. During an interview, Dr. Marvin Moser, White Plains (N.Y.) cardiologist, expressed concern over "the obsession of women with their husband's diet and cholesterol." He added, "If you or your husband is thin, eats sixteen eggs a week, and still has a normal cholesterol, don't worry—there's no reason to change your diet."

Recently a new element has been added to the cholesterol question, throwing wavering uncertainty into greater disarray. Although they were discovered over twenty years ago, the significance of two lipoproteins that help make up the total blood cholesterol level is only now being recognized. (Lipoproteins are fat carriers that travel with cholesterol in the bloodstream.) They are called LDL (low density lipoprotein) and HDL (high density lipoprotein), and according to the Framingham researchers, they are excellent predictors of heart disease.

The effect of the two is opposite, like the two ends of a seesaw. The higher the HDL level in your blood, the lower is your risk of coronary heart disease; and the higher the LDL, the greater the risk. The way HDL appears to work is to remove cholesterol from arterial cells, and to interfere with the entry of LDL into these cells. An average man's level of HDL is about forty-five milligrams percent in one hundred milliliters of blood, and a woman's is higher at fifty-five milliliters. Perhaps HDL is the mysterious factor X that protects a woman from heart disease; research is not far enough along to be certain.

Although many doctors are still doubtful about the significance of these findings, the Framingham group, leaders in HDL–LDL research, has marshaled some convincing facts:

Some families noted for their longevity have extremely high levels of HDL—seventy-five mg. per hundred cc. or more.

Marathon runners have much higher HDL levels than average. There is some evidence that getting people to run will raise their levels.

A study of sixteen Zen communes in Boston shows that those who are vegetarians and also eat fish have high levels of HDL.

Analysis of the blood of female participants in the Framingham study indicates that women with a triad of ills—obesity, diabetes and low HDL level—are at serious risk of developing heart disease. In fact, these factors combined appear to obliterate a woman's protection from heart disease altogether.

One finding that has compounded the confusion is an apparent linkage of moderate social drinking with high levels of HDL and with a slightly reduced risk of heart attack. Moderate drinking is defined as one or two drinks a day of beer, wine, or whisky.

Doctors are uncertain about whether to order HDL tests of an average patient's blood (the test is inexpensive), and if the result turns out to be low, what to do about it. There appear to be two circumstances under which such a test makes particular sense. If you are over fifty, the experts now believe that the total blood cholesterol level no longer predicts your risk for heart disease, but that the HDL level does. If you are under fifty, and your cholesterol starts to shoot up, a test of HDL may clarify its significance. "There are people who have a high total cholesterol," says Dr. William Castelli, director of laboratories of the Framingham study. "But when we look at their HDLs, it turns out that they are very high. Such individuals don't need treatment. They're better off than most people in the United States."

But if your HDL level is low, there's a good deal of uncertainty about what should be done to raise it. For a woman, the best advice probably is—exercise, and don't overeat. Diabetes, which many women develop in middle age, is linked with overweight, and so is high blood pressure. You don't need to turn vegetarian, but less meat and more fish and fowl is probably helpful.

Stroke

For a reason still unknown, women are not protected from strokes to the extent that they are from heart attacks. Starting at about the age of forty-five, the incidence of stroke rises steadily, although its main impact comes after fifty-five. Black men are the most at hazard, followed by black women, white men, with white women last. Stroke ranks third as a cause of death for women in the middle years, sixth for men (even though men actually suffer more strokes than women do). But the incidence of the disease and the number of deaths has decreased dramatically in the past fifteen years, particularly among black women. No one knows why, but better treatment of the high blood pressure that often precedes a stroke is probably part of the reason.

A stroke is like a heart attack that happens to the brain instead. Arteries nourishing the brain become clogged with fatty plaque, and eventually, when blood can no longer push through, a portion of brain is destroyed. In about one in ten cases, an artery actually ruptures, causing a cerebral hemorrhage, such as killed President Franklin Roosevelt at the age of sixty-three. Risk factors are the same as for a heart attack—hypertension, high blood cholesterol, smoking, diabetes—and multiply when two or more are combined. Even when the blood pressure is only slightly elevated, the risk of stroke increases.

To prevent a stroke, the usual advice to reduce the risk factors applies, with an additional point—stroke sometimes gives a prior warning. Fingers, hands or legs may feel weak or numb; voice may be slurred or words forgotten, vision may blur, or swallowing become difficult. These unpleasant symptoms usually last from five to thirty minutes, and represent a transient ischemic attack (TIA) or threatened stroke, in which blood flow to the brain is temporarily impeded, perhaps by a spasm, in an artery already partially clogged. Those who suffer one or more such episodes have one chance in three of suffering a stroke within the next few years. For a man who has had a TIA there's a new treatment that appears to prevent one stroke in two—four aspirins a day—but for some reason aspirin doesn't' seem to protect women.

Although the word conjures up a picture of a hopeless invalid in a wheelchair, stroke often isn't all that devastating. Half of those who survive a month recover completely or with only a mild disability, although rehabilitation may take as long as two years.

Diabetes

Diabetes is on the rise in the United States, particularly among women in the middle years, and even more likely among those who are overweight. But if you flinch at the thought of possibly having to give yourself an insulin shot, you can stop worrying. Adult-onset diabetes is quite a different sort of disease from that which develops in childhood, and insulin injections are not a common part of its treatment.

Although the basic problem in both is a high level of blood sugar (hyperglycemia), this is usually due only in the juvenile diabetic to an inability of the pancreas to manufacture enough insulin. The adult-onset diabetic produces some insulin, but often not enough or quickly enough. The insulin doesn't seem to perform efficiently in keeping the blood sugar level at normal limits.

We're all familiar with the classic symptoms of diabetes—terrible thirst, excessive urination, weight loss, fatigue—but when the disease appears in the middle years, the symptoms may be nonexistent or milder than these. Mary, who is forty-nine, was diagnosed as a diabetic two years ago. "I developed boils in the genital area twice in six months for the first time in my life," she says. "The doctor found that suspicious, particularly when I told him that my father was diabetic." Other signs that should alert a woman: itching, often around the vagina, blurring of vision, and also the typical excessive thirst and urination.

The routine test of your urine made when you visit the physician does not diagnose diabetes accurately; but unusual findings may suggest the need for a more sophisticated check. One of two tests is usually conclusive: a blood test taken several hours after you have last eaten; or a glucose tolerance test, which involves drinking a sugar solution, then having the blood examined periodically during a three- or four-hour span to observe how the body metabolizes the sugar.

You should talk to your physician about having one or the other of these tests if you have symptoms suggesting diabetes; if a close relative had the disease; if you are obese—twenty percent or more overweight; or have given birth to one or more babies weighing over ten pounds. Adult-onset diabetes is more likely to be inherited than the juvenile kind, but the pattern is not as simple or direct as previously believed. In one study, even though both parents were diabetic, only one-third of their offspring developed the disease.

Since it is overweight that appears to trigger diabetes in adults, the main treatment is reducing weight to a normal level. A mild modification of diet is advised, and refined sugars—candy, cakes,

ice cream—are usually prohibited. The daily calories should include about twenty percent protein, thirty-five percent fat (of
which at least two-thirds should be unsaturated), and forty-five
percent carbohydrates like bread, potatoes and pasta. "I had to
cut out sweets and also wine," Mary says, "but I only felt deprived for the first few weeks." Diabetics are also advised to take
regular vigorous exercise, which appears to reduce the need for
insulin, as well as helping to maintain normal body weight.

Unfortunately, although diet and exercise usually bring blood
sugar levels to normal, they do not necessarily eliminate the complications of diabetes: an increased risk of coronary heart disease,
of cataracts and glaucoma, and of changes in the eye retina that
might eventually lead to blindness. But the future for a middle-
aged diabetic isn't all that grim. Most experts feel that the later
one develops diabetes, the smaller the chances of serious eye complications; there are also new treatments for retinal changes
that offer fresh hope for diabetics with vision problems.

X
Cancer

Cancer is the leading cause of death among women in their middle years. This statement may be so frightening that some, ostrichlike, will shudder and turn the page. These are the women who fail to have a Pap smear or to examine their breasts monthly, because they're afraid of what they will find out.

Mature women will, I hope, grapple with the cancerphobia that grips us all to some degree, and read on. For when cancer is put in focus, much of the terror subsides. Although it kills more women aged thirty-five to fifty-four than other diseases, this is not because it is so prevalent, but because, during these healthy years, even fewer women die of other causes. The cancer death rate in these years is only one woman in every thousand.

Cancerphobia leads many to take a fatalistic attitude, to give a shrug of the shoulders and the half-joking comment, "Everything causes cancer these days. There's just nothing to do about it." This is a myth. "Everything" does not cause cancer. In fact, says Larry Agran, health advocate at UCLA, there are at most only a few hundred commercially significant chemicals in use that are carcinogenic (cancer-causing), and should be regulated or banned. And we *can* do something about it. Evidence is mounting that a person's own life style—the food she eats, the alcohol she drinks, the cigarettes she smokes, the quick suntan she seeks—are more hazardous than the occasional diet cola made with saccharin that she swallows.

The ways to fight cancer are through prevention—shunning the known risks and treating with caution those that are suspected; through detection when a malignancy is still small and localized; through prompt treatment with the most modern methods known. Learning about these things is certainly a more intelligent way to fight cancer than turning the page. You may even learn that, because of factors in your heredity and environment, your risk of getting cancer is lower than average. But suppose it's higher? Then there's more reason than ever to know what to do to protect yourself.

Cancer is uncontrolled growth. Although other cells in the human body have a limited capacity to reproduce, cancer cells go wild in useless replication. What triggers this process is not fully understood, although a number of specific causes—radiation, for example—have been identified. Probably what happens is that the body's immune system, its own police force that protects against foreign invaders like viruses or bacteria, is fooled into viewing a cancer cell as friend instead of foe. Cancer occurs only when the body's defenses have weakened, and one promising line of research is to bolster the immune system's defenses. One myth about cancer—that it is inevitable as people age—adds to the fatalism, but it is not true. Some changes eventually happen to everyone—the need to wear eyeglasses, for example—but cancer is definitely not one of these.

While the news about recent heart disease treatment is cheering, that about cancer over the past few decades is not. Although there has been spectacular success in battling a few cancers (childhood leukemia, thyroid cancer, and Hodgkin's disease, in particular), the overall incidence is not declining significantly, nor are survival rates increasing. In the middle years women are more vulnerable than men, but after age fifty for blacks and sixty for whites, more men develop cancer than women. Black women get cancer more frequently than whites, but in the past few decades their survival rates have shown slightly greater improvement.

More men than women die of cancer; women survive the disease better at every site. Survival appears to depend more than ever on how early the malignancy is discovered. Overall, survival for five years can now be expected in forty-one percent of cancers, a gain of only two percentage points in a quarter century. But when the disease has remained localized at diagnosis, the gains are more optimistic—improvements of five percent or more at several sites.

Despite the billions of dollars spent in recent years, why aren't we doing better in the prevention of cancer? This pertinent question is likely to have a dozen answers, depending on each expert's view of what causes cancer. Some sigh for the good old days when the conventional wisdom held that a virus was the cancer culprit. This was at least a known enemy, but now that support for the viral theory has waned (although viruses may play a part in some cancers), preventing cancer appears like trying to catch a mosquito in the dark. "It's the accumulation of very small amounts of materials in a person over a lifetime that ends in a tumor," says Dr. Donald Fredrickson, director of the National Institutes of Health. Finding the specific cause for a cancer is extremely difficult, he explains, because people are exposed to thousands of agents in their environment that are, at least, potentially carcinogenic.

Heredity is thought to be the direct cause of cancer in only one case in twenty, but a family susceptibility may be as frequent as one in three. This means that a person is two or three times as likely to develop cancer at a particular site if a parent or a sibling had it there. But it does not mean that a malignancy is sure to develop at this site or any other. And it may not be due to heredity at all, but to a common unhealthy life style in a family.

Recently cancer experts have become more strongly convinced of the importance of environment, either personal, social, or involving hazards at the work site, as crucial in the development of many cancers. The figure for industry-related cancers used to be one to ten percent of all cancers, but in a recent statement, Joseph Califano, Secretary of HEW, said that one in five cases would soon be work-related. Asbestos is probably the most serious industrial carcinogen; others are arsenic, benzene, vinyl chloride and petroleum distillates—all materials that for the most part are used in heavy, male-oriented industries. But now women are slowly beginning to enter these potentially dangerous areas.

More significant to women are the life-style carcinogens—cigarettes, alcohol, sun, air pollution, the food we eat and the way we prepare it. Although the connection between nutrition and cancer has *not* been proven, and although air pollution does not appear to be an important cause, the case against cigarettes, alcohol and sun exposure have been nailed down by fact piled upon fact, almost ad nauseam.

To repeat a few facts: about one in three women in the middle decades smokes cigarettes. More men smoke, but the gap is narrowing. And women smokers are lighting up more, going from an average of seventeen cigarettes a day to nineteen. Women who smoke heavily run a greater risk than men of developing lung cancer. It is now the second most frequent cause of cancer deaths among middle-aged women and third after the age of fifty-five. (Breast cancer ranks first between thirty-five and seventy-five.) Lung cancer rose a striking eight percent for white women and almost ten percent for blacks between 1973 and 1976.

Some women are concerned that years on the contraceptive pill may place them in special hazard now that they have entered the high-risk group. Although the Pill has been implicated in a host of other misfortunes, most reports of its association with cancer have been negative or inconclusive. Recently, however, a ten-year study from the Kaiser-Permanente health plan in Walnut Creek, California, described as "suggestive but far from definitive," has linked an increase in malignant melanoma, the most dangerous skin cancer, to use of the Pill. Kaiser researchers found that women who remained on the Pill for more than four years appeared to face almost twice the average risk of developing the often-fatal cancer.

Although melanoma is quite rare, accounting for only one percent of all malignancies among women, another Kaiser study has linked the Pill with the more common cancer of the cervix; further reports, however, suggest that the connection may turn out to be tenuous or even nonexistent. A few researchers have suggested a relationship between the Pill and breast cancer, but others have countered with the contradictory claim that because women on the Pill appear to get benign breast disease less often, they may also be less susceptible to breast cancer. In other words, don't damn the Pill until more evidence is in.

The relationship between the food we eat and cancer is not so easily proven, but diet, and particularly the American habit of overeating, has recently become a favorite target for many cancer experts. Food additives, such as saccharin and the nitrates used to preserve bacon and lunch meat, are now considered less significant a hazard than the basic components of the usual American diet, which is high in fat, meat and calories. According to Dr. Ernst Wynder, president of the American Health Foundation, half of the cancers in American women and a third in men are related to diet, particularly malignancies of the colon, the prostate in men, and the breast, uterus and ovaries in women. He blames not specific cancer-causing agents in foods but factors in the diet that set the stage for cancer. He believes, for example, that a diet high in animal fats increases the relative amounts of a hormone called prolactin, which has been found to be in some way connected with the development of breast cancer. He and others put the emphasis on reducing *all* fats in the diet, not merely saturated fats.

Then there are the blame-the-chef advocates, who hold that there is a relationship between the way food is cooked and the appearance of cancer. Charcoal-broiling on an outdoor grill is suspect, as is the cooking of hamburger in a frying pan or grill, with the heat source underneath, instead of in the broiler where the heat comes from above.

If you feel that this seems like insubstantial evidence, Dr. Sidney Arje of the American Cancer Society is inclined to agree. "There's simply not enough proof yet to jump on the bandwagon with those who say that one's diet can cause cancer," he says. "However, we are aware of links between certain foods and cancer. The best advice is—eat a balanced diet and *don't eat too much.*"

Breast Cancer

The best news about breast cancer is that surgeons—at least some of them—are finally looking at the woman who has the tumor and at the *kind* of tumor she has, and considering them both when suggesting—no longer ordering—treatment.

Women are becoming more vocal about what breast cancer means emotionally—not only their fear of the disease, but an extreme fear of mutilation and loss of feminine self-image. Dr. Oliver Cope, professor of surgery at Harvard Medical School, in his fascinating book, *The Breast*, says that when he tries to explain this to other surgeons, they chide him with being too sentimental. Then he asks: "If you had cancer of the penis and were offered two equally effective treatments, one involving irradiation, and the other excision of the penis, which would you choose?" "They don't answer," writes Dr. Cope. "They blanch, and the conversation ends."

Knowing more now than ever before about individual cancers and their differing spread potential, some surgeons are decrying the rigidity that rules only one kind of treatment acceptable, and turning instead to varying degrees of surgical removal, as well as to radiation and chemotherapy as adjuncts or alternatives. They are telling a patient about her options and asking her to participate in the decision.

Women are becoming bolder in seeking solutions if they must lose a breast, and if they feel its loss deeply, they are finding a plastic surgeon to reconstruct it later. Breast reconstruction after mastectomy has suddenly become respectable, even among physicians who used to humiliate a woman for even inquiring about it. It appears part of the same revolution that middle-aged women are making in other spheres: they are losing their timidity about speaking up. "This is important to me," they tell their doctors. "Why can't you postpone surgery for a few days, perform less than a mutilating operation, use other treatments, reconstruct my breast?"

Most women who do not have breast cancer know only the bad news: that it occurs as frequently as ever, and that survival lasts not much longer than it did thirty years ago. These are the facts we must all face: one in thirteen women will develop breast cancer during her lifetime (but, remember, twelve out of thirteen will not). It is a disease of women over thirty-five, and the leading cause of all female deaths from forty to forty-four, despite the fact that three out of four breast cancers occur after the age of fifty.

A diagnosis of breast malignancy is *not* tantamount to signing a death certificate. Among women of all ages and at all stages of the disease, two-thirds survive for five years; one-half for ten; and forty-five percent for fifteen. If the disease is still localized, confined to the breast when therapy starts, more than four in five survive for five years, three out of four for ten, and two out of three for fifteen.

What is your likelihood of getting breast cancer? Your chances of avoiding it are better than average if you started menstruating late, fifteen or older, and began menopause early, before forty-five. In other words, the shorter the duration of your reproductive years, the safer you are from breast cancer. This also holds true for women who had a surgical menopause, in which the uterus and ovaries were removed, before the age of forty-five, and particularly before thirty-five.

Your risk is also lower if you have borne children, particularly if you had your first pregnancy before you were twenty-two. If you are childless or postponed pregnancy until after thirty, then the risk increases. It doesn't matter whether you breast-fed your baby; this does not appear to affect the risk. And an aborted pregnancy is no more protective than one which never started.

Heredity affects your chances of developing breast cancer, but it depends on when a mother or sister got the disease, and whether it occurred in one or both breasts. If your mother, for example, developed cancer in one breast after the menopause, your risk is only slightly higher than average. But if cancer was diagnosed in both breasts before the menopause in a mother or sister (an uncommon occurrence), then your risk is far higher.

Obese women are more prone to breast cancer than those of normal weight, and in the past few years some experts have become convinced of a strong correlation with a high-fat diet. They cite the case of Japanese women who eat fish and rice, and have a very low rate of breast cancer. When they emigrate to the United States, the land of the cheeseburger and French fry, breast cancer increases. Race may also play a part, because black women have fewer breast malignancies than whites do. (This may also relate to the fact that although other diseases develop more often among the poor, breast cancer strikes the affluent more frequently.)

Benign breast disease—most commonly fibrocystic disease (it used to be called chronic cystic mastitis)—occurs most frequently among woman in their thirties, causing initial anguish followed by joy when no cancer is found. But how to lessen the initial anguish? Your own observations should help somewhat, although, of course, they *must* be confirmed by a physician, and sometimes by a biopsy. (One breast surgeon has recently urged his colleagues to plan the biopsy incision so that it won't leave an ugly scar. "I have seen too many patients who look as though a lawn mower had been driven across their chests," says Dr. Gordon Schwartz of Jefferson Medical College in Philadelphia.) These lumps hurt, particularly before the menstrual period when they grow larger. Neither of these symptoms is likely in early cancer. Sometimes they fill up with fluid, and after a doctor aspirates them with a needle the lump disappears, almost a certain sign of benignancy. You may feel several lumps on one breast, or even on both. A malignant lump, particularly to the practiced fingers, feels different: it is hard, nonmobile and not tender to the touch.

Doctors have usually considered fibrocystic disease a risk factor for breast cancer, but since close to one in every two women
has it at some time (just as they have benign fibroid tumors in
the uterus), some are no longer so certain. Many women with
lumpy breasts become so confused when they start self-examination (BSE) that they often just give up. One gynecologist told
me, "Women really don't know what the hell their fingers are
feeling, but they get upset, and they beg the gynecologist for another check. So the whole point of doing it yourself gets lost."

Though only about one in every two women sticks to this
schedule, a woman over forty should have her breasts examined
by a doctor once a year, and probably twice if she falls in the
risk category. She should examine her own breasts monthly, directly after her period. A careful check should take at least five
minutes and the local cancer society has a booklet telling how
to do it. If she no longer menstruates, she should pick a time—the
first day of the month is easy to remember—for the BSE. But only
one woman in four follows this advice regularly. "I feel squeamish
about it. I'd rather go to the gynecologist every three months,"
one told me. Another said, "I'm scared of what I might find." And
in two cases out of three, the doctor fails to tell her about BSE.
Despite this forgetfulness, women, not doctors, discover nine out
of ten breast cancers, usually by chance.

The breast is composed of fat, milk glands, ducts that carry
milk from gland to nipple, and fibrous tissue supporting the
breast. The more generous the fat, the larger the breast. Cancer
usually arises in the ducts and the glands, and benign breast
disease in the fibrous tissue. The breast is protected by its fat
and fiber from trauma; there is absolutely no evidence that a
bump or a blow will activate cancer. This is a point to remember
if your daughter wants to take up body-contact sports.

In addition to your own and the doctor's examination of your
breast for lumps, a special X-ray, called a mammogram, is a
diagnostic tool about which there is currently much confusion.
The recommendation of the National Cancer Institute is this:
if a woman of any age develops a symptom like a lump or discharge from the nipple, then a mammogram is an important tool
for diagnosis. But if she is symptomless and younger than fifty,
mammography should not be used for routine screening, since the
cancer-causing risk of the X-ray may outweigh the benefit of un-
covering an early malignancy. But after fifty, when breast cancer

is most common, many doctors advise that mammography should be used for annual screening. A woman in her forties should be screened annually if she, her mother or sister has already had cancer in a breast. At the ages of thirty-five to thirty-nine, routine screening should be restricted to women with breast cancer because of the chance a new cancer may develop in the second breast.

The NCI issued this directive to the twenty-seven Breast Cancer Detection Demonstration Projects that it sponsors jointly with the American Cancer Society; it is *not* a must for the individual patient and her doctor. In fact, some doctors believe that the danger from X-ray is now much lower than when the guidelines were approved in late 1977, because the newest machines give only a minuscule radiation dose to the woman being examined. Some private cancer-detection centers recommend a baseline mammogram for women over thirty-five, and others routinely screen younger women, at special risk because they are childless or had a late first pregnancy.

There are two other problems with mammograms: they are not as accurate as once touted, and the abnormalities they turn up are not always easy to interpret. It is believed that mammography may diagnose breast cancer two years before it results in a palpable lump, but whether all of these tiny malignancies eventually become overt, life-threatening cancers is not yet known.

If a mammogram is positive, the next step is a biopsy, the surgical removal of the lump, and its microscopic examination by a pathologist. Women should know about the important change in medical thinking regarding biopsies. Only a few years ago it was routine—whenever a suspicious lump was found on the breast—to send the worried women promptly to the hospital for a biopsy, to be followed immediately by removal of the breast if a pathologist, quickly examining a section of frozen tissue, pronounced it malignant. Several developments have cast serious doubt on this procedure. The first is a complaint from the patient herself who wants to make up her own mind about the nature of treatment *after* malignancy is diagnosed. The second is a growing belief that freezing may distort the tissue, especially when, discovered in a mammogram, it is smaller than one centimeter (two-fifths of an inch), making it difficult for the pathologist to interpret. An advisory committee to the NCI recommends that two pathologists be consulted about these tiny lesions *before* definitive surgery is started.

But many women are still being told by surgeons, who themselves may find the procedure of biopsy and breast removal more convenient, that it is safer for the patient. Their reasons? Temporizing even a few days with a fast-growing cancer is life-threatening; doing two separate operations and giving general anesthesia twice is unnecessarily hazardous. But these arguments are being refuted by other surgeons who point out that the biopsy can be performed under local anesthesia, and a delay of a week or even longer does not compromise a patient's chances for cure.

During that week, should the lesion prove malignant, important decisions must be made by a patient who only recently had no options at all. She expected the physician to perform a radical operation, the most frequent procedure for the past fifty years, a period without substantial improvement in survival. Now the options to be considered are: surgery, ranging from minimal to massive; surgery plus radiation and/or chemotherapy. No patient has the experience or the ability to interpret complex pathological findings by herself; but a few surgeons, and the number is growing, will now discuss the options with her, explain the odds, as much as they are known, that each choice gives for survival, and develop a plan of action that the patient finds acceptable.

If you are overawed by a surgeon's positive views, as most of us are, remember that there is no treatment even after all these years that is unquestionably correct. Remember, too, it is your body, not his. If loss of a breast destroys the joy of living, then you may lean toward a treatment that preserves the breast, although it may be described as a shade more hazardous to life. No two women, confronted with this unhappy problem, are likely to feel exactly the same way about it. These are their choices:

Surgery. Four operations are possible: lumpectomy, which entails removal of the malignant lump and surrounding tissue but not the entire breast; simple mastectomy, removal of the breast; modified radical mastectomy, in which the breast and the lymph nodes in the armpit are removed; radical mastectomy which cuts out the breast, the underlying muscles of the chest wall and the armpit lymph nodes.

Most surgeons have strongly opposed the lumpectomy alone unless the lesion is tiny (less than half an inch), and at the outer edge of the breast. Many believe that breast cancer is multicentric—occurring in several areas of the breasts at once—and cannot be cured by removal of a single lump. But more lumpectomies are being performed. Dr. George Crile, Jr., of the Cleveland Clinic has been lumpectomy's major advocate in the United States. In 1971 an editor and novelist named Babette Rosmond, than aged forty-seven, had a lumpectomy and wrote a book about it. When I checked with her eight years later, she said, "There's been no recurrence. I don't even think about it any more." (Although five-year "cures" are considered significant with other cancers, it is the general consensus that at least ten years should pass before a breast cancer is considered "cured.")

Simple mastectomy, although it entails loss of the breast, gives a better cosmetic result than the radical operations, because the lymph glands are left intact, and makes it easier for a plastic surgeon to reconstruct the breast later. In England it is often combined with radiation of these glands, and good five-year results are reported.

Although the glands under the arm, where breast cancer usually spreads first, are removed in the modified radical operation, the muscles of the chest wall are not. The chest looks better; the arm on that side functions better, and later reconstruction is possible. But those who advocate the radical mastectomy (named for Dr. William Halsted who first used it in the United States about ninety years ago) believe that removal of these muscles, making it possible to examine and excise more local lymph nodes, is safer for survival.

Women who are considering the surgical options must know that the Halsted operation is still the most widely advised. Some, but not all, studies show that its ten-year survival rates are better. Dr. Arje of the American Cancer Society told me, "The final word is not in. The American Cancer Society says that until we know better, experience shows that the best results are achieved with the radical mastectomy." When will we know better? impatient women ask. The National Surgical Adjuvant Breast Project, comparing different degrees of surgery, with and without radiation, has recently gotten under way in Pittsburgh.

Radiation and chemotherapy. A small group of nontraditional surgeons at such respected centers as Harvard and Yale has dispensed altogether with mastectomy in favor of removal of the malignant lump, followed by X-ray treatment, sometimes combined with chemotherapy. Dr. Oliver Cope, its leading advocate, says in his book, *The Breast:* "Major surgery as therapy [for breast cancer] has had its day. Mastectomy in any of its forms is on its way out." Dr. Cope himself performed his last radical mastectomy in 1960, although he has continued to treat breast cancer ever since.

As rationale for the iconoclastic viewpoint, Dr. Cope makes these points: radical mastectomy cures only those one-out-of-four patients whose cancer is confined to the breast region; radiation can do as well without mutilation; chemotherapy should be added if cancer cells have entered the bloodstream to spread elsewhere in the body.

The program in which Dr. Cope participates at Massachusetts General Hospital has four steps: removal of the cancerous tissue from the breast, which is accomplished by the biopsy, really what is known as a lumpectomy; extensive study for several days of the tumor by the pathologist; no further action if the malignancy has not invaded the rest of the breast; radiation to the breast and sometimes the lymph nodes, if it has invaded; chemotherapy, if it has spilled into the body. The treatment is predicated on the belief that there are at least fifteen types of breast cancer, ranging from the sluggish to the fast-spreading, and that each must be considered individually for the best results.

Chemotherapy. Research studies are going on in two centers—one in Milan, Italy, the other in Pittsburgh—to determine the value of starting chemotherapy with a combination of cancer-killing drugs, directly after a radical mastectomy, when spread to the lymph nodes has occurred. Results after four years from the Italian patients show that the treatment appears of definite value, with less recurrence reported, among women who are premenopausal. For those who developed breast cancer after the menopause, the difference in relapse figures is not as great. (Betty Ford, past her middle fifties at the time of her breast surgery, received immediate chemotherapy.) These powerful drugs must be given cautiously, because they kill normal as well as malignant cells. They also have side effects, including loss of hair, which make many women miserable, although hair grows back and other symptoms disappear once the treatment has ended.

Finally, research is now being pushed vigorously over a wide front to save the lives of more women who develop breast cancer. Another development that makes many almost as happy is the significant progress made by plastic surgeons in giving a mastectomy victim a new breast. Women are now talking openly, not only about their feelings of loss of womanhood, but about the practical limitations of the breast prostheses they have had to wear. "Imagine," said one during a panel discussion, "that every single morning, you must attach an extra thing to your body. A thing of considerable weight that must constantly be checked. Has it slipped? Is it too high or too low or too near the center? A thing you grow to hate, even while being grateful that it exists."

Breast reconstruction involves implantation of a mold of silicone under the skin and subcutaneous tissue of the mastectomy site, a procedure requiring two days in the hospital. A second operation is performed several months later to reconstruct a nipple if the patient desires it. Fears that the implant might reactivate cancer or hide a new cancer have not proved valid. Because it is contained in a mold, there is no danger of silicone breaking away and spreading into the body, as occurred in cosmetic operations to enlarge the breast some years ago. If you are facing a mastectomy and think you might want breast reconstruction later, you should tell the surgeon *before* he operates, because the more radical the operation, the less likely the possibility of reconstruction. Extensive radiation harming the chest skin may also interfere. Another factor is that if the nipple is not involved in the cancer, it can be "banked" by attaching it to the groin until reconstruction. Although many cancer surgeons still scoff at reconstructive surgery, it has become far more widely accepted in the past few years. But women must realize, as Dr. Reuven Snyderman of Rutgers Medical School, one of its pioneers, wrote recently, "We are not treating a cosmetic triumph, but rather making it possible for the patient to live without the burden of an external prosthesis."

Cancer of the Reproductive Organs

With a touch of macabre humor, a doctor says of cancer of the uterus, "Well, compared with breast cancer, it's no worse than a bad cold." What is really true and more optimistic about uterine cancer is that it is less common than breast cancer (one in twenty-five women will get it during a lifetime, compared to one in thirteen for the breast), that it is easier to detect in the early stages, and that it is far less lethal than breast cancer, with death barely a third as frequent.

Women susceptible to the two types of uterine cancer—malignancy in the cervix, or neck of the uterus, and in the endometrium, the lining of the uterus—are strikingly different in many ways. Those who develop cervical cancer are younger, usually in their forties, while endometrial cancer targets in on the age group of fifty to sixty-four, although some cases develop in the forties, particularly around the time of menopause. The poor and the deprived, black or white, are more susceptible to cancer of the cervix.

If you started to have sex at a young age, from fourteen to nineteen, married young, and have had many different sex partners, or more than four pregnancies, you are at extra risk for developing cancer of the cervix. This disease is frequent among prostitutes, rare in nuns. In fact, some researchers suggest that it has a venereal element, that a substance transmitted in sexual activity comes in contact with the cervix at a time when its tissues are particularly susceptible. It could relate to the sperm, or even to the cleanliness of the penis. Because Jewish women have a low rate of cervical cancer, it was long believed that circumcision of the husband was protective. This is no longer accepted, but other curious findings support the venereal theory. The second wife of a man whose first wife died of cervical cancer appears more susceptible to the disease. Women who use a diaphragm, which covers the cervix, or whose husband uses a condom, which covers the penis, may be less susceptible. And the wives of men with prostate cancer appear more likely to develop cancer of the uterus themselves.

The woman at risk for endometrial cancer is quite different: she is more likely to be overweight, childless, infertile, to have a late menopause or suffer from diabetes or high blood pressure. If a woman does not ovulate regularly, then her uterus is constantly stimulated with estrogen which builds up the lining of the uterus, without the balance of progesterone, the other female hormone, to break it down. This may set the stage for cancer of the endometrium.

While the incidence of cervical cancer has fallen, endometrial cancer has been on the rise in recent years. Most researchers blame the increase on the widespread use of estrogen to treat the symptoms of the menopause (see p. 81). This hazard does not seem to extend to the contraceptive pill, which is a chemical combination of estrogen and progesterone. Women are apt to misunderstand this; I spoke with one, for example, who at forty-three had just had surgery for cancer of the cervix, and blamed the Pill, which she had been taking for twelve years. She also blamed her husband: "I had to stay on the Pill because he was too *macho* to have a vasectomy when I suggested it." (This woman's case also illustrates the point that although certain factors predispose one statistically to a particular disease, it does not mean that, lacking those factors, you are immune. She is well-educated, married to a business executive who has been her only sexual partner for twenty-four years and has two children. She developed cervical cancer even though she had few of the characteristics that we have mentioned as being likely to make her a candidate for the disease.)

Because of clear-cut symptoms and easy diagnosis, the chances for cure of both kinds of cancer of the uterus are fairly good—about sixty percent for cervical cancer and seventy-five percent for endometrial. When endometrial cancer is discovered early, about eight out of ten women survive for ten years.

The figures, particularly for cancer of the cervix, could be even better. If every woman had a Pap test at regular intervals (once a year or perhaps slightly less often for those at low risk), the disease could be caught early and almost certainly cured. For the Pap smear the doctor uses a cotton swab to remove cells shed from the cervix and the uterus. Examination of the cells under a microscope is ninety-five percent accurate in diagnosing cervical cancer or the abnormal cell changes that may precede it. (A positive Pap smear does not necessarily indicate cancer. It may show cell changes that the doctor may wish to reevaluate at frequent intervals.)

Unusual bleeding or discharge between periods is a warning sign for cervical cancer, and should be checked. When the disease is diagnosed, hysterectomy, the removal of the uterus, along with radiation or chemotherapy in advanced cases, is the usual treatment, although in certain cases, less radical surgery is possible for a woman who wants to have more children.

A negative Pap smear should give a woman almost complete

assurance that she does not have cancer of the cervix. Close to one out of two women think this includes endometrial cancer too, but it doesn't. The smear is considered only about forty percent effective in detecting cancer of the body of the uterus. A woman in the menopausal years, from forty-five to fifty-five, should be particularly alert to irregular vaginal bleeding—spotting between periods, unusually long or heavy periods, and bleeding after the menopause. Unfortunately, these are also typical signs of the menopause itself. "After the menopause, bleeding is cancer until proved otherwise," says Dr. Arje. "The group we're concerned about are those aged forty-five to fifty-five who are bleeding and we're not sure why."

Formerly, when a woman this age or older reported unusual bleeding to her doctor, he used to have no choice but to admit her to the hospital for a dilatation and curettage. Now several tests are available that can be made in the doctor's office, involving suctioning or washing out cells and tissue from inside the uterus. Women who are at higher risk for endometrial cancer are advised to have such a test at the time of the menopause, and particularly if suspicious bleeding occurs. Although such bleeding could have other benign causes, it should *always* be reported to the gynecologist. Hysterectomy, sometimes with radiation, is the treatment for cancer of the endometrium.

When the gynecologist puts two fingers of one hand inside the vagina, and presses the abdominal area with the other hand, you may wonder what he or she is probing for. One organ doctors can feel, or palpate (and it may give you a brief twinge of discomfort), is the ovary, and they are checking for *ovarian cancer*. It's not a common malignancy, perhaps one-third as frequent as cancer of the uterus, but it kills just as many women. Those in their fifties are most susceptible, particularly when close relatives have also had a malignant ovary. Childless women have a somewhat higher risk, black women lower than white.

The problem with ovarian cancer is that there is no test to discover it in the early stages. Even when a gynecologist feels a suspicious mass during the pelvic examination, there's one chance in two that the disease has already spread outside the organ. Survival rates are dismal; about one-third live for five years. And the symptoms are vague—gastrointestinal complaints, abdominal distension—usually dismissed as "something I ate" or "I guess it's the menopause." There may be better news, however. Instead of using surgery alone, doctors are now being advised to start radiation or chemotherapy early when metastases may still be small. One drug, also used in breast cancer, appears effective against cancer of the ovary.

XI
Middle-Age Spread

Ask a woman over thirty-five how she feels about her figure and she is likely to explode in a caterwaul of complaints. These are the aspects that bother her most:

I'm putting on weight for the first time in my life. "I never had a weight problem until three years ago," says a divorcee of forty-four. "Now if I even sniff what's cooking, I seem to add a pound."

It's so much harder to lose. "I used to take off five pounds in three days by eating only one meal a day. But for the first time it doesn't work any more." This from a forty-two-year-old housewife and amateur athlete.

I weigh the same but it's all in the wrong places. "I've got a fat rear end and waffly bumps on my thighs. I just hate them," complains a secretary aged forty-five. She first noticed the change a few years ago "when I put on a bathing suit and looked yucky." Others talk about a spare tire around the middle, a bulging stomach, heavy hips. "All of a sudden I have no waistline," one says, "and I'm four inches bigger around the thighs."

These are all common experiences. At least one American woman out of every two gains during the decade before the menopause. A recent federal study charts the inexorable climb for a woman of average height (five feet three inches): in the child-bearing decade between twenty-five and thirty-five she weighs 139, but in the next ten years she puts on a hefty nine pounds.

She adds another two between forty-five and fifty-five, and three more by her mid-sixties. But by age sixty-five the gain has ended, and a slight decline starts that continues into old age. If it's any consolation, statistics show that the biggest rate of gain comes early—between the mid-thirties and the mid-forties—and then slacks off. During these years, for a woman of this height and a medium frame, a "desirable" weight, according to Metropolitan Life Insurance Company tables, should range between 110 and 122.

What she is accumulating is fat, and at the same time she is losing muscle mass. Before the age of thirty-five, one-third of a woman's poundage is fat; by age fifty-five it has crept up to forty-three percent. Extra fat is deposited under the skin on her belly, hips, buttocks and waist. She literally becomes thicker through the middle. Although there is little change in fat deposits on arms and legs, the swelling trunk makes the extremities look smaller in proportion.

Many women, in despair about their weight gain, find it particularly irritating that their husbands don't suffer the problem to the same extent. "He always maintains his weight without any difficulty, darn him," says one. "He keeps in shape. He has marvelous self-control," grumbles another. The fact is that it's easier for men not to get fat. Statistics show that they gain only up to the mid-forties, while women put on weight for two further decades. At all ages after puberty, male bodies contain less fat, more muscle. (But female fat is what makes feminine curves.) And when men do gain at middle age, the weight is deposited differently, over the diaphragm (the beer belly) rather than lower down in the abdomen, as in women. There's a genetic factor, too, in a female's fat deposits. Some women have flaring fat on the thighs, almost as if they're wearing riding pants; their sisters and mothers are likely to have the same contours.

At any age the basic reason for weight gain is depressingly familiar: people eat more than they burn up in activity. But at middle age there's a special explanation—the basal metabolism rate (which regulates the speed at which the intake of food is turned into energy) starts to slow down. According to one estimate, the rate falls by about two percent per decade starting at twenty-five: there is some evidence that the drop becomes more precipitous during the forties. Recent research suggests what may be happening: two hormones normally prod the cells to release fat and send it to the blood, where it is converted into energy, but as one gets older, the fat cells become less responsive to these hormones—at least, that's what occurs in rats, and probably in people too.

And for women in particular, there's a double-whammy. Without an infant to get her up during the night, without a toddler to chase after, her level of activity decreases. If she's a housewife, she may keep her home just as neat, but she performs each chore at a slower pace. If she has a job, it's likely to be one that keeps her sitting all day. Trudy, who is forty-five and recently took her first job, says," I used to keep moving in the house and the garden, but now I don't get up from my desk for hours on end."

Increased tension engendered by the new challenge of job or school is a secondary factor. Lorna is fifty and started graduate school eight years ago when the first of her three children went to college. "I took thirty points and gained thirty pounds—a pound a point. I guess it was my way of working through anxiety." A woman is more likely than a man to act out emotional problems, such as tension, mild depression and lack of self-esteem, by overeating. But she should be skeptical about swallowing the physician's favorite explanation—that she overeats because she feels useless and bored. Doctors are apparently the last to know that a majority of women in the middle years are holding down jobs *and* running a home.

Whatever the secondary reason for weight gain, every woman past thirty-five must face the fact that because of her slowing metabolism, her calorie requirements are less than they were in her twenties. Even if all she does differently is to eat one extra cookie a day, she can look forward to a weight gain of about ten pounds a year. (A plain cookie is worth about one hundred calories. An intake of 3,500 calories, or thirty-five cookies, equals one pound of body weight. Thus with one additional cookie a day she will gain a pound every thirty-five days.)

Professional advice on optimum food intake is only now beginning to take this into account. The National Research Council's recommended dietary allowance (RDA) suggests that a woman drop an advised daily intake of two thousand calories to 1,800 after she passes the age of fifty. Many nutritionists consider this change too little and too late. More realistically, the Food and Agricultural Organization of the United Nations suggests a calorie reduction of 7.5 percent for each decade beyond the age of twenty-five. If one follows the FAO recommendation, an appropriate number of calories would be 1,850 a day at age thirty-five, 1,700 at forty-five, and about 1,600 at fifty-five. (One can drop 150 calories by cutting out one and a half tablespoons of butter, a tablespoon or so of salad oil or a cupcake.)

But a numbers game is rigid and simplistic, and fails to take into account a woman's frame and her level of activity. A larger, heavier woman burns up more calories from the same amount of exertion than does one who is petite and small-boned. And if two women have the same build but one is an exercise nut while the other sits still all day, their caloric needs differ.

Most important, a numbers game fails to take into account each woman's individuality: where she gains her ego-satisfaction, whether eating is a positive pleasure, what meaning a trim body holds for her. One woman may equate getting old with getting fat and view both with horror. Another may accept the whole process with more serenity. Each should make her own value judgment before initiating a painful change in her diet, as long as there are no health problems related to her overweight. Here are a few examples of such judgments:

Pamela, an outstandingly successful lawyer, is in her sixties and plump. She is also the most beautiful woman I know, with a rounded face that is barely lined. Although she is not a heavy eater, she often lunches or dines with clients, a time when it's more important to be mentally sharp than to count calories. Pamela is probably thirty pounds overweight, but she has made her peace with a heavy body, and enjoys the adulation her lovely face receives.

Divorced twice and in her late fifties, Dorothea worries about her financial future. She wants to hold on to her job for another decade and she'd also like to find a man. Tiny, with a youthful body and a pert face, she believes these are important assets for both goals. Although an active feminist, Dorothea remains emotionally wed to her mother's counsel that a woman should always look her best—and that means thin. "I'm painfully figure-conscious, although I sometimes wish I weren't."

Joan is fifty-two, twice-widowed and a teacher in an alternative school. By traditional standards, she appears to be the opposite of chic Dorothea. I have never seen her wear makeup; her hair is drawn back simply from her face, obviously without benefit of hairdresser. But recently she has started to date again, and she is giving her body a critical look. "On the whole I'm pleased with it. It's well-muscled, with a strong frame. But I've always had a weight problem. I weigh myself every day, and if I've gained, I hate myself for the next twenty-four hours. I may not win the battle against fat, but I'm going to die trying. Why? It's a matter of self-image; I intend to keep on liking myself."

Betty, fifty-one, the mother of two grown sons, says, "I have more time—and inclination—to take care of *myself* these days, now that the boys are on their own. The fact is, I feel better when I'm thin. Aside from the cosmetics, I get less winded and feel more energetic and I *know* I'm in less danger of heart attack and a lot of other problems."

Understanding her own motivation, each of these women has charted a personal course with which she feels comfortable. This appears to be infinitely wiser than mindlessly falling into one extreme or another—getting sloppily fat without thinking, or starving oneself because it's high fashion. Some women even grow to hate themselves because they can't slim down enough to reach the standards that a youth culture demands. But, for many, these may be impossible standards that run contrary to one's own physiological and psychological needs. Every woman should make up her own mind about losing weight, untangling the popular dream of being fashionably skinny from her own vision of a good life and an acceptable body.

But isn't it unhealthy to be overweight? That depends on how much. A few extra pounds may be unattractive to your own eyes, but it takes twenty or thirty pounds before you risk being a candidate for serious disease. At that point you are not overweight but obese, which is usually defined as twenty to thirty percent over "normal" weight. Actually, there is no norm, but physicians usually use as a rough guide the "desirable" weight tables of the Metropolitan Life Insurance Company, which take into account different body frames. Obesity is widespread among middle-age women. According to one estimate, three out of every five women in their forties are overweight, and two in five are obese. (Some doctors are now questioning the validity of standards from which such a high percentage of the population appears to stray.)

Osteoarthritis, the joint disease that many develop during the middle years, is aggravated by a heavy body that puts excess pressure on the joints. Women who are obese *and* have a family tendency to diabetes, develop this disease after forty at a much higher rate than men do. High blood pressure, another condition that runs in families, may be triggered by excess weight that is put on in young and middle adulthood, though not, according to a recent report, by weight gained after the age of fifty. High blood pressure also responds to weight loss, but, says Dr. Lot B. Page of Tufts University Medical School, "Taking off excess weight is less effective than not having gained it in the first place."

It is also less safe. Excessive fad dieting can harm your health. Some doctors still prescribe amphetamine pills for weight control—and some women still grab for them like candy—although the pep pills may produce psychological dependence, prolonged depression and acute anxiety. They may even lead to brain damage. Diuretics (water pills) are another potential hazard. These drugs drain fluid from the body, thus giving the appearance of weight loss, but the fluid is quickly replaced. They can be hazardous, because they also drain essential minerals. One woman I know wanted to look fashionably thin for an important party. She swallowed a handful of water pills and landed in the hospital instead of at the party.

The danger of an extreme fad diet is illustrated by the liquid protein tragedy, a "last chance" diet that turned out to be indeed a final chance for at least fifty-eight Americans, mostly women, who died after trying it in 1977 and 1978. The diet is a modified fast in which the only calories consumed are eight daily tablespoons of liquid protein. Although liquid protein diets are still being advertised, their use has dropped sharply. But according to a recent poll, there has been a rise in total fasting to lose weight— an even more dangerous procedure unless undertaken with strict medical supervision. Other fad diets, although not lethal, are likely to short-change the dieter of such essential nutrients as carbohydrates, calcium, iron, vitamin A and trace minerals.

If you've made your own value judgment, and want to keep a trim figure without being fanatic about it, these are some points to bear in mind:

Pare down the day's menu just as soon as you've noticed the scales nudging upward by a few pounds. Muriel Stone, assistant director of nutrition at The New York Hospital, thinks that the first three to five pounds are crucial. "Lose them while it's still easy," she says.

Shave your caloric intake to 1,200 calories a day, *but not less.*

Most women lose weight at that level, says Dr. Henry Jordan, the University of Pennsylvania psychiatrist who helped develop the behavior modification treatment for dieters. A 1,200-calorie diet can be nutritionally complete: anything lower should not be attempted without medical supervision.

Don't expect to lose more than a pound or so a week. This can be accomplished by lopping off 500 calories a day. But don't haunt the scales; two weeks may pass before you see them moving downward. Weigh yourself weekly on Wednesdays, so you're not discouraged by a weekend gain.

Don't cram all your caloric goodies into one sitting. Whether you eat twice a day or spread out into five small meals is not important, says Dr. Jordan, but you should choose the number that you're comfortable with and make that a consistent pattern. Some doctors frown on skipping breakfast, but Dr. Jordan says, "There's nothing magic about having breakfast if you don't want to." Other physicians advise against a heavy evening meal. "There is good evidence," says Dr. Lyn Howard of Albany Medical College, "that fewer calories are stored as fat when eating is followed by exercise." If you eat a big dinner and then go to bed, you have less chance of burning off the calories you've taken in.

Exercise should be a part of your life style, even when you merely want to keep your weight stable. Don't expect to lose weight if you start exercising without cutting calories, but you can expect to get rid of flab, retarding the process that turns lean muscle into fat as the years pass. If you diet *and* exercise, the pounds are likely to drop off faster than if you just dieted. They will, however, drop off in equal proportion throughout your body. Women may wail, "I wanted to lose off my thighs, and instead my face got thinner," but this isn't true. Face and thighs have both slimmed down; it's just more noticeable on the bony face than on the padded thighs.

Many women are unhappy over unsightly ripples of nubbly fat that appear on their thighs: "It looks bumpy, like the skin of an orange," one told me. This condition has excited special attention since it was named "cellulite" and given a French accent. Cellulite "experts" have made a pile of money treating it with pills, massage and special creams. Recently I saw a woman in the shower at the YWCA rubbing her thighs vigorously with an abrasive sponge. "Someone told me it would get rid of these bumpy things," she explained, "but I haven't seen any improvement."

Despite the fancy name, cellulite is fat that is laid down in a particular contour, says Dr. Bernard Simon, chief of plastic surgery at Mt. Sinai Medical School in New York. It probably runs in families. Special creams and massages are a waste of time and money. The only treatment, according to Dr. Simon, is to exercise and to lose weight, reducing the fat and firming up the muscles.

Trimming the calories isn't all there is to a weight-loss plan. If it were, a day's menu could include two hot dogs, a small bag of potato chips, a piece of mince pie à la mode, and two Cokes, and still remain within a 1,200-calorie limit. Nutritionally such a menu would be a disaster. "The biggest mistake is to consider only calories, and forget about the other aspects of nutrition," says Patricia Wolman, a Brooklyn College nutrition professor. To keep healthy a woman needs a balanced intake of protein, carbohydrate and fat, in foods that include essential vitamins and minerals. "And on a 1,200-calorie diet, you practically need a calculator to figure it out right," she adds.

The trick is to choose foods that are nutritionally rich and calorie-poor—skim milk, for example, fish, a baked potato which, served plain, contains only about a hundred calories, thirty less than a cup of lettuce with Italian dressing. And since we require about fifty different nutrients, a week's menus should include a wide variety of foods. The wisest course is to consult a nutritionist, since doctors are notoriously ignorant about nutrition. You can also join a group like Weight Watchers, or ask your local chapter of the American Heart Association for advice about prudent dieting.

With two exceptions, a woman's nutrient needs do not change after the menopause. Because she is no longer losing blood every month, the iron requirements advised by the National Research Council drop from a daily eighteen milligrams to ten. But a premenopausal woman on a low-calorie diet should ask her doctor about an iron supplement, since it is almost impossible for her to take in enough iron on 1,200 calories.

Calcium is the other crucial mineral that must not be skimped after the menopause, when osteoporosis, a thinning of skeletal bone, may become a hazard (see p. 198). Skim milk, or milk products like yogurt and cottage cheese, should be a part of her reducing diet.

Complicating matters is the development during the middle

years of an intolerance for certain foods, for which doctors have no ready explanation. Although it varies from person to person, the foods most often complained about are onions, garlic, cabbage, coffee, dishes rich in butter or heavy with spices. "What happened to my iron stomach?" one woman, forty-four, wants to know. "I have gas and heartburn, and I burp, particularly when I eat peppers and fried foods." "When there's garlic in the food —and how we used to love scampi!" says another, forty-two, "I get sweats and palpitations. At two-thirty in the morning, my husband and I find ourselves sitting up in bed and rumbling at each other."

Because of the discomfort, many women are changing to simpler meals. Often they're cutting down on meat, and serving more fish, vegetables, whole grains. "The doctor told us to cut the cholesterol," one says, "so now I only serve red meat once a week. My college son calls it 'eating healthy,' and I think he's right. My husband and I both feel better for it."

Some are also flirting with the radical chic in nutrition—megavitamins, high-fiber-content foods, macrobiotics, organic foods. Although the pros and cons of many of these food fashions are beyond the scope of this discussion, two are pertinent to the nutritional needs of midlife—vitamin E, because its proponents promise that it will cure the hot flashes of menopause, enhance sex drive and retard aging; and the high-fiber diet, because of claims it will cure constipation and diverticular disease, both problems of midlife and later.

Vitamin E is found in margarine and other vegetable oils, in whole grains, green vegetables, dairy products, meat. The National Research Council recommends a daily consumption of twelve international units for an adult woman, and nutritionists believe that most of us get at least that in our diets. But thousands of women also swallow vitamin E capsules in doses ranging from four hundred up to a thousand units daily. "I take lots of vitamin E," a woman of fifty-four told me. "I've found it oxygenates the blood. I was getting hot flashes a few years ago, but vitamin E made them all go away."

Because vitamin E is fat-soluble, extra amounts remain in body tissues and are not excreted rapidly, as are water-soluble vitamins. Yet no scientific evidence of damage from overdosing has yet been documented. Many doctors, however, remain skeptical about its benefit. They point out that it's hard to evaluate vitamin

E's effect on sex drive because of the self-persuasive factor. If you think it will help you, it probably will. As for retarding aging, Dr. William Adler of the National Institute on Aging says, "I put this idea in the same category as laetrile." And according to *The Harvard Medical School Health Letter*: "Most of the claims made for vitamin E are either excessive or false. However . . . there is enough suggestive evidence for some benefits to merit further research."

The high-fiber diet has been blessed with even broader claims than vitamin E. In 1970 a British physician suggested that a diet heavy in roughage might reduce the incidence of cancer of the colon, number three cancer killer among middle-aged women. Since then advocates have hailed the high-fiber diet as the scourge of overweight, constipation, heart disease, appendicitis, gallstones, diverticulosis, hiatus hernia.

Dietary fiber is the indigestible portion of a plant, consisting of cellulose, pectin, mucilage or other chemicals that pass unchanged through the gastrointestinal tract, where they absorb water, and thus make the stool bulkier, softer, quicker and easier to pass. Foods high in fiber include whole-wheat bread, some breakfast cereals, peas, baked beans, nuts and peanut butter.

Many of the claims have now been sorted out, and fiber appears to be of definite benefit in constipation, an increasing problem as people become older. Because its use minimizes straining at stool, it is also likely to reduce hemorrhoids and possibly even varicose veins. Doctors who used to treat diverticular disease with soft, bland diets have made a ninety-degree turn, and now advocate plenty of fiber instead. In this disease, which afflicts two in five Americans over the age of forty, pouches are formed on the intestinal wall, a condition called diverticulosis. Often they become inflamed (diverticulitis), produce cramping pains and even lead to blockage that requires surgery. Physicians now think that a high-fiber diet may reduce symptoms, and even prevent diverticular disease from occurring at all.

But as a nostrum for other serious diseases, current research turns thumbs down on dietary fiber. Cancer specialists believe that too much fat in the diet is more likely to cause colon cancer than too little fiber. Studies have failed to show that fiber enhances the removal of cholesterol from the body, reducing the risk of heart disease. And the only way it seems to promote weight loss is because of its bulk, which makes the dieter feel stuffed sooner.

The other day on television I heard a commercial that urged dog-owners to buy a new food, tailored to the needs of the pet who had reached seven years—canine middle age. It made me start thinking about the possibility of a special diet based on the changing needs of women during the middle years. But the fact is that nobody knows very much about a woman's nutritional needs, nor is anyone trying very hard to find out. Dr. E. Neige Todhunter of Vanderbilt University, one of the rare experts in the field, puts it bluntly, "Nutritional requirements for women have received little investigative attention except during pregnancy and lactation . . . More research is needed."

XII

Changes in
Skin and Hair

"I know I'm pretty, and I guess I'm vain. I suppose that's why I've gotten so bothered recently about the bags I've noticed under my eyes." With her curly brown hair and rosy cheeks, Ellen, forty-four, is indeed very pretty. She lives in the suburbs with her husband, who is four years older, and the youngest of their three daughters. The older two are away at college.

Now she is weighing her assets with the thought of getting a job or starting a business. But Ellen's appearance, always assumed as a plus, is arousing an itch of concern. "I'm going a little in the face, drooping a bit," she observes. "I look at myself and say, 'Oh, God, I've got Daddy's bags under the eyes.' I'm sure everyone notices it. I've seen a friend put a finger up to her own eyes, as if she wants to smooth out the dark circles under mine. Maybe I'm imagining it, and yet it happens time and again."

Ellen is hardly alone in her concern. Trudy, who is forty-five, thinks she still looks younger than her age, but dreads tomorrow, a time at which "your skin just seems to disintegrate. It looks old, and you can't hide it. It's there on your face for everyone to see." And Rosa, at fifty-six, speaks dismally of "fantastic" changes in recent years: "My skin is so dry, and I've got liver spots on my hands and arms, and even one on my forehead. And around the chin and under the eyes, I just seem to sag."

Too busy with small children, these women may not have no-

ticed it at thirty but that's the age when the skin starts to lose
the glow of youth, particularly in the exposed places: face, neck,
hands. There are the laugh lines, charming at first, but worrisome
as they deepen; then the crow's-feet around the eyes, the purse-
string lines circling the mouth: "I told myself I was never going
to get those lines, and now I have, and they bother me," says
Louise, forty-five. There are dark circles under the eyes, signs of
a late night at first, then, apparently there to stay. And for some,
small pouches of fat, accenting the circle.

Then there are the spots, tan, red and brown, that seem to appear from nowhere overnight. They include freckles that no
longer fade in the winter; "liver" spots that have nothing to do
with the liver; raised rough areas that resemble baby warts.

And the hair. It grows where it didn't before, and doesn't grow
where it used to. It changes color, and for the worse. It's sparser
and sometimes it's coarser. Inexplicably, a hair suddenly sprouts
on the chin. Underarm and pubic hair start to thin. Fingernails
grow more slowly. And a plus, sweat and its odor start to lessen.

If a woman's face is her fortune—and that's what our mothers
and our grandmothers taught—then we're rapidly becoming
bankrupt. Too many women half believe that as the appearance
of youth vanishes, it will become impossible to snare a man or
hold the one you've got, make a friend, find a job, get a raise,
secure happiness. An acquaintance of mine tolerates an unusual
number of prominent wrinkles for her age—fifty-two—because of a
recent second marriage in which she feels secure. "The wrinkles
really blossomed about eight years ago when I was divorced,"
she confides. "And in a way they helped precipitate the breakup.
I decided I'd better get moving while I was still attractive, or
I'd never have a chance to find another man."

What happens to skin and hair during the middle years? Are
these changes inevitable? Can we stop the clock? And if not, how
can we come to terms with the sags and bags that unfortunately
rhyme with "old hag"?

The skin does not cover your face, limbs and torso merely to
look soft and touchable. The largest organ of the body, it is the
sealed envelope protecting the inner you from the environment.
What happens to it as the years pass is related to two factors:
a heredity that you can't change, and an interaction with the
environment, particularly with the sun's rays, that you can.

Everyone's skin ages sooner or later. It becomes looser, dryer, less elastic, like an old rubber band that has lost its tautness. When one woman was a child, she took great delight in standing before a mirror and contorting her face into ridiculous shapes, mouth widened, cheeks scrunched up, forehead tightened into menacing lines. She laughed when her mother warned her to be careful or it would stay that way. Forty years later, she told me recently, "My mother turned out to be right."

If you habitually squint to see better, grimace in distaste, laugh broadly, frown in concentration, scowl in anger, then these are the likely parts of your face to develop lines that deepen into furrows as your skin loses tone and elasticity. Facial exercises don't help; they may even compound the problem. Some beauty specialists advise their clients to modulate their facial expressiveness in order to delay the appearance of these character lines. It makes a certain amount of sense, since doctors know that if one side of a face is paralyzed, that blank, expressionless side looks more youthful. So here's a tip (even though it's one that I personally view with distaste): look bland and immobile if you're determined to appear younger. Another tip is more practical: if you smoke, you're likely to develop lines around the mouth and eyes that nonsmokers don't get.

Heredity determines what kind of skin you start out with, whether it's dry or oily, fair or dark, taut or loose on your facial bones. Whether it will show wrinkles at forty or at seventy, however, depends to a considerable extent on whether you've had a lifelong love affair with the sun. There is no longer any scientific question about it: like love and marriage, sun and wrinkles go together. Burning ultraviolet rays make your skin leathery, cause premature aging, encourage the emergence of the reddish-brown blotches that are the despair of many. Most of the half-million Americans treated annually for skin cancer are reaping the unpleasant rewards of years of sun worship. There are over 5,000 new cases of melanoma, the lethal skin cancer, diagnosed in women each year, and it is more likely to develop on sun-exposed parts of the body. In the San Francisco Bay area, and possibly elsewhere, melanoma is on the rise among women. Although a melanoma is a cancerous mole, ordinary moles do not multiply from sun exposure. They are, in fact, about the only surface growths that tend to lessen in number as the body ages.

If you want to protect your skin from aging and cancer, the obvious solution is to stay out of the sun or cover up with hat, parasol, long sleeves, stockings and gloves, or the kind of bathing costume your great-grandmother thought stylish. You can avoid such a drastic step if you learn a few facts about the sun's dangers, your own particular susceptibility and the protection offered by new chemical preparations.

It is the ultraviolet rays of the sun that do the damage, and their effect is related to the amount of melanin (pigmentation) in your skin. If your complexion is dark, you have some natural protection; and if your skin is black, you have a great deal. You'll acquire wrinkles much later in life than a white-skinned person. The sun is most formidable as our enemy close to the time of the summer solstice, May to July, for those who live in the northern hemisphere, and at the midday hours. Ultraviolet rays are more penetrating at higher altitudes; on the beach where the sand reflects the rays, even if you're sitting under an umbrella; and on the ski slope, where the snow has the same effect. You're better off if it's overcast, but not much, because seventy to eighty percent of the burning rays can penetrate the clouds. These rays will penetrate more if you've just emerged from the surf and your skin is wet; also if you've lathered yourself in oil.

Although sun*burning* is your enemy, *tanning* can be a friend: essentially it is the addition of more of the protective pigment, melanin, to your skin. "A tan is nature's sun screen," says Dr. Norman Orentreich, New York dermatologist and an authority on aging skin. The trick is to know your own skin and stay in the sun uncovered only long enough to produce a light blush, which will turn into a layer of tan. If you're a blonde, says Dr. Orentreich, the limit is about five minutes before you ought to cover up with a hat and a sun block, an opaque substance like zinc oxide or titanium dioxide that absorbs ultraviolet rays.

There's a good deal of confusion these days between sun blocks, sun screens and sun-tan lotions, all chemical mixtures that are bought in a drugstore and slathered on during the summer months. When to use one or another depends upon your coloring, and how much exposure reddens your skin, a question about which you're the expert observer. There's a wide range, from the fairest skin that always burns, and never tans, to the darkest that rarely burns, usually tans. Although brown and black skins neither tan nor redden with normal exposure, a light-skinned black woman can burn; and even if her skin is dark, sun damage can follow excess exposure. The significant word is *cumulative*. If you've been a sun-worshipper for years, some damage is inevitable, and you should be extra cautious from now on.

The sun-tan lotions that have been on the market for years promise they will give you a tan and avoid a burn, but they won't do it, unless you have a skin that is likely to tan in any case. The sun screens, available for the past half-dozen years, do a better job. The best of these contain alcohol and para-aminobenzoic acid (PABA), and they reduce the burning effect of the sun's rays by half. This simply means that an hour's exposure with the screen will produce the same burn that occurs after thirty minutes without it, warns Dr. Albert Kligman, dermatology professor at the University of Pennsylvania. In other words, if you're very fair, use a sun screen by all means, but you must still limit your sun exposure to very brief periods. Sun screens should be applied an hour before going outdoors, and reapplied after you've swum or sweated.

Many sunscreens now being marketed are graded for different complexions, labeled with three letters, SPF (Sun Protection Factor), and a number. SPF 6, for example, is for the most sun-sensitive skin, SPF 2 for the darker skin that seldom burns. The idea is to switch back and forth from one strength screen to another, depending on your coloring and degree of prior tan. But even those with darker skins are likely to need the strongest screen at their initial exposure. And blonds and redheads with very fair skin will need to cover up or use a sun block, which literally does block ultraviolet rays, if they want to minimize wrinkling and prevent skin cancer. Many dermatologists are convinced that no one should sunbathe and everyone should use a protective screen, even after the skin has tanned.

The flat liver-colored spots and the raised scaly lesions that may already have turned up on your hands, face, neck or chest, the areas constantly exposed, are the cumulative result of too much sun. The former are often blotchy freckles, and the latter result from superficial thickening of the top skin layer, the keratin. More than half the population over forty-five has already developed a liver spot or two. Some of these progress to become solar keratoses, which are not only unsightly but can, in about one case in four, eventually turn into skin cancer. A solar keratosis shculd be removed. This is a painless procedure, done in a few minutes by a dermatologist in his office, and entails either cutting, freezing or burning off the bump with an electric needle.

The second goal in battling aging skin is to keep the water content of skin cells from evaporating. This function is normally performed by the epidermis, the paper-thin outer layer that constantly flakes off and regenerates itself. But as a woman becomes older, the replacement rate slows down, and the keratin, the top epidermal layer no thicker than plastic wrap, is no longer as smooth, or as efficient in moisture retention as it used to be.

The first step is to wash the face briskly with soap and water, which most dermatologists recommend over cleansing creams for the ordinary skin. Dr. Kathleen Riley, dermatology professor at the University of South Carolina Medical Center, believes many women have to be "deprogrammed" by their doctors. "Some haven't washed their faces in years," she says. "The suggestion that they apply soap often causes hysterics."

Vigorous washing with a rough cloth removes dirt, flaky skin, excess oil. Dr. Orentreich believes a woman can achieve an even more significant effect if she washes with an abrasive cleansing puff made of polyester fiber web. The process is called epidermabrasion, and Dr. Orentreich says that it produces a mini-rejuvenation of the skin's top layer. (Don't confuse this with dermabrasion, a surgical procedure used by dermatologists and plastic surgeons, and described on p. 187.) "Stimulating the skin by abrading it," he says, "helps the epidermal layers to replace themselves more quickly, the way they do naturally in younger skin. It removes surface sun-damaged material, stimulates an increase in blood supply, and scrubs away senile blackheads, which appear after forty or fifty on the forehead." For men epidermabrasion of cheek or chin is unnecessary; daily shaving has just about the same effect.

The time to pat on a moisturizer is after the face is thoroughly rinsed but still damp. These products do not add moisture to your skin, but seal the skin surface so that water in the cells does not escape. Some dermatologists believe that ordinary Vaseline is just as effective a moisturizer as an expensive cosmetic cream and less likely to irritate a sensitive skin.

Although her skin shows little sign of aging, Barbara, a psychologist who is thirty-six, started using a moisturizer last year, on the advice of a nurse at her health maintenance group, and she's probably wise to do so. Gail, fifty-three, busy and athletic, grumbles over the time her new facial routine takes. "I used to pride myself that I could bathe, dress, and be out of the house in seven minutes. No more. Since my skin started looking dry, I've been spending half an hour over it. I use body lotion after a bath, which I never used to. I put on a moisturizer, rub off the excess, and then add a light cream foundation. Because my skin is fair, I apply sun screen before I play tennis. And that means I have to carry a towel to mop up the lotion as it mixes with sweat and drips on my clothes."

Is it worth it? Dr. Riley believes that cosmetics advertisers "are selling the American woman a bill of goods" by insisting that their products will serve as a fountain of youth. And Dr. Kligman has coined the term "acne cosmetica" to describe the pimples and blackheads that he says one in five women experience from their thirties on, due to ingredients in commercial cosmetics. The use of moisturizers is widely accepted, but other products, and particularly their lavish claims, are viewed with considerable skepticism by dermatologists.

One bit of advice on which there's wide medical consensus: Shun a face cream that contains estrogen. The ingredients are listed on the label now, thanks to a new regulation from the Food and Drug Administration. "All my laboratory research suggests," says Dr. Orentreich, "that female skin ages faster than male, because estrogens thin the skin while androgens, the male hormones, thicken it." And thicker skin, while it's not as soft and pretty, is more impervious to lines and wrinkles. By the time of the menopause, when female estrogen production declines, the damage has already been done, Dr. Orentreich believes.

Giving a woman androgens to supplement the small amount her body manufactures might be helpful to her skin; unfortunately, it would also have other masculinizing effects. For one thing, this male hormone is the cause of male baldness, a middle-age occurrence that women largely avoid. During and after the menopausal years, women are indirectly affected by the androgen they secrete, which is about one-tenth the amount men produce. When estrogen production starts to flag, the balance between the two hormones changes. That's why those coarse hairs occasionally appear on a woman's chin.

Paradoxically, other body hair tends to diminish, starting about five to ten years before the menopause. Women with a heavy hair growth under the arms and on the legs find they have to shave less. Later pubic hair thins out. "I used to have to pluck a few hairs from my eyebrows every day," one woman, aged forty-five, told me. "Now I don't bother more than once a week." And another only shaves her legs every two to three months.

Scalp hair also thins on many women, but the process often doesn't start until after the menopause, long after men are in despair over a receding hairline. Whether you will lose hair from your head, how much and when is related to your heredity as well as your age. The process could be slowed down or even stopped if you took supplementary estrogen by mouth, though not by smearing on a topical cream. But most dismiss this as a frivolous reason for ingesting a drug that could cause cancer (see p. 82).

If you're disturbed about the thinning of your hair, counting a day's loss on your brush may reassure you that all is well. Hair growth is seasonal, and when the leaves fall in October and November, every woman is likely to shed more hairs than she did in May. Out of an average 100,000 scalp hair follicles, the tiny tubes from which hair grows, nine-tenths are in a growing stage at any one time, a period that lasts for about three years, and one-tenth are in a resting period of three to six months. Hair falls out during and just after the resting phase, as its attachment to the base of the follicle weakens, or it is pushed out by a new hair emerging underneath it. If you count about a hundred hairs or so on a clean brush in one day, you are losing only an average amount; you might lose as few as fifty in spring and as many as one hundred and fifty in the fall.

If your hair has started to thin, these facts may guide you in what or what not to do about it:

Wash it as often as you please. Hair follicles are not harmed by a daily shampoo. Shampooing does, however, loosen hairs that are ready for shedding. If there appear to be excess hairs in the shower drain when you wash on a Monday, you're merely losing hairs that would normally have been shed on Tuesday or Wednesday.

Grandma was wrong in her advice about brushing a hundred strokes a day. Normal brushing to groom your hair is fine, but excessively vigorous brushing can pull hair out by the roots before its "shed" time.

Today's natural style—wash and blow-dry—is a lot better for a woman's hair than styles that pull on it, like braids, upswept hair-dos or those requiring frequent use of curlers, bobby pins or tightly inserted combs.

Don't waste your money on beauty products that claim to nourish, stimulate or revitalize thinning hair, or on salons that promise miracles from a unique massage or dandruff treatment. The hair shaft is not alive. No treatment will affect it at all. Ordinary dandruff does not cause hair loss. A conditioner or protein rinse is useful, however; it coats each shaft and makes it appear thicker. The number of active hair follicles lessens with age in most people, and no chemical has yet been discovered to reverse this process.

There's also no food or pill that helps common hair loss. Don't dose yourself with tranquilizers to calm "nerves" that may be accelerating hair loss; there is no firm evidence that emotional tension promotes it. Extra vitamins don't help, either, unless the loss is due, as it rarely is, to nutritional deficiency. In fact, unusually high doses of vitamin A may cause hair to thin temporarily. If you're concerned about nutrition, taking a one-a-day vitamin pill is all you need, according to Dr. Orentreich.

If you're really worried about hair loss, it's wise to check with a doctor about your general health. Anemia and thyroid imbalance, both correctable, are two conditions that may cause thinning. Stringent weight-loss diets may also result in temporary loss of hair.

Coloring or bleaching of your hair is not responsible for its thinning either. Dyes and bleaches, applied repeatedly for years, are likely to cause hairs to break. And because hair grows only about four inches in a year, lots of broken hairs may make it look sparser. The breakage, however, does not affect the roots.

Whether or not to hide the gray is a problem almost every woman faces during her middle years. Depending on heredity, graying starts for some at thirty, for others at fifty, but the change is almost inevitable. Graying occurs when the color cells at the base of each hair follicle stop producing pigment. Pulling out each gray hair as it appears may be emotionally satisfying, like hitting your head against a wall in frustration, but in about three months another hair, just as gray, will grow out of the same follicle. Plucking does actually destroy about one follicle in every hundred, a fact to remember if you habitually thin your eyebrows. Eventually some hairs may not grow back. There's good news too. Gray hairs are coarser, with more body. And they are also less likely to thin out.

Among the vast majority of the women who talked with me

about their middle years, the decision to dye was almost a knee-jerk reaction to the first gray, although some tried frosting as an interim solution. "I started coloring when I had nine gray hairs," one woman, forty-five, told me. Others used words like "traumatic" or "mortifying" to describe their emotions.

When I asked why they objected so violently, the answers were vague: "It's drab"; "I'm not old enough"; "It wouldn't fit my coloring." Apparently few had thought over the alternatives, although several commented on how distinguished men looked when they grayed.

To a woman, they grumbled at the inconvenience: "It's a bloody nuisance." Natalie, forty, observed the gray only a few months ago, and has so far had her hairdresser dye it twice, a dark brown with reddish highlights. "It's really not like me," she said. "I hate looking artificial, I don't feel comfortable having to wear a hat on the tennis court. I guess the hairdresser pushed me. She just talked me into it."

Rosa, fifty-six, who says she has dyed her hair "for a thousand years—well, it's been twenty at least," first went to the hairdresser every seven weeks for a tint. "Now it's every four, and in between I have to touch it up with a pencil, and to bleach eyebrows to match. Sometimes I wish I'd never started, but the thought of stopping now is just too traumatic. I say to the hairdresser, 'I'm bored. Should I let it grow out?' and she answers, 'Never. It would make you look ten years older.'"

Women should be wary of these scare tactics often used by their hairdressers. Skeptical buyers of clothes and furniture, we are apparently too emotionally involved with our looks to discount the arguments of someone who stands to profit from hair dyeing. Hairdressers, too, are likely to pooh-pooh the recent report from the National Cancer Institute that chemicals used in many hair dyes may be carcinogenic (cancer-causing). Yet it must be taken seriously by women who dye or are considering dyeing their hair.

These are the facts: it is well known that dye applied to the scalp easily finds its way into the bloodstream; some women notice that it even discolors their urine, an indication that large amounts are entering the body. Darker coloring shades contain more of this chemical than the lighter colors: one way to avoid the hazard is to bleach or streak the hair with peroxide or henna. The FDA has now ordered warning labels to be placed on all products containing the suspect chemicals; and several leading hair-dye manufacturers have changed their formulations to remove the suspect chemicals.

Yet although I asked specifically, not a single woman told me that she had stopped dyeing her hair because of the cancer hazard. Charlotte, forty-four, a natural brunette, started coloring her hair blue-black at sixteen, and switched a decade ago to strawberry blond. "I'm not worried about the cancer scare," she told me. "I figure if it's going to kill me, then at least I'll die looking young."

But is looking young really what it's all about for a female? Some women have begun to wonder. Lorna, who is fifty, has dyed her hair since she was thirty-five. "Last summer I came out of the closet and let it go gray. I'm really enjoying it. To me it's a statement. It's my way of saying—this is what I am. I no longer have to go the youthful route." And Joan, who is dating again after being widowed twice by the age of fifty-two, has become philosophical about her thinning hair. "The fact is that I've always had thinnish hair. So why does life have to be perfect?"

Yet even when they don't aim to set back the clock, many women still don't feel philosophical at all about those gray hairs. "It's not the gray that bothers me, but the mousy look it brings," explains a forty-two-year-old who was once a natural blonde. "I don't care about looking young, but I still want to look attractive, and that just takes more of an effort now."

Another finds that graying hair doesn't fit her self-image. "I'm a hiker and a tennis player, and I hope the word that describes me is 'vigorous.' Gray just doesn't connote vigor to me, and that's why I keep on coloring."

There seems to be a real dichotomy here for women who want to look attractive, as we all do, but are not overconcerned with hiding their years. Some consider their gray hair a positive statement; others like themselves better when they camouflage it. Perhaps it's because one's hair—the "crowning glory" of the nineteenth-century novels—is so central to appearance. No facial feature so strongly defines a face as the hair which frames it.

Although she may consciously deny it, every woman over thirty-five is deeply affected by the implications of this country's youth cult. It's natural to want to look as attractive as possible, but must the two words *youth* and *beauty* be the only possible combination to aspire to? Isn't there a season for everything—for youth with its soft, firm skin and agonies of self-doubt; for the bloom of motherhood; and for the softer tones of middle age? In her book, *The Wonderful Crisis of Middle Age*, the psychologist Eda LeShan quotes a woman as saying, "Isn't it terrible to look in the mirror and know that nothing good will ever happen to you again?" Although few of us are so full of self-shame, many—perhaps most—dislike what they see in the mirror in their forties and fifties.

Isn't this just one more area in which women have been sold a bill of shoddy goods? We've bought it from the large companies who skillfully evoke fear by suggesting that our hands aren't as young as a daughter's, our face isn't as youthful as a husband's, and those nasty dry lines around the eyes will never win a lover or a job. We've bought it from film and television which apparently require a Betty Furness to have copper-colored hair, but allow a Phil Donahue to be pure white. And we've bought it by not questioning the conventional wisdom, which holds that after thirty or forty, deception about her appearance is a womanly duty.

Susan Sontag suggests that women ought to begin to rethink what being feminine is all about: "The single standard of beauty for women dictates that they must go on having clear skins. Every wrinkle, every line, every gray hair is a defeat . . . all women are trained to want to continue looking like girls." The ideal of femininity is static, an appearance of eternal youth, Ms. Sontag writes. But masculinity, dynamic, equated with doing, credits a male with "character" when his face shows lines and furrows. She suggests that just as blacks suffer a damaged self-image from a society whose ideal of beauty is white, so do women from a society that equates beauty with youth.

Yet it is not society but middle-aged women themselves who are their own worst enemies. This is indicated in a study made by Carol Nowak, Pennsylvania State University psychologist. Dr. Nowak asked men and women of varying ages to judge the youth and attractiveness of persons whose faces they were shown in a series of color photographs. She found that *only* the middle-aged women, whose average age was forty-eight, misjudged consistently: if the photo showed a plain young woman, they guessed her age as older than it actually was; if she was older and attractive, they judged her as younger. They said that graying males "appear distinguished" and graying females are "old-looking." A woman with wrinkles, sags and bags was called "ugly"; a man with similar changes had "character." No other group—men, young women, elderly women—showed distorted vision to such an extent.

"Beauty and youth, then, are the winning combination," Dr. Nowak concluded. "It seems likely that, for women at least, there is a 'crisis point' in midlife where they truly do feel less attractive . . . and less good about themselves."

Although Sontag and Nowak are both correct, I'm inclined to think that their wringing of hands may be excessive. Although women *are* more concerned than men about facial aging, a growing number are now just too busy to agonize over it. They're going to school, advancing in a job, playing tennis, and although they believe they look worse, many paradoxically seem to like themselves better.

On her fiftieth birthday one woman looked in the mirror and announced to her husband and daughter that she was now "an aging beauty." They all had a good laugh, but there was some truth to the joke. "I know that the purse-string lines that I've had for a decade around the mouth," she said later, "and the furrow between the brows that showed up last month may not be pretty. But they're me, and if they betray my age, well, what is there to lie about?"

Many women are now heeding the plea from Susan Sontag for another female option: Women "can let themselves age naturally and without embarrassment, actively protesting and disobeying the conventions that stem from this society's double standard about aging . . . women should allow their faces to show the lives they have lived. Women should tell the truth."

Is Cosmetic Surgery for You?

Well, why not? That's what many women with aging faces are asking these days. Why not have a face lift, get rid of baggy eyelids, smooth the wrinkles with a chemical peel, even erase the stretch marks on the abdomen?

There isn't any reason at all why not—if you're realistic about the results you expect, if you have a fistful of money (usually in four figures, paid in advance), several weeks of time and are willing to suffer a little pain and plenty of discomfort.

Although women aren't heading for the surgeon's knife quite

as fast as they're dyeing their hair or having their teeth capped, cosmetic surgery has now become respectable. Once it was for the rich, the famous and the film colony, and even these kept it a secret, checked into the hospital under a false name, and lied blithely when asked.

In the past thirty years the number of cosmetic operations has multiplied about sixteenfold, and is still growing at the rate of five to ten percent a year. Part of the reason is that antibiotics and skilled techniques have made the surgery safer and more effective. Another part is the American cult of beauty and youth. Yet neither is the complete explanation. An important new factor is the strengthened view that women in late middle age and the early years of old age remain part of the vital mainstream of life, no longer relegated to the back shelf. "My grandmother started dressing all in black at the age of forty," says one woman, herself forty-five, a jogger, gardener and golfer. "At seventy-six my mother went to Europe with me." Even in their late fifties and early sixties, women remain in the labor market in huge numbers. Right or wrong, they believe that competence is equated with looking young.

Whether one approves of it or not, Betty Ford's highly publicized face lift at the age of sixty tells us something about ourselves and our changing mores. "I wanted a nice new face to go with my beautiful new life," she said. "My children thought it was silly, but I told them—wait till *you're* sixty!" These are important statements for Mrs. Ford's own generation, and for yours that follows. First, if you're having cosmetic surgery to solve your personal problems, you've put the cart before the horse. Don't expect a "nice new face" to lead to a "beautiful new life." Make the new life first, and then add the surgery to embellish it.

If cosmetic surgery is on *your* mind, there are the points to consider:

The benefits. A New Jersey divorcee, fifty-nine, decided to leave the insurance business for a less taxing career closer to home. "I felt I would have a better chance of getting a good job with a younger face. Although I felt bouncy and energetic, everything had sagged like crazy." First she had her face lifted and the crepey wrinkles removed from her eyelids; then she went job-hunting. Now she has a new job and another plus: "I just feel more secure about myself."

Another woman went on a physical fitness kick and emerged

twenty pounds slimmer, firmly muscled, brimming with energy. "But when I got out of the shower after a five-mile jog or a half-mile swim, and looked in the mirror, there was that old droopy face. It didn't fit my body or the vital new me." She decided on cosmetic surgery to please herself. (One warning for dieters: lose the weight first, then have cosmetic surgery. The ping-pong type of weight loss and gain can be disastrous, particularly to a face lift, says Sylvia Rosenthal in her book *Cosmetic Surgery: A Consumer's Guide.*)

"The best candidate for cosmetic surgery is an emotionally healthy well-integrated woman who just wants to look better," says Dr. Bernard Simon, who heads the plastic surgery department at the Mt. Sinai Medical School in New York City. "With her active life, she has to make an effort to fit the surgery into a busy schedule. Her face is not her raison d'être, although its sagginess bothers her. She's no more narcissistic about her appearance than any woman who asks a hairdresser to style her hair more becomingly."

A woman should forget about aesthetic surgery if she is doubtful of its benefits: "I'd like to get rid of the saggy skin under my chin," one says, "but what difference would it make?" She should not have the operation if her expectations are unrealistic: "I look forward to a face lift as a ticket to the altar," says a divorcee. She should also forget it if she's trying to suppress moral qualms about face surgery. One woman told me that at the age of forty-eight, she and a friend had consulted a surgeon about a face lift, and been advised to go ahead. "Then my friend developed cancer. She kept thinking it was a punishment for her vanity. I didn't agree, but still I wondered." Eight years have passed; the friend has died, and she is still wondering.

The timing. This decision is a bit like the familiar monthly agonizing over a haircut. Should you trim it often so it never looks overgrown, or wait until it's really wild and make a dramatic change? The answer for a face lift (and probably a haircut too) is to wait until it's worth doing, but not too long. "You're not ready for it if your chinline and your face are still firm," says Dr. Simon. Though actresses have the operation earlier, the average patient is in her mid-fifties and most would probably benefit from their late forties on. If the skin hangs in folds but still retains some elasticity and a little subcutaneous fat, you're a good candidate, according to Sylvia Rosenthal's guide.

Permanence. The classic comment about youth-enhanc-
ing surgery is that you can expect it to turn back the clock, but
not to stop the ticking. In other words, the surgeon's scalpel can
remove many of the effects of aging, such as sagging and loss of
elasticity, but it cannot stop the relentless momentum with which
these effects continue. Expect five, eight, even ten years of benefit,
followed by a gradual undramatic return to the crepey look. All
other things being equal, surgery performed during your forties
will last longer than if it is done in your sixties, because the
younger skin will age more slowly. But individual factors are important. Your heredity, skin tone, weight, exercise, eating and
drinking habits and emotional trauma all affect the face lift's life.
"Human tissue," says Dr. Thomas Rees, chief of plastic surgery
at Manhattan Eye, Ear, and Throat Hospital in New York, "is
not like sculpting in clay or wood."

Hazards. Never forget that this is an operation, not a
beauty parlor facial. All surgery entails some risk of infection,
hemorrhage, blood clot or nerve damage. The frequent use of local
anesthetics lowers the risk somewhat. Still, women with diabetes,
high blood pressure, extreme obesity or a bleeding tendency
should consult their personal physician before going ahead.

When skin and tissue are cut, they heal by scarring; there is
no such thing as scarless surgery. But plastic surgeons are clever
at covering up their tracks. Incisions are made back of the hairline, close to the ear, in natural skin folds, so that they are barely
noticeable, especially after a few months have passed. Black
women, who are more at risk for thick unsightly scars, are less
likely to have the wrinkled and saggy skin that improves with
cosmetic surgery.

Probably less than five percent of face lifts and eye operations
fail; the sags and bags return in less than a year. Provided the
surgeon is technically able, no one quite understands why this
happens. If it does, a second tuck may set back the clock for a
longer time.

The surgeon. He should be chosen with the same meticulous care one would use in selecting a doctor to perform open-
heart surgery. The reputable cosmetic surgeon is a diplomate of
the American Board of Plastic Surgery, which means that he has
the same lengthy training as a general surgeon, plus two to three
extra years in plastic surgery. It's wise to check on your prospec-
tive surgeon's qualifications in the *Directory of Medical Special-*

ists, on the shelf of most public libraries. His hospital affiliation is another tip-off. Find out whether he practices on the staff of a leading, preferably a teaching, hospital, or whether he operates *only* in a small private hospital. Remember too that able surgeons do not advertise, nor do they guarantee results.

Although the face lift is thought of as *the* operation to set back the facial clock, cosmetic eye surgery is actually the most frequent, the most dramatically effective, and the longest-lasting. The procedure, called a *blepharoplasty*, smooths out crepey, droopy eyelids, removes bags under the eyes, and when necessary, raises the eyebrows. Because the upper-eyelid skin is the thinnest on the body, it is often the first spot to wrinkle. Pouches of protruding fat may form, sometimes even obscuring vision. Surgery removes excess skin and fat, giving a smoother tauter look. Bags under the eyes rarely recur, and the eyelid corrections last as long as ten to fifteen years.

The operation, which takes one and a half to two hours, is generally performed under local anesthetic, and can be done in a doctor's office. Swelling and discoloration (but little pain) can be expected to last about ten days, and patients are advised to stay out of the direct sun for several months. The thread-thin scars are barely noticeable after a few months. Don't expect to feel completely normal quickly. One woman says it took six months before she felt her eyes really belonged to her again.

Ophthalmologists as well as plastic surgeons perform this operation. In fact, if the overhanging lid is so droopy that it produces a hooded effect and interferes with vision, consultation with an eye surgeon is advisable. Whether you choose a plastic or an eye surgeon, his expertise is crucial. The function of the lid is to cover and protect the eye, and if the surgeon should err by lopping off too much, it could leave the eyeball exposed.

Expect the operation to cost between one and two thousand dollars, *payable in advance*. This is the accepted procedure with all cosmetic surgery. Your health insurance may pay part of the bill *if* an eye specialist says that your vision was impaired by the droopy lids.

When is the time for cosmetic eye surgery? When slackness of the skin and bagginess of the eyelids is not a temporary condition relieved by rest, or when it becomes increasingly difficult to camouflage the condition by cosmetics, advises the American

Academy of Facial Plastic and Reconstructive Surgery. The condition is common after the age of fifty, even earlier in families in which deep pouches under the eyes are hereditary.

Repair of the eyelids is sometimes done in conjunction with a face lift, as in the case of Betty Ford, who lost her droopy lids at the same time her jowly chin was tightened. Many surgeons, however, prefer these to be separate procedures. If you're planning only one procedure, advises Sylvia Rosenthal in *Cosmetic Surgery*, choose blepharoplasty: it's the single most effective way to look younger.

Although men have the eyelid surgery almost as frequently as women, ten women have a face lift for every man who does. As skin and underlying muscles lose elasticity, your size-twelve face is wearing a size-sixteen skin. The surgeon, like a meticulous seamstress redraping a dress, detaches the skin of the face and neck, tightens underlying muscle and tissue, shifts and rotates the skin, then trims away the excess. Jowls, wattles and crepey skin on the neck give way to a trimmer, tauter jawline, and facial skin no longer droops.

There are some changes that a face lift does *not* accomplish. It does not remove wrinkles, but if they are associated with a generalized sagging, it makes them smoother and less conspicuous. If you are plagued, as many women are, even in the mid-forties, by fine lines radiating out from the lips, into which lipstick often bleeds, a face lift will not help. Neither will it smooth out the horizontal worry lines on the forehead, the vertical lines between the brows, or those running diagonally from nose to mouth. It won't affect the eyelids and under-eye bags, of course, unless the extra eye procedure is added.

The operation is tedious, taking two and a half to four hours, and is usually performed with a local anesthetic after a patient is sedated. Expect to remain in the hospital three to four days, and to look passable in about two weeks. Fine scars will be inconspicuous, since they are hidden under the chin and hairline, and close to the ears. Average cost is about $2,500, although some women pay as much as $5,000 or as little as $1,500; the hospital bill may add several thousand more and only a few medical insurance plans pick up any part of the tab.

If you don't think your facial skin needs redraping, but merely smoothing and resurfacing, *dermabrasion* or a *chemical face peel* are the appropriate procedures. Both make wrinkles lighter and shallower, soften facial scars, including those made by adolescent acne, and take away freckles. These procedures are performed by dermatologists, sometimes also by plastic surgeons. They work on the same principle—that if the top layer of the dermis is scraped or burned away, the skin as it regenerates will become smooth and unwrinkled, an effect that is likely to last for several years.

According to Dr. Norman Orentreich, the New York City dermatologist who helped develop the dermabrasion technique currently in use, this procedure removes one-third to one-fifth of the dermis, creating a controlled wound. The skin is planed away with a rotating wire brush, and if the entire face is abraded, the operation takes about forty minutes. It is usually done with a local anesthetic in the doctor's office, though sometimes in a hospital. As the skin heals, it is covered by a thick, soggy crust that peels away in about seven to ten days. At first the new skin is pink and tender but it gradually reassumes normal color. After dermabrasion or a face peel, a woman must stay out of the direct sun for a full year, unless protected by a sun screen.

From the description, it should be obvious that a motor-powered wire brush, unless it is carefully handled by a competent, experienced operator, can wreak real damage, even destroying the full thickness of the skin. Just as in cosmetic surgery, you should choose a specialist who uses this technique frequently, not one for whom it is a couple-of-times-a-year sideline to a dermatology or plastic surgical practice. This advice should be even more strongly emphasized for the face peel. Instead of a wire brush controlled by a doctor's hands, the peel uses a caustic chemical solution called phenol (carbolic acid) to remove the upper layer of dermis. It is actually a controlled second-degree burn—controlled only if the operator is skilled. *Never* go to a layman for chemosurgery. Some surgeons think it is more effective than dermabrasion in lightening crow's-feet, purse-string lines around the mouth and forehead wrinkles, but most agree it is also more hazardous.

Writing in *The Menopause Book*, Dr. Mary Catherine Tyson, an internist at Mt. Sinai Medical School in New York, advises that blue-eyed blond women are the best prospects for successful chemical face peel; those with darker coloring are more at risk. Black women should *never* have a face peel; it may cause unsightly scarring and areas of depigmentation. "In my opinion," she adds, "the face peel is almost always inadvisable . . . Burning one's face is not a trivial decision . . . Some faces so treated look taut and strange and oddly shiny."

For a woman who wants the works, it is feasible to have eye surgery and a face lift, followed several months later by derma-brasion or a face peel. Now there is still another wrinkle (or anti-wrinkle in this case)—injections of liquid silicone to plump out any facial lines or wrinkles that remain after the other proce-dures. This material is similar to the medical-grade silicone used in solid form to augment the breast, and to correct chin, nose and ear deformities. The consistency of mineral oil, it is injected painstaking drop by drop deep into the tissue through a fine needle. Sometimes it takes several visits over a month or longer to fill out a single wrinkle, with a cost of $60 for each visit.

A woman considering the use of medical silicone should be warned that it is a questionable procedure for the following rea-sons:

It is an experimental drug, and has not been licensed by the FDA for general medical distribution.

It requires unusual experience and patience from the doctor administering the silicone. If a few drops too many are injected, they may drift to other locations, and can never be completely removed. At one time liquid silicone was used by unscrupulous surgeons to augment breast size, and results were often disastrous. (The solid gel now used for breast implants is considered quite safe because it remains separate from the body, forming no bond with human tissue.)

Liquid silicone injections are useful in rare cases in which facial atrophy occurs. A group of doctors, sponsored by the American Society of Plastic and Reconstructive Surgeons, is now investigat-ing its values and hazards in treating this deformity. Their find-ings will not be known for several years.

Cosmetic surgery of the body is mainly useful for those women who want to look acceptable in clothes and don't mind the scars that their garments hide. After repeated childbirth, particularly in-volving unusually large babies, and with extensive weight loss, some women develop extra folds of skin that hang loose from the abdomen. Others have pads of bulging flesh resembling riding breeches on the outside of the leg just below the hip, or batwing deformities, with flesh hanging pendulously from the upper arm.

Lipectomy is the name for surgery that contours these un-sightly pads; essentially it's like a face lift applied to part of the body. Major surgery performed in a hospital under general anesthesia, lipectomy has problems of infection, slow wound healing, lengthy recovery, extensive scarring. Last year a California woman died of overwhelming infection following an abdominal lipectomy performed by a general surgeon. Because of extensive upper-arm scarring, repair of a batwing deformity is seldom done by American plastic surgeons. Some use dermabrasion to lighten stretch marks on the body that appear after pregnancy or extensive weight loss, or surgery to tighten split abdominal muscles and remove excess stretch-marked skin.

Cosmetic surgery is respectable today. And yet columnists and the public did not treat Betty Ford's face lift with the compassion they gave to her breast cancer and her bout with drugs and alcohol. Some accused her of trying to become a plastic doll. One of the gentlest and most thoughtful comments came from Ellen Goodman, columnist of the Boston *Globe*. It is worth quoting, because it has meaning for all women who want to set back the clock with cosmetic surgery:

"It's not that I blame Betty Ford for wanting to look 'better' or younger. But I wish women didn't have to fight to stay young out of fear of turning ancient . . . I am struck by how difficult it still is for women to age gracefully. It is still assumed that age gives 'character' to a man's face and 'ruins' a woman's . . . If the cultural process were a gentler one, then women perhaps could grow ripe with the sense of generating rather than deteriorating."

At age fifty-four, Lauren Bacall was asked whether she had ever had a face lift. "Can't you see I haven't?" she answered. "I'm never going to have one. This is my face and I'm going to live with this face. It's me, Betty Bacall—by myself and part of myself, wrinkles and all."

XIII

The Backs
and the Bones

Is arthritis in your future? The answer used to be a firm *yes*, but now the medical experts are not so sure. And even if it is, they add, it probably won't be the bad kind. Yes, you're likely to get more aches and pains in the joints, occasional stiffness in the neck or lower back, even a pinched nerve or the dull throb of bursitis in the middle years and later. But the ominous phrase "crippled by arthritis" will be reserved for only a few. And you can prevent some of the garden-variety joint pain by moving your body more and better, starting right now.

Arthritis, or joint inflammation, is a wastebasket word that covers a hundred or more different medical conditions. The two most prevalent are rheumatoid arthritis and osteoarthritis, frequently and inaccurately lumped together. Women develop more of both types, but rheumatoid arthritis, which has nothing to do with aging, frequently shows up in the twenties and thirties, while the milder osteoarthritis, also called degenerative joint disease, doesn't develop until the forties, fifties or even later.

Only about one or two percent of the American population will ever get rheumatoid arthritis, a serious disease that can rack the whole body with fatigue, fever and severe joint pain and can even be crippling. If you're into the forties and you haven't got it yet, the chances are diminishing that you ever will.

But if one were to X-ray the entire adult population, the degenerative joint changes of osteoarthritis would show up in an occasional woman in her late thirties, perhaps one in four in the forties, half by age fifty, and almost all in the sixties. This doesn't necessarily mean that the victims are even aware of the changes. "There is little correlation," says Dr. Emmanuel Rudd, consulting medical director of the Arthritis Foundation, "between what the X-ray shows and the patient feels." He cites the case of a ballet dancer in her sixties: "X-rays indicate she will never walk again, but she has good muscles because of her work and manages remarkably well."

Osteoarthritis, about which surprisingly little is known, used to be dismissed as a wear-and-tear disease of the joints. The theory was that the mechanical parts of a joint, particularly those in the knee and hip that bear the weight when a human is in an upright posture, simply wear out with advancing age, and nothing can be done to prevent it. A "youthful" joint (the area where two bones meet) is protected with layers of smooth elastic material called cartilage or gristle that allow the surfaces to slide smoothly across each other. But as the years pass, the cartilage often becomes pitted and frayed; then bone ends become thicker, with bony spurs sometimes developing; surrounding ligaments and membranes may thicken; and muscles may tense, go into spasm, and weaken. Inflammation, which is the key symptom of rheumatoid arthritis, may not be present at all. Although pain is a feature of both, in osteoarthritis it comes in spells, and may eventually disappear.

But with too many unanswered questions, researchers have started to wonder about the wear-and-tear theory. The consensus now is that some forms of osteoarthritis may be inherited; others may follow congenital or acquired joint abnormality—the trick knee of the football hero, for example; and both are probably worsened by a bulging abdomen, muscles weakened from disuse, and the joint distortions caused by fashionable shoes. Thus the cheerful news that painful osteoarthritis is not inevitable and may in some cases be prevented or ameliorated.

The most prevalent site for osteoarthritis in women simply doesn't fit the theory of wear and tear on weight-bearing joints. Occasionally in the late thirties, and more frequently in the forties and fifties, redness, swelling, tenderness and aching develop in the end finger joints nearest the nail. Although the pain abates, usually within months, bony enlargements of the joints, called Heberden's nodes, appear, giving the fingers a knobby appearance. Occasionally the middle finger joints or joints of the toes may also be affected. Don't confuse this problem with gout, another form of arthritis that men get more often, usually in the joint of the big toe.

There appears to be no direct association between the appearance of Heberden's nodes and the menopause, although they often turn up at this time. Nor is there a relationship to household chores such as scrubbing; rich as well as poor are susceptible. If your mother has Heberden's nodes, you may develop them too, for they appear to run in families. They do not cripple; they do not worsen; but they do look strange.

Although many other joints are unaffected, osteoarthritis also favors the hip and knee (Grandma called it "housemaid's knee"), particularly among heavy women whose weight forces these joints to carry an extra load. Athletes develop osteoarthritis in the same joints, and so do others who have been injured in an accident. Doctors now believe that some cases may actually be traced to infancy, when hip dislocations suffered during birth are so mild that they go unnoticed. Eventually the damage takes its toll in the start of degenerative arthritis. Alert to a future danger, some hospitals now keep an eye out for hip dislocations among the newborns in the nursery, and treat them early.

Doctors also speculate that an inconsequential sports injury, such as a twisted knee or a wrenched hip, untreated in youth and often forgottten, may eventually result in osteoarthritis serious enough to require surgery forty or fifty years later. Eighty thousand joint replacement operations are performed each year on the hip alone, usually on persons in their sixties. Some of these might have been prevented if a minor injury had received proper care many decades earlier.

When osteoarthritis develops, apparently without cause, in the middle years, doctors call it primary; when it follows injury or abuse to a weight-bearing joint, it is secondary. But as more knowledge is gained and more questions asked, the line between the two keeps blurring. Are the joints of some arthritis sufferers imperfect from birth, and is this the result of heredity or congenital injury before or during birth? How do poor posture, flat feet, obesity contribute to osteoarthritis? Why do some people, despite signs of joint degeneration revealed by X-rays, sail through life with barely a twinge? These questions remain unanswered, but they suggest that the simplistic and negative explanation of aging may short-change the sixteen million Americans who develop osteoarthritis.

Doctors may be stumped by the real cause of degeneration in finger, hip and knee joints, but the puzzle is child's play compared to the aching back. In this common problem twenty-four vertebrae and their joints, twenty-three cartilaginous discs separating the vertebrae, as well as supportive muscles and ligaments in back, hips and abdomen, may act in concert or alone to become the villain in the piece. When the human animal first stood up on her hind legs, the strain on the spine, running from head to buttocks, made back trouble almost inevitable.

The popular explanation, a slipped disc, is far from accurate. A disc, in fact, really doesn't slip at all; it bulges and sometimes ruptures, causing some, but far from all, of the grab-bag complex of problems called back pain. The disc is a kind of joint, made up of a ring of cartilage surrounding a capsule of gelatinous material, that acts as a shock absorber. One disc is positioned between each of the spinal vertebrae to give supple motion and flexibility to the spinal column.

Degeneration of the discs usually starts by the thirties, even among persons with no symptoms at all. It is part of the aging process, but how much trouble it causes, and where and when, is also related to a woman's living pattern. A typist with myopia strains her neck—the cervical spine—all day as she leans forward to peer at her copy. One woman I spoke with was fifty-two when she had surgery on her lower back, the lumbar spine. But her back trouble went back twenty-eight years, to when a weight gain of forty-five pounds in the first of three pregnancies aggravated a slight spinal curvature. Another woman, laid up at fifty-four with severe back pain, had adopted two toddlers when she was thirty. Using back and abdominal muscles unaccustomed to the load of lifting a two-year-old started a process that laid her low twenty years later.

Acute back pain may follow when a bulging disc finally ruptures, spilling out its jellylike substance, increasing the friction of uncushioned vertebrae rubbing against each other. More often, discs just thin and flatten out, ending their role as shock absorber. Much back pain is unrelated to discs, but is caused by strain put on the complex web of muscles and ligaments in the back, hips and abdomen that support the spine. Neck and lower back pain often appear in spells, with weeks of discomfort followed by gradual easing, then surcease that may last several years. Even the pain of a ruptured disc comes to an end as time passes and the extruded material shrinks in size. For these and other reasons, surgeons are reluctant to operate on painful backs, except in cases where pressure on a nerve may be causing permanent damage.

Despite a future that may promise disc degeneration and osteoarthritis of the spine, an aching back is by no means a necessary corollary. It may be eased or prevented entirely by following these admonitions:

Stand up straight. "The worse your posture is, the more likely you are to develop arthritic changes," says Dr. Willibald Nagler, chief of physical medicine and rehabilitation at The New York Hospital. Don't slump with your head forward like a turtle, or stand swaybacked, belly bulging. Strong stomach muscles will keep a female abdomen from sagging, and help support her back. Women in their thirties should start stomach exercises now (see p. 116). Even better, they should never stop the exercise regime advised to restore the musculature made slack by childbirth.

Keep your weight down. Overweight aggravates osteoarthritis, particularly among women in their forties and fifties. It puts a strain on back, knees and hips, the weight-bearing areas susceptible to joint degeneration.

Sit properly. Use a straight hard chair for prolonged sitting, and rest your spine against it. This is important while you are at work and watching TV. Typists do better placing their work on a desk stand that allows them to keep the head upright. Dr. Bernard Jacobs, an orthopedist at the Hospital for Special Surgery in New York, points out that people tend to forget the importance of a car seat that supports the driver's back. He recommends bucket seats designed in consultation with an orthopedist as the best. A driver should sit close enough to the wheel so that her legs are partly bent when working the pedals.

Sleep on a bed with a hard mattress, or insert a thin plywood board between mattress and box springs. Some doctors deplore reading in bed because they say it strains the neck muscles. Dr. Nagler thinks it's okay if you're propped up properly, pillows positioned so that head and neck do not droop forward. Don't sleep without a pillow (this bends your head backward), or on too thick a pillow, which bends it forward.

Wear medium heels. Both high heels and flats can throw your back out of balance.

Carry bundles close to the body to protect the spine, one cradled in each arm if possible. To pick up anything, even a scrap of paper, bend your knees, and squat, using your leg muscles, not the spine, to do the job.

Is a woman a superstitious fool for wearing a copper bracelet on wrist or ankle as a protection against arthritis? Although it is a totally unproven remedy, doctors now think it possible that the copper, absorbed through the sweating skin, may be mobilized to help defend the body against an attack of rheumatoid arthritis. But if you're nearing fifty and you've never had rheumatoid arthritis, it's osteoarthritis that should concern you, and a copper bracelet is valueless except as an ornament.

If you develop mild arthritic pain, home treatment for a few days may be as beneficial as dashing off to the doctor. This includes aspirin, which is anti-inflammatory as well as a painkiller; hot baths, a heating pad, plenty of rest. An orthopedic or cervical collar is an excellent crutch to have handy if your neck hurts or feels stiff. By limiting the motion of the cervical vertebrae, it may cut pain quite effectively.

The physician whom you may consult is likely to prescribe an anti-inflammatory drug stronger than aspirin, which may have potentially serious side effects. "These drugs are useful in a spell of illness to help nature do the healing," Dr. Rudd says, "but I think they're overused. It's more important to learn the proper way to move than to swallow a pill." Traction that stretches muscles and ligaments in the affected area is another resort, as is the use of a cane or crutch to protect a painful weight-bearing joint. A cane relieves a painful hip of close to one-third of its load. If you think it lines you up with the elderly, invent a silly decoration like a sprig of flowers taped to the handle, to show yourself and others that you're young in heart.

The long-term value of an injection of hydrocortisone into the painful joint, a treatment that doctors have used for the last thirty years, is now being investigated. Usually it relieves pain promptly, and its effect may last as long as eight weeks. But a recent study shows that although a joint injected with a placebo improves more slowly, it gives no more pain after four weeks than one treated with cortisone. Pain relief from the placebo injection also lasts up to eight weeks. Specialists are now advising more conservative use of this powerful drug.

Another group of painful conditions called soft-tissue rheumatism rises sharply in incidence among women during the middle years. It includes bursitis, tenonitis, fibrositis and tennis elbow. All involve local inflammation of tendons, muscles and ligaments that support joints of the finger, shoulder, elbow and hip. They are not true arthritis; they may occur once and never return; and they are usually caused by extra strain on soft tissue that may have suffered some age-related changes. By middle age some fraying occurs in a tendon, reducing its ability to withstand unexpected violent stress. "If a woman unaccustomed to regular exercise paints her kitchen ceiling," says Dr. Nagler, "she's liable to wind up with tenonitis—tendon inflammation—in her shoulder. Her unused muscles are just unprepared for the job she's pushing them to do."

A dull, steady ache in the shoulder, the kind that can keep you awake at night, is usually diagnosed by the victim as bursitis, though it can also result from damage to other soft tissue, such as a tendon. Like a disc, a bursa is a cushioning device, a small sac containing slippery fluid. It is located at potential friction points between adjoining tissues within the joint. Pressure or injury can trigger bursa inflammation, made more acute by calcium deposits in the area. Bursitis usually affects a shoulder, but may occur in other joints, hips and elbows in particular.

Tennis elbow, another soft-tissue inflammation, is not a form of bursitis but a first cousin that affects muscles, ligaments and tendons in the elbow joint. Only one-third of its victims are tennis players. Overuse of the forearm in playing tennis, shaking hands repeatedly (a politician's hazard), doing handiwork involving a screwdriver can all cause the condition.

Writing in *The New York Times*, Jane Brody, medical columnist, describes the victim of tennis elbow as a person of either sex, aged about thirty-five to fifty-five. "This disorder," she says, "seems to represent a lost ability of the body to repair wear and tear on the elbow, an ability that declines in the third decade of life." To prevent the disorder, tennis players are advised to warm up slowly, wear an elastic bandage on the playing arm, avoid a wooden racket, use light balls with plenty of bounce and switch to a two-handed backhand.

When soft-tissue rheumatism is acute, an injection of an anti-inflammatory drug kills the pain, but as with osteoarthritis, does not cure the underlying condition. You may be ecstatic over the instant relief the injection brings, but if the pain returns, don't pressure your doctor for repeated shots. Two or three injections are okay during an acute phase, but repeating them on a regular basis over months or years carries some hazard to the joint.

The main thing to remember in order to prevent these miseries that afflict joints, muscles and other tissues that keep your body moving smoothly, is that nothing works quite so efficiently as you're getting older. Your back muscles are stiffer, abdominal muscles flabbier and both have lost some elasticity. Cartilage wears down, tendons fray, discs deteriorate. As a youngster, you could hole up in the library for three weeks writing a term paper, and when it was finished, celebrate with three fast sets of tennis. Chancing on-again, off-again exercise like Sunday gardening, once-a-year snow shoveling, a single weekend of cross-country skiing, should no longer be your thing. Now you must keep in trim at all times by regular use of muscles, joints and tendons ranging throughout the body. Like Alice in Wonderland, you have to keep moving in order to stay in the same place.

Osteoporosis

What do an astronaut and a woman past the menopause have in common? The answer is osteoporosis, a condition in which skeletal bone thins, becoming less dense and more prone to fracture. Forced inactivity, as when you are confined to bed for weeks or months, may also cause osteoporosis.

Although it may start in some women by the mid-thirties, the bone disorder accelerates during the decade following the menopause, affecting one in four women, and one in ten severely. Men develop osteoporosis too, but it starts about fifteen years later and is less than half as frequent. Symptoms include back pain, rounded shoulders, loss of height and later dowager's hump. But the most serious effect is the fracture of brittle bones, most frequently a rib, wrist, vertebra or hip, often after only minimal trauma. Wrist fractures start to rise in women after the age of forty, and after fifty the upward curve becomes precipitous.

Although no one is certain why this happens, the blame is usually placed on the loss of estrogen that occurs with the menopause, on inadequate intake of calcium or on both. The estrogen theory holds that when the metabolic balance between the secretion of male and female sex hormones is upset by the menopause, the body may lose some of its ability to absorb the calcium ingested in the diet. Calcium is vital to the continuing process of breakdown and regeneration of human bone, and many nutritionists think that adult women don't get enough of it. Some also suggest that periodontal disease, in which teeth loosen and fall out, starts with damage from osteoporosis to the bony tooth socket. Dentists disagree (see p. 211).

But that's nothing new. Practically everybody involved in the treatment of osteoporosis disagrees about everything. Doctors do agree about one thing, however: which women are most at hazard. Black women rarely develop the signs of this bone disease. White women who are large-boned and overweight are also less susceptible. The disorder seems to favor fair-skinned, dainty, fragile-looking women. And although symptoms may take ten years after the menopause to show up, they turn up faster, in three to six years, in a woman who has had her ovaries removed before the age of forty-five, thus suffering an abrupt and complete loss of estrogen. Those who have taken cortisone drugs for arthritis or other diseases are also more likely to develop osteoporosis.

Lack of exercise appears to play an important part. The serious calcium depletion that showed up in astronaut bones during the last eighty-four-day Skylab mission was probably caused by weightlessness and lack of strain to the skeletal system because of enforced physical inactivity in a confined space. Further proof of the hazards of a sedentary life style comes from X-ray studies of the finger bones of five thousand persons. Bone density was greater in the more frequently used fingers of the right hand, while in left-handed persons the reverse was true.

The real muddle is how to treat osteoporosis. The Food and Drug Administration guardedly describes Premarin, the leading estrogen medication for menopausal symptoms, as "probably effective" in slowing down the disease. But recent studies indicating that estrogen could prevent bone deterioration have led a committee of experts appointed by the federal agency to advise a change in labeling that would call Premarin "effective." The committee suggests an okay on use of the drug or a synthetic estrogen, but only for women with X-ray evidence of bone loss or fractures. But wheels at the FDA grind slowly, and at this writing, close to a year after the recommendation, the FDA has still not come to a final decision.

The question is, Is the benefit worth the risk? Estrogen drugs have been shown to increase a postmenopausal woman's chance of developing cancer of the endometrium, the lining of the uterus (see p. 155). Yet for some women the risk isn't quite as overwhelming as it seems. Those who have had a hysterectomy need not fear endometrial cancer, because they no longer have an endometrium. Younger women who had their ovaries removed along with the uterus are thus most at hazard from osteoporosis and least at hazard from uterine cancer, and most likely to benefit from taking estrogen. And if a woman's blood pressure is normal, if she's never had thrombophlebitis, or shown symptoms of arteriosclerosis, her risk of taking estrogen is not so great—or so the doctors figure at this time.

As for the postmenopausal woman with an intact uterus, the course of action she and her doctor chooses depends on whether she is at extra risk for osteoporosis, and whether she is showing early symptoms, such as back pain, from the disorder. X-rays are of limited value in early diagnosis, since they do not show up the presence of osteoporosis until after considerable bone deterioration has already taken place. Where there are symptoms a low daily dose of Premarin is advised by some physicians, with a regime of three weeks on the drug and one week off each month. Studies suggest that this dosage will *prevent* further bone deterioration, but will not reverse damage that has already been done. Women who take Premarin for osteoporosis should be checked frequently by their doctor, and have periodic biopsies of the uterus. (See p. 150 for a description of this procedure.)

To further complicate this tangled tale, some experts don't see any need to use estrogen at all in the prevention of osteoporosis— provided a woman is willing to take about one and a half grams of calcium daily, either in tablet form or in her diet. Dr. Uriel Barzel of Albert Einstein Medical School in New York, chairman of a recent international osteoporosis conference, prescribes calcium and exercise for his patients. "With the menopause, the need for calcium seems to increase in many women," he says. "Taking estrogen appears to reduce this enhanced need, and thus to protect a woman from calcium deficiency. My gut feeling is that she should take more calcium instead. If for some reason she can't do this, then she should take estrogen."

Dr. Barzel suggests that about the time of menopause, a woman should take stock of how much calcium she consumes in her diet. The National Research Council recommends 800 milligrams daily for an adult, and they may soon raise this figure to 1,200 for post-menopausal women. Studies show that the average woman takes in a bare 500 milligrams, or half a gram of calcium daily. "When females grow up, they stop drinking milk," says Dr. Anthony Albanese of the Burke Rehabilitation Center in White Plains, New York. "They avoid whole milk because it's fattening, and they don't like the taste of skim milk."

If you drink two glasses of milk a day, or eat its equivalent in yogurt, cottage cheese, custard and other milk products, or in sardines and red salmon, also rich in calcium, then you're taking in only a little more than half a gram of calcium a day. You should aim for a gram and a half, says Dr. Barzel, and if you can't get it from your diet, talk to your doctor about taking calcium tablets as a way to prevent or retard the serious problems of osteoporosis.

Dr. Barzel sums up the confusing picture neatly: "Although estrogen has a place in therapy for some women with osteoporosis, calcium alone appears to be quite adequate as a primary treatment, provided enough is taken every day." He adds one bit of further advice: Don't act like an astronaut. Get up and *exercise.*

XIV

Eyes and Teeth

Preserving Your Eyes

Women now in their forties grew up at a time when Dorothy Parker's witty couplets were being quoted as gospel. Few have forgotten that "men seldom make passes / at girls who wear glasses." And if Dorothy Parker didn't tell them, their mother did. "It was always made perfectly clear to me," says one woman who put on her first glasses at the age of eight, "that it was highly undesirable for a female to need spectacles."

Small wonder, then, that when a woman in her forties finds the newspaper a blur unless she holds it at arm's length, she tries to deny the growing disability. Few even know the word *presbyopia*, the gradual loss of ability of the eye's crystalline lens to effectively change focus from far to near objects. To view a book at reading distance, about fourteen inches away, the lens accommodates by becoming rounder and more powerful, in an automatic contraction of eye muscles that takes less than a second. At its highest efficiency in early adolescence, accommodation then starts a slow decline as the lens becomes stiffer, its muscles less supple.

This is not your misery alone. Both men and women go through this change, but it is so gradual that it goes unnoticed until mid-life. "I hate it. I can't tell you how it bothers me," says Trudy, forty-five. "It's the first sign of aging. And I was always so proud of my eyesight. I was the one who could always see everything. Two years ago I gave in. I bought jazzy-looking Christian Dior glasses, but when I put them on, I know everybody's thinking— She's *old*."

Christine, forty-four, admits that she stalled off an eyeglass purchase for two years. "Finally I didn't enjoy reading any more. Then my husband started wearing glasses, and that made me feel less peculiar about myself. It helped when I sneaked his old pair onto my night table. It's not just vanity. It's disbelief—how could this be happening to my good eyes? I have a friend who's avoiding the problem now just as I did. When I suggest she try on my glasses, she says firmly, 'I have perfect eyesight.'"

Behind this anguish lie several common misconceptions:

"Now that I've lost my twenty-twenty vision, my health must be going downhill." When you develop presbyopia, you still have twenty-twenty vision. This is only a shorthand way of saying that when you are tested on a Snellen chart, placed twenty feet away, you can read the letters that any normal person can read at twenty feet. This doesn't presuppose health or its lack. Your nearsighted friend who's worn glasses all her life is probably just as robust as you are.

"Eyeglasses make you look ugly and old." Maybe so, but neither Gloria Steinem nor Lesley Stahl appears to be handicapped. Luckily, your need for glasses coincides with a fashion revolution in their design. Women never had a wider choice in size, shape or color of eyeglass frames. And if you're bothered by bags under your eyes, you'll discover that the new glasses camouflage them beautifully.

"I don't bother with my glasses because I know the more I wear them, the more I'll need them." This reasoning is tempting, but it's nonsense. There is no evidence that wearing glasses worsens eyesight. The reason that you become dependent on your glasses is that you see better with them.

In the age range of seventeen to forty-four, fewer than one in two American women wears eyeglasses, but between the mid-forties and fifties, the percentage soars to eighty-six and to ninety-four by age sixty-five. About two in every five women start to shop for their first pair of glasses during their middle years. The first thing to do is to have your eyes tested by an ophthalmologist, a physician who specializes in eye problems, or an optometrist, a professional who measures the extent of vision defects and prescribes glasses for them. I suggest starting off with an ophthalmologist, who will then be available to prescribe medication or treatment should medical problems develop later.

After examining your eyes, either professional will write out an eyeglass prescription and send you to an optician to have it filled. Here the choice is yours in the style and shape of the frames, and also between plastic and shatterproof glass for the lens. Both are safe under most circumstances, but plastic is lighter, a consideration if you've chosen huge contemporary frames. Glass does not scratch as easily, or build up static electricity, a magnet for gathering dust, as plastic does.

As to cost, half-glasses are the least expensive, but they're popularly known as granny glasses, enough reason for many women to avoid them. All eyeglasses are expensive; a bill upward of fifty dollars is no longer a shocker. But if you're considering the top-price, name-designer frames, remember that presbyopia is progressive and you'll probably need stronger lenses within a year or two. Unless your old frames are too flimsy and bent out of shape, you can use them with new lenses. After a decade or so, your eyesight is likely to stabilize, and you won't have to get new glasses so often.

If you've got the miseries over starting to wear eyeglasses, those who've always worn them for myopia (nearsightedness) or hyperopia (farsightedness) are squirming too. They face the question, Will I need bifocals? Many consider the glasses with the line across the middle a final tip-off to aging. "The doctor said I needed bifocals," Eve, forty-seven, a kindergarten teacher, told me. "And I answered, forget it. I just wasn't going to do it. I don't want to look like a little old lady."

Some who are nearsighted are delighted to find that for a time, occasionally as long as a decade, they no longer need glasses at all for reading. But if one is farsighted, presbyopia compounds the problem, requiring one prescription for close work and another for distance vision. The answer is either two pairs of eyeglasses or bifocals. Marjorie, a freelance bookkeeper, got bifocals soon after her forty-ninth birthday. "I take three courses at our local college, and between looking at the blackboard and taking notes, I was switching my glasses on and off every second minute. Getting used to bifocals put me in a foul temper and I still avoid them whenever I can."

One fact about bifocals should be clear. "They are glasses of convenience," say Dr. Leonard Flom, a Fairfield, Conn., eye doctor and officer in the American Association of Ophthalmology. The convenience is yours. If you prefer switching between two pairs of glasses to wearing bifocals, that's your choice. Remember too that if you wear bifocals and like to read in bed, you may want an extra pair of reading glasses to keep at your bedside because the angle of vision won't work too well with bifocals.

A solution that an occasional woman adopts is to wear contact lenses to correct faulty distance vision, and reading glasses for close work. One of these is Constance, fifty-six, divorced for the past fourteen years. "I use my contacts just out of vanity and only when I'm on a date," she says. "Then I can pull out my reading glasses to read a menu just like everyone else. But when I'm not trying to impress a man, I wear bifocals." Why not bifocal contacts? A very small percentage of those already used to contact lenses can manage these, but many ophthalmologists are doubtful about their effectiveness.

A new product has recently been introduced that eliminates the line between the two lens sections in bifocals by gradually increasing corrective power without abrupt change in magnification. "There's little or no medical advantage to the seamless feature," says Dr. Flom. "Many people find them harder to adjust to than ordinary bifocals." Nevertheless, promoted as "a lens that doesn't tell the world you're getting older," this product meets the objections of the youth cultist in all of us.

Does your debut with spectacles mean an added annual or semiannual checkup with still another physician? No, it doesn't. An increase in blurring will warn you when you need a change of glasses. Once you've passed thirty-five or forty, however, it's wise to see an eye doctor every two years to guard against the onset of *glaucoma*, a serious disease that becomes more common in middle age. Glaucoma can blind you, but it's neither as frequent nor as sudden in onset as some scare propaganda suggests. Those over forty have about a one-in-fifty chance of developing it. Blacks are at greater risk. The hazard increases if you have diabetes, or if a member of your immediate family has glaucoma. Cortisone drugs may sometimes precipitate the disease; some blood pressure medications may accelerate its damaging effects.

When the circulating fluid that washes over the eye lens is blocked from its normal drainage, it can cause abnormally high pressure within the eyeball, squeezing the blood vessels that nourish the optic nerve. This may result in glaucoma. If it progresses unrecognized, nerve cells within the eye may be damaged, peripheral or side vision diminished; tunnel vision and eventually blindness may follow.

But long before it destroys eyesight, the increased pressure can be diagnosed by an instrument called a tonometer, in a brief examination not much more onerous than a routine check on blood pressure. Some family doctors now include a glaucoma check in a regular physical exam, but the test is mostly still performed by eye specialists. Make sure you have a tonometer diagnosis every second year, as you already make sure you get an annual Pap smear. If you fall in a high-risk category you should start the test younger and have it more often.

A simple but tedious treatment, a pill or an eyedrop used several times daily, will be prescribed if the tonometer shows you have glaucoma. The medication reduces the pressure but does not cure the disease; if it is skimped on or forgotten, pressure will rise again. Another apparently effective drug used to treat glaucoma is marijuana, or cannabis, its principal ingredient. One note of caution: Be sure to tell your family doctor if an ophthalmologist has diagnosed you as having glaucoma. Some drugs that he may prescribe should be used with caution or not at all in glaucoma patients.

Chronic open-angle glaucoma, the form of the disease that nine out of ten people develop, gives little or no warning, although it builds up over months or years, not days or weeks. The following occasional symptoms are cause for suspicion: your eyesight seems to be worsening, and frequent changes of glasses don't help; you have difficulty adjusting to the dark, as when you enter a theater; you see rainbow-colored rings dancing around lights, like the halos that Van Gogh depicted in his later works (doctors speculate that he had glaucoma).

Don't confuse these last, however, with the occasional appearance of tiny wiggling black spots that may dance across the field of vision as one looks at a light background, such as a white wall or blue sky. These are *floaters*, annoying visitors that may first appear in midlife but are seldom a cause for alarm. The only exception is a sudden increase in their number, a shower of black specks accompanied by light flashes. If you see these, better consult an ophthalmologist promptly. It could be the first sign of *retinal detachment,* a potential problem for the aging eye that occasionally occurs earlier.

Cataract, an opacity of the lens, is another problem unlikely to surface before old age. Fewer than one in ten develop a cataract in their sixties. It's even rarer at younger ages, except for those who have diabetes, injure an eye or are exposed to intense heat or radiation, although occasionally a baby may be born with cataracts. A group of studies, still controversial, suggest that microwaves may initiate cataract formation earlier than usual.

In this disease the lens, normally transparent like clear glass, becomes cloudy and milky in appearance, and starts to blur. Physicians no longer counsel waiting until the cataract is "ripe," but operate when everyday activity is impaired despite the aid of eyeglasses. Cataract surgery is successful in ninety-five out of a hundred cases; it usually requires five days or less of hospitalization.

Are all these threats to normal vision inevitable with aging? The answer is yes to presbyopia, a definite no for glaucoma and maybe for cataract. Researchers speculate that if one lives long enough cataracts will eventually develop, but even some ninety-year-olds don't have them.

None of these vision impairments can be blamed on one's use or misuse of the eyes—on poor light, eyestrain, reading in bed. Yet good illumination is more important than ever in the middle and later years. Avoid glare, to which your eyes are becoming increasingly sensitive. Switch your sixty-watt bulbs to seventy-fives and the seventy-fives to one hundreds. If you are right-handed, light should come over your left shoulder and be diffused evenly over the area in which you are working. Keep a second lamp burning in a room, so that when you look up, your eyes are not forced to adjust abruptly from bright to dark.

Preserving Your Teeth

On the dental front, there's good news and bad news as you move into middle years. When you visit the dentist, look for less drilling but more scraping. As your teeth become more resistant to caries, the soft tissues surrounding and anchoring them become the target area for serious problems. Periodontal or gum disease is the major reason for tooth extraction, which starts to accelerate at an unpleasant rate in midlife. Seventy percent of all teeth are lost after the age of forty.

This does *not* have to mean you. You may remember with a shudder the troubles your parents had when they were fitted with dentures, but your generation is better off. The techniques of making and fitting dentures have greatly improved. More important, increased knowledge about preventive dentistry in the last decade or so is paying off; the number of toothless Americans is now happily on the decline.

Gum diseases are *not* caused by the aging process itself. Gingivitis, or gum inflammation, is present to some degree among most teen-agers. Close to one out of two persons over twenty has already lost a tooth or two. The progression of gingivitis to periodontitis, the form of gum disease that leads to tooth loss, is not inevitable. Anywhere along the line the process can be halted and reversed if you and your dentist work at it together. But the longer you wait, the more painful, expensive and time-consuming it becomes.

Strong, healthy teeth can remain firmly fixed in your mouth only so long as they are surrounded by healthy gums and connective tissue, and anchored in a strong bony socket. You are likely to notice the first hint of trouble: your gums look an angry scarlet; they're puffy and spongy instead of pink and firm. They bleed a little when you brush. The important thing to remember is that *normal gums do not bleed.*

The reason for this irritation is dental plaque, a gummy substance formed by colonies of bacteria that set up housekeeping in your mouth. If plaque, which forms daily, is not removed by brushing and other dental hygiene measures, it starts to coat teeth and gums, then hardens into tartar or calculus, particularly along the gumline. (Benjamin Franklin called this condition "tooth fur.") Plaque and tartar, mounding up in layers, are highly inflammatory to gum tissue. Soon the inflammation becomes chronic and destructive. The edge of the gum starts to detach from the teeth, and deep pockets filled with bacteria and pus form between the two. Parts of the membrane circling the tooth disintegrate, and bone is lost from the tooth socket. This stage is called periodontitis; many are more familiar with its former name, pyor-rhea. The result: as the tooth's supporting structures weaken, like the foundation of a house attacked by termites, the tooth becomes loose and wobbly, and eventually falls out.

In some people the process is swifter, more destructive than in others. Diabetes is likely to make gum disease more severe; so is physical or emotional stress. Heredity plays a role. Then there are plaque traps—old worn-out fillings, particularly those below the gumline, numerous crowns and inlays, broken edges of de-cayed teeth, poorly fitting partial dentures, teeth that are crooked or crowded. Most of us accumulate more of these hiding places for bacteria as we get older, particularly those who are careless about regular dental visits.

I asked Dr. Sigmund Stahl, chief of periodontics at New York University Dental School, what preventive measures against tooth loss a woman of thirty-five or forty should be taking. These were his suggestions:

Learn how to wield a toothbrush to remove plaque, a chore that must be repeated daily. The most important time for brush-ing is at bedtime, because during the night the secretion of saliva, which washes away harmful mouth bacteria, decreases. All avail-able surfaces should be brushed thoroughly with a brush that is soft, multitufted and small enough to reach into crevices. It may be manual or electric, whichever does a better job for you. Be sure to toss out the toothbrush and get a new one every three or four months. Your dentist or dental hygienist has probably taught you the proper technique, with bristles held at an angle and pointing toward the gumline. Avoid abrasive toothpaste or powder, and don't count on the paste to do your job; it does not prevent plaque formation.

The second important plaque fighter is unwaxed dental floss. One dentist has suggested a middle-age motto: "If you've got 'em, floss 'em." If you floss regularly, working it between the teeth and moving it up and down in a sawing motion, it will remove plaque that your toothbrush can't reach. A Water Pik helps wash away food particles that may attract plaque; it is also useful for those with dental work. An interdental stimulator, the rubber tip at the end of some toothbrushes, massages the gums as well as removing food debris. How long to brush? Some dentists say fifteen minutes is average, but Dr. Stahl's advice is: until the job is done. For the conscientious, use of a disclosing tablet, a wafer that stains red the plaque that you've missed, will tell you when to stop.

It's a formidable task, and Dr. Stahl is pragmatic about it. "Dentists recognize that brushing is time-consuming and relatively ineffective for the results you get," he says. "Not everybody can use dental floss. You've got to follow the technique that works best for you. If it did the job, I wouldn't care if a patient used her fingernails. And if you find it just too much hard work, then go to the dentist more often. That's a trade-off that appeals to some."

Women (and men even more so) tend to slack off on their dental visits after the age of forty-five, just when they need them most. You should go to the dentist twice a year, more if he advises that tartar is forming in your mouth faster than he can get rid of it. He or the hygienist will scrape away the accumulated tartar with a special instrument, particularly below the gumline and at crowns and roots.

Be sure your dentist uses a periodontal probe, an important diagnostic tool, as he checks out your mouth. Inserted between tooth and gum, a procedure that's not painful, the probe measures the depth of the pockets that may have formed between the two. When they are numerous and deep, the process that destroys membrane and bone has probably begun. Don't merely assume the dentist has used a probe, but ask him directly. "The sad fact is," says Dr. D. Walter Cohen, dean of the University of Pennsylvania School of Dental Medicine, "that the periodontal probe is missing from most dental offices."

How about X-rays? "As little as possible and as often as necessary," Dr. Stahl advises. This means a full set of X-rays every two years, and spot pictures in between of teeth that appear suspicious to the dentist. Even after the childbearing years, your chest and abdominal area should be covered by a lead apron when you're being X-rayed.

Some dentists advise a diet high in fibrous foods, including apples and celery, which exert a cleansing action on the teeth, and low in soft foods, such as white bread, that cling to the teeth. Dr. Stahl disagrees. "Eating apples won't remove plaque," he says, "nor does what you eat, unless you're extremely malnourished, have any effect on dental tissues. There's also no scientific data to show that taking large amounts of vitamin C will help your mouth and gums, as some have claimed—unless you have scurvy."

Some nutritionists think that destruction of the bony tooth socket, a development that leads inexorably to tooth loss, is linked with osteoporosis, a bone disease prevalent among postmenopausal women in which skeletal bone weakens and becomes brittle (see p. 199). They believe that a diet high in calcium may retard the process. Dental researchers doubt it. They hold that although osteoporosis may affect the jawbone, it is a parallel process and plays no role in gum disease.

If these differences of opinion are confusing, it's because the experts admit that they're confused. "Periodontal disease has many causes," says Dr. Edward Tonna, a bone biologist at the New York University Dental Center, "and there's a great deal about it we still don't understand." The course of the disease, for example, is often unpredictable. Do angry bleeding gums suddenly become pink and healthy because of a woman's vigorous nightly battle against plaque, because other factors have strengthened her resistance to bacterial invasion, or because the bacteria themselves have become less virulent? Why do some people die in their nineties with a full set of natural teeth, and others lose teeth at an alarming rate in their forties?

Periodontal surgery has had a vogue among the well-to-do; it has been a status symbol, like dental braces for an eleven-year-old. But whether you need it or not depends on the depth of the periodontal pockets measured by the dentist's probe. The purpose of surgery is to make these pockets shallow enough so that toothbrush and dental floss can keep them free of plaque. Various techniques are used to lift the gum, clean out diseased tissue from the pockets, and resculpture bone and gum so that they again fit tightly together. Performed under local anesthesia, this is a tedious, unpleasant and expensive procedure, with cost varying from $500 to $5,000, depending on its complexity.

If your dentist says that you need a tooth pulled, you should be aware that new techniques now make it possible to retain a tooth even after it has become wobbly. Yanking the teeth is quicker and cheaper, but many can be saved by splinting a wobbly tooth to its firmer neighbor, while periodontal treatment continues to reverse the process of bone destruction. More radical procedures like bone grafting are even having some success. You're wise to question a surgeon when he recommends an operation, and in the same skeptical spirit, you should ask a dentist about alternatives before he starts wielding the dental forceps.

For the future there's hope that such drastic measures may someday become obsolete. Researchers in preventive dentistry are hot on the trail of new discoveries—a chemical to stop plaque formation, a way to manipulate the body's defenses more effectively, a vaccine against plaque-causing bacteria.

But right now there's no alternative to the nightly bouts at the wash basin with toothbrush and dental floss and/or Water Pik, tools that one dental school dean admits are "primitive, crude and difficult." Your dentist's warning that you'd better brush if you want to keep your teeth isn't merely conjuring up a bogey man; for many of us, it's the unpleasant truth.

XV
Memory and Stress

"I walked over to the refrigerator to get out the jam for breakfast. Then I just stood there, hand on door. I couldn't remember what I was fetching."

"I have to make a supermarket list, or I'll come home with half the items missing. The trouble is that sometimes I forget to bring the list."

"I particularly wanted my husband and my boss to meet at the office cocktail party. When I started the introductions, I got a sinking feeling. My boss's name had just vanished from memory."

"The aging mind has a bagful of nasty tricks, one of which is to tuck names and words away in crannies where they are not immediately available," wrote the humorist E. B. White. What worries many women is that their minds appear to have started aging so early. Those quoted above who forgot the jam, the list, the boss's name, are all in their forties and fifties. Their question —Am I losing my mind, becoming stupid? Is this the start of senility?

The answer is an emphatic no. Conventional wisdom holds that youth has the corner on brains as well as beauty, and that by middle age the mind is already on the skids. Not so, say the experts. Intellectual ability *does* decline, but much later than previously thought. Some aspects do not appear to go downhill at all, vocabulary, for example. The most pronounced losses are in speed and in memory. "To the age of fifty and even beyond," says Dr.

Jack Botwinick of Washington University in St. Louis, "there is little or no decrement in intellectual performance."

Some women are hesitant about returning to school in their middle years, because of concern about how well they'll do. Older students are "highly susceptible to the feeling that they can't keep up with the young," observes Dr. Lee McEvoy, a psychologist at the University of California at Los Angeles. But experience proves them wrong. College deans report that the middle-aged student does as well and often better than the youngster.

"Of course, I worried in advance," says Polly, who started college at eighteen, then married, had a baby, divorced and finally got her degree at forty-one. "But I learned that I'm a lot sharper mentally now, although I may not be as quick in answering questions. I work harder and more effectively than I used to."

Some move at a rate that is nothing short of spectacular. One divorcee, raising two teen-age children, holding a full-time job, nevertheless completed her last two years of college in a single year, and with a perfect grade average. Her explanation? "I guess something clicked."

"It's the motivation of knowing where you're going and why," explains a woman, fifty-two, now in law school, where she ranks eighth in a class of two hundred. Mother of five sons, she says, "I am now the most resented member of the family because I've proved that if you really try, you can do it. My kids think this is revolting."

Researchers are only now beginning to study the middle years. Although they know that a decline in memory and in speed of response are clearly apparent by the seventies, they cannot yet pinpoint at what age these start, and how quickly they accelerate. It is known, for example, that simple reaction time increases by twenty-five percent or more between the ages of twenty and seventy. If a lightning-quick response is a factor in performance on a test given to young and old, the oldsters get clobbered. But when does the slowdown begin? According to industrial studies, a production worker is likely to improve in both speed and accuracy until close to the age of forty-five; after that accuracy remains high, but speed stabilizes or slowly declines.

When speed is not a factor, memory loss appears to remain mild until the sixties or seventies. In one study, persons of different ages listened to the recitation of a string of letters, and were asked later to repeat them. Averaging the results, those in the twenties repeated 6.7 letters; the number went down in the thirties to 6.2; and up slightly in the forties and fifties to 6.5. In the sixties there was a sharp drop to 5.5, and in the seventies to 5.4. In another memory test, no rise was noted among persons in their fifties. Subjects were asked to look at a geometrical design and then reproduce it from memory. Results showed virtually no decline in the thirties and forties, a modest loss in the fifties and sixties, and a substantial drop in the seventies.

If you're forty or older and think you're getting forgetful, take these factors into account before you jump to the conclusion that your mind is on an inevitable downhill slide:

Memory loss is often a self-fulfilling prophecy. "When you're young and forget a name or a place, you just shrug and say, 'Something drove it out of my mind,'" says Dr. Lillian Troll of Rutgers University. "If the same thing happens when you're older, you blame it on your age."

Depression may be a factor. When persons over fifty were evaluated by the psychiatry department at the University of Chicago, those who were depressed complained most bitterly about a failing memory. Testing showed that some of these actually functioned better than those with fewer complaints and a cheerier mood.

Differences between individuals are great. If you're sharp when you're young, you're likely to keep on being sharp when you're older. The Gerontology Research Center (GRC) has studied the same subjects for a considerable time, testing them repeatedly over periods ranging up to fourteen years. "In every age group, even the oldest, we found some individuals whose performance did not decline and are indistinguishable from young adults," says Dr. David Arenberg, chief of the learning and problem-solving section. More than one out of every four men in the late seventies performed as well as they had six or seven years earlier. Although it is assumed that female memory ages in the same pattern as male, there is little proof so far whether this is so because, until recently, only men were studied.

However, a deeper understanding of the memory process is developing. We are gradually learning what makes it work smoothly, and what causes it to falter; strategies are being formulated to counter the deficit that grows over the years. The memory is like a huge storage area—the basement storeroom, for example, where you keep your overflow groceries. When you were three or even eighteen, there weren't many items on the shelves in the memory storeroom. Now it is bursting at the seams with names, dates, faces, places, the impressions and experiences of forty or more years. Nothing that was ever put in has disappeared. The only trouble now is how to get it out. You struggle without success to remember the name of a high school classmate, for example. Finally, after you've given up, gone to bed and apparently forgotten about it, it suddenly and almost miraculously reappears in your consciousness.

The trouble lies, not with the memory storeroom itself, but with the process of retrieval, the plucking of a single item out of the jumbled room. Once an item has been stored in long-term memory, perhaps only thirty seconds after it was perceived, the task of retrieving it is believed to be, at least by some researchers, the same as if it had been there thirty years.

Psychologists cite these factors as contributing to a decline in memory over the years:

The memory storage closet becomes crowded. The more items it contains, the harder it becomes to find any single one. "It's a kind of overloading. There's just not so much to sort out when you're young," says Dr. Troll.

People organize their memory storage less effectively as they get older. Young people automatically use codes when they store an item, and retrieval cues to help them hunt for it, strategies that older people appear less adept in. It's easier to find a jar of applesauce in the basement provision closet if you've put all the fruit on one shelf, away from the vegetables and cereals, and memory storage is not so different.

Distractibility becomes more of a problem with age; people react less efficiently to competing stimuli. When you were a young mother, attention riveted on the new baby, you weren't likely to forget any step in the infant's schedule. Now when you're fixing breakfast, your mind churning with other problems—a term paper due, a son's heavy drinking, a husband's unaccustomed grouchiness—you become distracted from the task at hand. That's when you stand hesitant in front of the refrigerator, forgetting the jam you started to fetch.

You get out of the habit of working at remembering. At a time when you need to try harder, you slacken your efforts, partly because you anticipate failure.

Yet a special attempt can be vastly rewarding. One woman,

fifty-nine, toured the Galápagos Islands near Ecuador last year with a group of sixty-seven strangers. "I'm the kind of person who forgets to listen to a name when I'm introduced," she says, "probably because I'm self-consciously concentrating on the impression I'm making. This time I determined not to blow it.

"Every night I checked the passenger list of the small boat on which we were cruising the islands to confirm the name of a person with whom I had lunched or dined. I used tricks to connect a name with a face—his mustache, her pixie haircut. By the end of the two-week trip, I knew almost all of them by name. Success made me feel good. I liked my traveling companions better for it, and I think they liked me better, too."

The memory tricks she employed are called mnemonic aids, aids to memory. These are the tools that a forty- or fifty-year-old needs to start using to help train her memory for the later years. The most obvious strategy is to make a list. There's no need to recall something you don't really need—a telephone number, for example—so long as you write it down. "Lists help enormously," says one forty-year-old. "I'm better organized than when when I was younger."

Most people can develop their own strategies to aid the memory if they consciously try. "I always had an excellent memory," says Rosa, fifty-six. "Now when I can't remember a word I want, it makes me angry, impatient. Years ago when I was teaching nutrition students, I made it a point to remember their names. I've started to use the same memory devices. You have to work at it; it needs discipline; but it really helps."

It's also important to make a special effort to keep one's mind flexible, open to new techniques in order to develop creative mnemonic aids. Like an aging rat running through a maze, people tend to become set in their habits. If doing a task a certain way worked well in the past, then as you grow older you're likely to keep on doing it in the same way. We should instead strive to keep curiosity alive. Even if a certain route to the seashore is the way you've always made the trip, vary it occasionally by venturing on a back country road. Then if the old route becomes blocked by a detour sign, you're less likely to panic and get lost. Being mentally adaptable pays off and is a lot more fun.

To keep yourself mentally limber, stay in touch with young people, whose curiosity is infectious. Don't try to fashion them over in your own cautious image, but emulate their tendency to experiment with something new. Travel also helps to stretch the mental muscles, gives you new situations to cope with, particularly at late middle age when handling stress is starting to become increasingly difficult.

Drink and Drugs

Stress, and an impaired ability to cope with it that sometimes starts in middle age, appears to be the villain in the crippling twin addictions that may peak at midlife: alcoholism and popping prescription pills, particularly tranquilizers. Turning sixty, Betty Ford admitted that her dependence, intensifying for years, was finally out of control. For many women her story had a depressingly familiar ring: beginning with medication for physical pain (arthritis in her case); discovering its magic in easing emotional turmoil like loneliness, low self-esteem and the burden of bringing up virtually single-handed the four children of a politician-father. Then the knockout blow, mix-matching the drugs with liquor in the heavy-drinking atmosphere in which political families socialize.

Alcoholism is now becoming a woman's problem. The figure used to be one female alcoholic to every four males, but the ratio is changing rapidly. One out of every three new members of Alcoholics Anonymous is now a woman, and experts believe that the male-female alcoholic balance has come close to fifty-fifty. Some aspects of excess drinking are worse in women. They are twice as likely as men to suffer a double addiction that includes drugs. Their heavy drinking starts at a later age, but they catch up fast, reaching a peak in the forties. A second peak may come some twenty years later when elderly widows, alone in a cramped apartment, discover the solace of nipping at the bottle.

No one can find any single reason why some women drink to excess, nor even pinpoint the woman who is vulnerable. The old stereotype of the bored housewife sousing in private is now being questioned. Many alcoholics are housewives, but many also hold down jobs. Research now suggests that the stress leading to dependence on the pill container and the whiskey bottle may be entwined with the problems of being a modern woman, and particularly with the midlife leap to greater independence and assertiveness.

"It is my sincere belief that most American women are losers, sometimes through lack of opportunity, more often by choice," says Marianne Brickley, mother of six, recent alcoholic and wife of the former lieutenant-governor of Michigan. "Many of us don't know how to win or when to compete, and we are not programmed to try . . . The 'I do' at the altar is the 'amen' to the decision-making era of our lives." Mrs. Brickley suggests that many women start to drink heavily as their husbands become busier, more successful, more alienated from their marriage. The woman "is feeling left out of her husband's life . . . Many times I hear a man describe his wife as 'the little woman'—and in many cases, that's exactly the way she feels."

Women often say that they start hard drinking because liquor makes them feel more feminine—prettier, sexier, more loving and desirable. Crisis points for tipping the bottle are divorce, hysterectomy, menopause, events that force them to question their femininity. An alcoholic "overbuys the feminine role but it does not seem to work out for her," says Dr. Edith Gomberg, professor of social work at the University of Michigan. Such a woman may find the transition to midlife painful and difficult. She wants to remain dependent when less dependence is called for, to feel needed when no one needs her—because she lacks faith in her ability to take control herself. Essentially she is the woman who misses out on the goodies of the middle years.

Often there's another switch she can't make either: the transition from altruism—appropriate when there were little ones to look after—to egoism, the more self-fulfilling role of middle age. Dr. Hans Selye, the Canadian doctor who developed the modern concept of stress, said in a 1978 interview in *Psychology Today*, "Human beings . . . are born egoists—they necessarily have to look out for themselves first." Some, however, try to adopt "altruism and endless self-sacrifice" as a way of life. "The danger is that altruism carried to an extreme—constantly putting other people's good before your own—violates our nature . . . and leads to constant . . . stressful frustration and resentment."

Women like Catherine, fifty-seven, a former alcoholic and pill addict who now counsels other alcoholic women, feel guilty because they aren't more altruistic, aren't a better mother, wife or daughter. They are also angry and resentful because these roles are thrust upon them to the point where they threaten a fragile ego. When I first met Catherine, she was a picture-book

wife and mother with two beautiful children and a handsome
husband, herself a former Junior Leaguer, pretty and vivacious.
But she didn't always sleep well and the family doctor gave her
an open prescription for sleeping pills. When an unplanned third
child was born, she felt tense; her gynecologist promptly scrib-
bled a prescription for a tranquilizer. There was social drinking
occasionally to excess: this was fashionable in the Connecticut
suburb where she lived.

Then came overwhelming stress, almost impossible to handle
soberly when pills and liquor, the means for blotting it out, were
so temptingly close. There was a fourth pregnancy when she was
thirty-eight. Her oldest child was fifteen and her youngest seven
at the time; an auto accident killed her mother and seriously injured her father; a surprise announcement came from her husband that they were moving to Baltimore, where he had accepted
a new job. "First he took the job, and *then* he talked to me about
it. It meant leaving my father, for whom I felt responsible. Our
oldest was president of her high school class. I never felt comfortable in Baltimore. Between the move, the new baby, the loss
of friends and of identity, I was always fatigued, the kind of
enervation that leads to a nip before the guests arrive for dinner."

There were several hospitalizations, "but no doctor ever said I
was an alcoholic. In fact, one assured me that I wasn't. Another
suggested I stop drinking, but didn't tell me how. Finally I
reached an AA-oriented therapy group where there were plenty
of double-addicted women like me. I faced up to my alcoholism, a
necessary first step to successful treatment. This was the kind
of therapy I should have gotten ten years earlier. I was sober
for a year and a half when my shaky marriage collapsed."

Like Catherine, other alcoholic women often have trouble recognizing and being treated for their addiction. They hide it themselves because of the double-whammy attached to being female
and a drunk. Society may no longer frown on the drinking
woman, but it still censures her for getting drunk. It treats her
spouse more tenderly. When a woman has an alcoholic husband,
she is often pointed to as the cause. But when *she* has the
drinking problem, her husband is regarded with sympathy, and
she is condemned. For every ten wives who see an alcoholic husband through his illness, only one husband remains with an alcoholic wife.

Finding adequate treatment is another hurdle. Because different problems underlie alcoholism in men and women, programs ought to be tailored to the special needs of each sex. But one study of halfway houses for alcoholics revealed that more than half were for men only, nine percent limited to women, and among the rest that were coed, eight out of every ten beds were occupied by alcoholic men.

Middle-aged women appear to be catching up to men in alcoholism, but they are galloping far ahead in sedative abuse. "They grab tranquilizers by the handful as if they were popcorn," one doctor told me. While doctors may disapprove, they also bear a heavy responsibility for female pill-popping. Often when a woman is having trouble with alcohol and talks to her doctor, he prescribes a tranquilizer to calm her nerves. Before long she's hooked on both.

According to the National Commission on Marijuana and Drug Abuse, tranquilizers are prescribed for women twice as often and for twice the length of time as for men. A steep rise in their rate of use comes in the thirties and forties. White men or blacks of either sex who overdose with a chemical smorgasbord are usually in their twenties, but white women who die of drug abuse—commonly a combination of alcohol and a sedative or tranquilizer—have a median age of forty-three.

The simplistic explanation of why doctors prescribe more tranquilizers for women is that they visit the doctor more frequently, and talk more openly about their emotional problems. But that can't be the whole picture. Women make fifty-eight percent of the doctor appointments, but, one study shows, receive seventy-three percent of the prescriptions for mind-altering drugs. Doctors, most of whom are male, are more likely to dismiss a woman's physical complaints as "all in her head" and to take a man's seriously. If they judge that a patient is overreacting to a minor complaint, the way to get rid of her is to prescribe a tranquilizer. "I think a physician makes a very quick assessment based on his ideas that a man has to go to work, but a woman has nothing else to do, so let her be quieted down," says Dr. Rose Laub Coser of the State University of New York at Stony Brook.

A few years ago Linda Fidell, a California psychologist, studied the use of mind-altering drugs, mostly tranquilizers, in a group of middle-class women, who were overwhelmingly white, married and mothers. Close to half took tranquilizers, usually supplied by a family doctor. Those with jobs, about half of the sample, were given the drugs as often as the housewives. But what was most curious was the lack of discrimination in the kind of drugs the physicians prescribed. Major tranquilizers, like Thorazine, are generally considered suitable for a psychotic; they are widely used in mental hospitals to treat schizophrenia and other serious mental disorders, and they may cause serious physiological side effects. Among the Fidell group—a sampling of 465 ordinary women in a suburban community—those who voiced the most complaints, physical and mental, were the ones most likely to be given a prescription for a mind-altering drug. But the doctors did not appear to discriminate between drugs; if a woman reported that she felt jittery, had a stiff neck and an upset stomach, she was just as likely to get a prescription for a powerful major tranquilizer, such as Thorazine, as a woman who reported paranoid symptoms or acted psychotic.

One reason women use tranquilizers is to treat insomnia, but as they get older, it may not be insomnia at all. "When my three kids were little," one suburban woman, aged fifty, says, "I seemed to need nine or ten hours' sleep a night and seldom got it. Sometimes my husband and I would give ourselves a treat. We'd spend a weekend in a New York hotel, put a sign on the door, 'Do Not Disturb,' and just sleep the morning away. Now that the kids are grown and I finally have the luxury of sleeping late on a weekend morning, what happens? I wake up early. I just don't seem to need more than seven hours now."

As one gets older, the fourth stage of sleep—deep and dreamless—diminishes markedly; people awaken more during the night, and early-morning sleep becomes fitful. A seven-year-old is likely to sleep ten hours a night; but only seven hours at the age range of twenty-five to fifty-five; and six and three quarters when she reaches sixty-five. These are natural developments. Older people need less sleep. But when the pattern begins to change in the late middle years, some interpret it as insomnia and rush for the tranquilizer bottle.

If you awaken more frequently during the night, if your sleep seems shallower but you feel no less rested in the morning, then it is unlikely that you have insomnia. Once you realize that it's normal, you'll get used to the changing pattern. If you do try tranquilizers or sedatives, use them only for a few days, perhaps to help you blot out temporary stress that intrudes on your sleep. Sleeping pills are seldom effective for more than two weeks at a time, and sometimes for only a couple of days. One problem is tolerance: you need more pills to get the same soothing effect. The pills are likely to distort the natural sleep stages, cutting down the period of REM (rapid eye movement) sleep when you dream. If you stop after long reliance on a pill, you'll probably suffer a rebound effect; the insomnia will return worse than ever. This symptom of drug withdrawal is more frequent if you're dosing with sedatives than with tranquilizers, but it occurs with both. When you limit yourself to intermittent use on the rare occasions when sleep is really elusive, you'll avoid these problems.

To avoid getting hooked on drugs and alcohol, bear these points in mind:

Early middle age is a danger point when social drinking may subtly shift into alcoholism. By late middle age, fifty-five and over, tolerance diminishes both for alcohol and tranquilizers. You think you're holding your liquor fine: your voice isn't even fuzzy, but your reactions are sluggish, and that's dangerous if you drive. A small amount of alcohol provides a bigger bang as you get older, even though you don't realize it.

Don't assume that every problem of living has a medication to solve it. The temporary crutch only postpones the day when you will have to face the problem, now made worse by putting another monkey on your back. One woman who started drinking heavily in her forties, then switched to tranquilizers to calm her boozing jitters, had to face up later to her trouble. "I was full of self-pity and resentment. I had expected my husband to take responsibility for making me happy. And when I learned that life wasn't just a bowl of cherries, I couldn't handle it. I had no self-esteem. I thought I was stupid." Now in her fifties, she hasn't had a drink or taken a pill for five years. She has a job and "I've discovered that I'm not stupid. I'm really very bright."

Recognize a drinking problem and seek help. How can you tell? If you are beginning to destroy yourself socially, maritally, psychologically or physically, and still keep on drinking, then you are an alcoholic. Dr. Joseph Pursch, chief of the Navy's Alcohol and Drug Abuse Center at Long Beach, Cal., who offers this definition, adds, "An ex-alcoholic is in the same category as an ex-virgin. It's impossible to go home again after certain things have happened in one's life, and alcoholism is one of those things." In other words, no more drinking—ever.

Tranquilizers are powerful drugs. A supply in your medicine

chest doesn't give you the license to play doctor, dispensing a handful to a friend or to your teen-ager with pre-exam jitters. If your doctor prescribes a tranquilizer, ask him why. How is it likely to help? If there's a good reason, seek his aid in using the smallest effective amount over the shortest period of time.

Should you need outside help, Alcoholics Anonymous now has a sizable minority of women members and a few all-women chapters. Women for Sobriety, a female group started in 1975, has several hundred self-help units throughout the country. Send a stamped, self-addressed envelope to Box 618, Quakertown, Pa. 18951 for further information. To seek information about Pills Anonymous, a group patterned after AA, write to 443 West 50th Street, New York, N.Y. 10019.

If you no longer sleep as long or as soundly as you used to, don't automatically grab for the bottle of pills. When insomniacs are monitored during the night, many are found to be getting enough sleep. Instead of tossing and turning in bed, practice relaxing, muscle by muscle. It's better to turn on the TV or read a book than to lie in the dark, clenching your teeth in frustration. Exercise during the day may help you to sleep at night. After-dinner coffee may hurt, making you jittery, even though it never used to. Eliminate an afternoon nap to help you sleep better at night. If you're getting less sleep than you used to, it may be all that you need. And think of all the wonderful things to do with the gift of extra time.

Depression

Middle age is not prime time for depression. Current research suggests that women are more likely to suffer depression from eighteen to thirty; that married women are more susceptible than single, except for the recently divorced; mothers of preschoolers are more depression-prone than mothers of adolescents; and empty-nest mothers the least prone of all. Nevertheless, some women suffer depression in middle age. At all ages up to fifty-five, twice as many women are depressed as men, and this stage of life is no exception. After fifty-five, according to one study, men catch up; depression rates are high for both sexes from the mid-sixties to mid-seventies, and then slacken off.

Clinical depression does not merely mean feeling blue; we all have days when the zing seems to have gone out of life. When these feelings persist, affect body as well as mind, cripple daily activities, lead to hopelessness and despair, they are labeled depression. A depressed woman is sluggish, with no energy, little appetite, disturbed sleep, lost sexual drive.

When depression hits at middle age, it is not *because* of this stage of the life cycle, but almost *in spite of it*. Its victims are likely to be women who have never felt good about themselves or their life. Marjorie Fiske Lowenthal and her colleagues describe such a woman in *Four Stages of Life*: she views her children's imminent departure as a mere punctuation mark to a drab and unrewarding existence. "I just live from day to day," she says. "After Judy [her daughter] leaves, I don't care what happens to me any more because my life is just not that important."

Among women close to the empty-nest period who were studied by the Lowenthal group, those who were depressed felt little sense of control over their lives; they were unsure of themselves, uneasy over their abilities, in despair over their marriage. A significant number took the troubles of every family member as their own. They worried about a husband's health, a parent's loneliness, a child's failure. When her son got sick and had to drop out of school, one said, "He was very unhappy. *When he is unhappy, I am unhappy.*"

These are the women, says psychologist Lillian Troll, who "put all their eggs in the one basket of motherhood." Pauline Bart, in her study, "Mother Portnoy's Complaints," describes them as women who have "overprotective or overinvolved relationships with their children." She adds, "You do not have to be Jewish to be a Jewish mother, but it still helps a little."

Women who are susceptible to depression in the middle years are not essentially different from those who sink into its lethargy earlier. They live by the traditional femininity taught them as girls—helplessness, passivity, dependence. They expect their husbands to make the decisions and are shattered if death or divorce destroys this prop. They live through others, their spouses as well as their children. They feel guilty if a healthy egoism—"I want something for myself"—sneaks into consciousness. When one woman played tennis well on a day that her husband's game was ragged, she said, "It made me blue. I didn't think I was allowed to be happy when he wasn't."

Low self-esteem is central to their personality. "Ask yourself this question," suggests Dr. Lenore Radloff, of the National Institute of Mental Health. "When something happens to you, good or bad, how do you typically explain it? If you're successful and you call it luck; if you fail and blame yourself, then you may have the kind of personality that is prone to depression."

Another facet, familiar to the divorcee, is the concept that life is worthless without a man. "The belief that you can't be happy without a man is central to the thinking of depressed women," says Dr. David Burns, a psychiatrist at the University of Pennsylvania Medical School. "It's also a belief that most females learned in childhood."

The woman who is depressed feels helpless and hopeless because she views herself in the control of others, of her husband, employer, children, parents. This is probably why depression is less frequent in midlife, a time when a healthy woman holds the reins firmly in her own hands, exchanges her go-for role for enhanced self-interest, learns to speak up for her own needs and take credit for her achievements. Yet even healthy, effective women can falter. One, a speech therapist who had nurtured a husband and two sons, spun into depression when she had a hysterectomy at the age of fifty. "I couldn't tell my husband how low I felt," she says, "and that was the worst. I just was afraid he would stop loving me if he knew I could no longer cope."

Scientists have recently discovered that moderate and severe depression are accompanied by biochemical changes in the brain, and believe that it is these changes that affect sleep and appetite, cause lethargy and lack of interest in sex in a depressed person. A group of prescription drugs called the tricyclic antidepressants appear to reverse these chemical changes, reducing insomnia, improving the appetite and making a depressed person appear brighter and perkier.

Women for whom antidepressant medication is prescribed should also know the limitations of these drugs. They don't do much good for most people unless taken in fairly large dosage, yet the elderly must be treated cautiously. Consult a physician who is familiar with these drugs—a psychiatrist or a family doctor with an interest in emotional problems. They are slow-acting. Two to three weeks may pass before a patient starts to feel brighter. They should not be stopped when the symptoms—insomnia, lack of appetite, lethargy—start to pass; maintenance doses continued for six months or more appear to guard against relapse.

Moreover, the antidepressant drugs do not change a woman's mind set, the self-disgust, devotion to self-sacrifice, feelings of helplessness that underlie the depression. Psychotherapy helps, particularly a version called cognitive therapy, pioneered at the University of Pennsylvania, which teaches a depressed woman how to combat the negative feelings that trigger depression. Lengthy psychoanalysis that probes the dim recesses of childhood is *not* considered a treatment of choice for depression.

How can a woman avoid depression? The experts make these suggestions:

Get a job. A National Institute of Mental Health survey showed that working wives suffered less depression than housewives, though more than their working husbands.

Have a confidante, a supportive person with whom you can talk honestly. Women under stress are more likely to find solace from a friend rather than a husband or family member.

Practice speaking up for what you want. Some find that it's necessary to take a course in assertiveness-training in order to counteract that sacrificial-Mom attitude. (If at Thanksgiving you give the rest of the family the white meat, crisp skin, second joint, plump legs, saving the scrawny back and neck for yourself, then you'd better practice up on self-assertion.)

Take credit for your own successes. Try to act less helpless. Learn to change a tire, fix a clogged toilet, and then enjoy your new skills.

Underlying the problems discussed here—depression, alcoholism, tranquilizers—is a common denominator, an inability to cope with stress. What we should cultivate, says Dr. Hans Selye, is *eustress*, a pleasant stress that enhances living, the stress of a passionate kiss instead of the tension of sitting in a dentist's chair.

How to do it? Not by avoiding stress, which is impossible, says Dr. Selye, but by recognizing our own nature and organizing life to fit it. He believes that there are two kinds of individuals— race horses, who thrive on a vigorous busy life style, and turtles, who prefer a tranquil environment. Unpleasant stress that harms body and mind comes only, Dr. Selye says, when one violates the inner self. The race horse, eager to run, might still overstress herself with too much frenetic activity, or practice overcontrol be-

cause she thinks it's ladylike to act like a turtle. Both ways according to this thesis, are harmful. These days when careers are
in, a turtle might feel guilty if she didn't strive for one, when
what she really wants is a routine job and the joy of puttering
in kitchen and garden.

In other words, don't handle life's demands by being a chemical glutton—dulling yourself with liquor and pills; don't drift
into depression because you feel helpless to face stress. Instead,
be self-aware and practice a life style, either busy or contempla-
tive, that fits your own inner being.

XVI
The Future

The problems of aging are the problems of women, for we are the survivors. Women over sixty-five constitute the fastest-growing segment of the American population. At the turn of the century more men lived to old age than women. By 1930 the scales were even. They have been tipping ever since. Now the over-sixty-five population includes sixty-nine men for every hundred women, and the gap keeps widening.

Gerontologists, now more aware of the survivorship qualities of the female, are asking, Why do women live longer? They are tossing out the clichés about the weaker sex, and beginning to wonder if it's not a matter of the survival of the fittest. The idea is growing that women have more stamina and emotional reserve than men. When women age, they are better able to care for themselves physically, while many older men fumble around the house. Often more expressive, women usually have more friends and they apparently can cope with loneliness.

It has been assumed that widowers remarry because there are fewer of them, and they have more opportunity. But that isn't all; they may rush into a second marriage because, unlike women, they can't hack it alone. Kurt Back and Joanna Morris, Duke University sociologists who studied men and women aged forty-six to seventy, came to this conclusion: "Women seem to be better adapted than men to changes in the rhythm of life."

Yet despite these strengths, many women feel fearful about the future. "The idea of being lonely—that scares me," one woman says. And from another, "I couldn't stand being incapacitated." "My grandmother became senile, and that frightens the living daylights out of me," says a third. These are fears that we all share.

Yes, it's true that some of these things happen to some people. But the notion that after passing sixty-five, every woman's life becomes gray shading into black is a myth. "There is a stereotype abroad in this youth-oriented culture that old age is a disaster," says Dr. Francis Braceland, psychiatry professor emeritus at Yale University. "The aged are considered to be decrepit, infirm, querulous, poor and useless; but ninety-five percent do not conform to this stereotype . . . The largest segment sails on as if aging has brought little change."

For one thing, a woman of sixty-five is no longer elderly. Writing in 1922, a psychiatrist placed the start of senescence in the forties. In 1935, when the Social Security Act became law, it moved upward to sixty-five. "At present, it would seem more realistic to regard seventy-five as the beginning of old age," says Roy Hamlin, research psychologist with the Veterans Administration. "Before long eighty-five may seem reasonable."

Psychologist Bernice Neugarten has coined a new word to describe the junior senior citizens in our midst, the "young-old." Their age is fifty-five to seventy-five; they are mostly healthy (less than one in four have a disability that interferes with normal activity); they are still married, and living with a spouse in their own household. She believes that the number of young-old will grow larger as we move into the twenty-first century.

In her Boston *Globe* column, Ellen Goodman suggests that young-old women are now groping to establish their own identity. She pictures the period as "a new awkward age that arrives when they are older than Jacqueline Onassis and younger than Maggie Kuhn [leader of the Gray Panthers] . . . pregeriatric and postmenopausal." For these women, "Youth is unbecoming but old age is still premature."

It is highly likely that our generation, now in the middle years, will nail down that identity, expanding the horizons for the young-old so that the "golden years," an overworked cliché, will cease to be a bad joke and become reality. For we have advantages for enriching these years that our forebears lacked. We have so shaped middle age that it is more vigorous, productive and fulfilling than ever before. Our health is good; many of us are still jogging, swimming, playing tennis, postponing the muscular atrophy that used to typify the after-sixty-five years. We are out in the world, unlike our mothers, whose horizons often did not stretch beyond the family. Even when the job we hold is routine, we experience the ego satisfaction of earning our own way. We enjoy new sexual rights, particularly the right to orgasm, and we are unlikely to surrender them. We should not, therefore, be afraid of the coming years.

The first task is to take the fear out of aging by dispelling some of its myths—the cobwebs that foster prejudice against older people, and make the aged themselves as contemptuous of their own status as are their bitterest critics. The myths that do the greatest harm are these:

All old people are alike. "Older people actually become more diverse rather than more similar with advancing years," says Dr. Butler. This is a time when chronological labels are meaningless because of the wide spread in rates of physiological, psychological and social aging.

No two people age at the same speed; each individual organ has its own rate of slowing down. The difference depends on heredity, lifetime environment, life style, personality. One woman's hair turns gray in her twenties, another in the fifties, and an occasional person hardly grays at all. Before you make a snap judgment about a person in her seventies, eighties or nineties, think of feisty Margaret Kuhn, seventy-three; vigorous Georgia O'Keefe, the painter, ninety-one; and Pablo Picasso, who died in his nineties and was continuously and intensively creative. Their pattern of aging is unique, and so no doubt will yours.

When you're old, you're sick. This dangerous myth holds that debilitating disease is inevitable among the elderly. Too many physicians, believing the myth, use it as an excuse not to treat ailments that can actually be cured or alleviated. Even now when you complain of fatigue, pain, dwindling sexual enjoyment, your doctor is likely to answer, "But what do you expect at your age?" "To equate chronic illness with aging is like equating juvenile delinquency with adolescence," points out Dr. Roy Hamlin.

Dr. Butler cites the tale of an old gentleman, aged a hundred and one, who consulted his doctor about a pain in his left knee.

"For heaven's sake, at your age you've got to expect some pain and discomfort," the doctor said. The old man responded angrily, "Now look here, my right knee is also one hundred and one and *it* doesn't hurt. How do you account for that?"

You'll be neglected when you get old. According to the stereotype, the elderly are shunted off into nursing homes to die alone without care and love. But nursing homes are *not* the inevitable junk-heap for the aged. Only five percent of the nation's over-sixty-five population reside in them, usually the very old who have outlived their close kin.

Ethel Shanas, University of Illinois sociologist, has effectively demolished the cruel myth that American daughters and sons do not care for their elderly. Fewer old people live with their children today, she says (eighteen percent compared with thirty-six percent twenty years ago); but the reason is not callous neglect but mutual pleasure. Most parents, as well as their offspring, prefer their independence; and many are healthy and wealthy enough to manage in their own digs.

Three out of every four elderly parents have a child living no more than a half-hour away, and many live only down the street from each other. Relationships with these children have not deteriorated in twenty years, according to three surveys cited by Dr. Shanas. In 1975 three out of four older people told an interviewer that they had seen at least one of their children within the week, a figure close to that reported in 1957. Only one in ten had not seen any children for a month, a number that has not changed over twenty years.

As a woman in the middle years, the responsibility for your parents falls largely on your shoulders. What Dr. Shanas is saying is that *you* are not neglecting your parents, and you can have confidence that if you need them, *your children* will not neglect you. Nor do today's adult children dump their parents into institutions, she adds. "Placing an elderly relative is the last, rather than the first resort of families . . . They have exhausted all other alternatives . . . and made the final decision with the utmost reluctance." The dominant family form for old people, Dr. Shanas concludes, is the modified extended family—what she calls "intimacy at a distance."

Old people inevitably become senile. This may be the cruelest myth of all. As long as it is widely believed that aging and brain deterioration are synonymous and irreversible, research into the cause, prevention and cure of a serious but by no means inevitable disease called senile dementia will be stymied. So will treatment of the hundred or more illnesses that look like senile dementia but aren't. Many of these are readily curable, sometimes even by the simple measure of a few good meals with a dash of tender loving care.

Senility is a wastebasket designation, a convenient way to dismiss all old people who appear forgetful, confused, disoriented. Many illnesses may cause these symptoms: among them, alcoholism, depression, excessive medication, walking pneumonia, congestive heart failure, diabetes, anemia, malnutrition. In one case, when a woman of eighty-three, who lived alone and cared competently for herself, suddenly became confused and helpless, her neighbors tried in vain to get her physician to pay a house call. "She's senile. She'll have to go to a nursing home. Stop bothering me," was the doctor's irritated reply. Finally they persuaded a nearby hospital to send an ambulance. At the hospital, physicians diagnosed her "senility" as influenza. After a week of bed rest and treatment, she was sent home, as lively and chipper as ever.

"A national catastrophe," is how Dr. Richard Besdine, chairman of an NIA task force on reversible dementias, describes such misdiagnoses. He estimates that these medical errors may account for 300,000 wasted lives and 100,000 needless institutionalizations. How do they happen? When a fifty-year-old has a heart attack, Dr. Besdine explains, the symptom, chest pain, is unmistakable. But with the elderly, the only symptom may be confusion.

Senile dementia is a disease: the progressive, relentless deterioration of the brain, affecting memory, personality and judgment and eventually leading to death. Recent research suggests that only one in twenty persons over sixty-five has the disease in a severe form, and perhaps another one in ten to a milder degree. A rare ailment of the middle years called Alzheimer's disease appears to be an earlier form of senile dementia. Current speculation links its occurrence to a slow virus that may lie quiescent in the body for many years, and only become virulent when prodded by the physiological changes of aging.

Mental deterioration may also be caused by hardening of the arteries that feed blood to the brain, a condition that limits the amount of oxygenated blood the brain receives. This is *not* thought to be related to the mild memory difficulties experienced in late middle age. Researchers now believe that it is a rarer cause for brain deterioration, less severe, and usually accompanied by other signs of artery disease, such as hypertension. The cause for most senile dementias is unknown.

The theory that patients with senile dementia suffer from an enzyme deficiency that causes depletion of an important neurotransmitter in the brain is now being considered with cautious optimism by scientists. They are feeding choline, a common food substance found in egg yolk, and also in meat and fish, to sufferers from senile dementia. Preliminary results are reported to be good in patients who have the disease in an early state.

Some scientists hold that if one eats a large omelet, extra choline will appear within hours in the brain. The work is still highly experimental. It appears to bring no change to those with normal memory, and only one experiment suggests it may aid the minor memory faults that accompany aging. Even if it only admits a chink of light into the darkness that blocks our understanding of senile dementia, it is an encouraging development.

Senility is *not* the future fate for most aging Americans. "If you think you're going senile," says Harvard's Dr. Besdine, "then you probably aren't. Having the intellectual facilities to worry about it means you're likely to be okay."

If aging isn't inevitably disease, senility and loneliness, then what is it? What happens, says Dr. Nathan Shock, scientist emeritus of NIA's Gerontology Research Center, "is that you lose your reserve capacity. This is the essence of aging . . . you find that you can't play as fast a game of handball as you used to, and the time comes when you must face up to it . . . On the other hand, it's a mistake to face up to it too much, to give in and stop playing handball altogether."

No one really knows what causes aging. One theory holds that it is a wear-and-tear process, that the human organism just slows down and gives out like an aging piece of equipment. Another holds that it is genetic, that every species has an ordained life span, modified in each individual by her own heredity. This is probably true. The life span of a rat is three years; a horse, twenty-five; an elephant, seventy; and a human, about a hundred. Among other mammals, as well as man, females live longer than males. Humans with long-lived parents and grandparents survive on an average about six years longer than those whose parents died before the age of fifty. But heredity is modified by environment, by stress and other trauma to which each individual is subject.

Right now the immunity theory of aging is a hot topic among scientists, partly because it includes the possibility of taking action, of treating people to ward off some of the diseases that become more virulent over the years. Immunity is the process by which the body's white cells battle foreign invaders, gobbling them up and forming antibodies to destroy them. Immunity declines with age (although more slowly in females), and this is probably why old people die of pneumonia and other bacterial and viral diseases. One diminishing ability is the recognition of invaders as foreign; some scientists speculate that this may explain the increase in cancer and in auto-immune diseases like arthritis in which the body mistakenly fights its own tissue as foreign.

A decline in immune function starts in the thirties and forties, perhaps even earlier; it does not begin with the onset of old age. The thymus gland in the chest, which controls one aspect of immunity, shrinks after puberty; the level of thymic hormone starts decreasing at about the age of thirty, and by sixty it can no longer be detected in the blood of some people. At The New York Hospital, this decline in thymic hormone is being studied in six hundred elderly volunteers, under the direction of Dr. Marc Weksler, head of a newly established division of geriatrics and gerontology. One finding is that there is a marked difference in immune function among the elderly. "Some are immunologically young, others middle-aged, and still others bereft of function, immunological cripples," Dr. Weksler says. Is this difference significant to longevity? The researchers have a hunch it is, but they do not really know yet.

One question is basic: Can these immunological cripples be treated with thymic hormone, and will it bolster their immunity to disease? "This is our dream," says Dr. Weksler, "like giving insulin to a diabetic." But it lies in the future, perhaps your future.

Other recent discoveries about the immune system may have practical application right now. Stress harms immune function by releasing hormones that can destroy the disease-fighting white blood cells. Older people do not adapt as well to stress, to heat or cold, to heavy exercise, to emotional trauma. Many believe that divorce in a sixty-year-old probably causes more havoc than divorce at an earlier age. "Stress allows you to become more susceptible to infection, perhaps even to the common cold," says Dr. William Adler, of the Gerontology Research Center. Diet may also play a part; it is known that malnutrition harms immune function. To help keep your immunity level high right now, Dr. Adler suggests, "You should choose a reasonable diet and avoid stress. These are the elements of life style to adopt in middle age."

Most women now in the middle years have little desire to set a record for longevity. Their goal is not to add more years to life, but more life to the years. This is what is starting to happen now. Although the number of old people in the population is on the rise, there is no lengthening of the age span, but instead a broadening of its base. The number of centenarians is not increasing, but there are a lot more sexy sixties and swinging seventies around.

If you are in the forties, or even the thirties right now, with old age almost thirty years away, you need not worry about this goal for the future. For if you live fully today, if you learn to dare, to flex mental and physical muscles, to stretch out toward your own full potential, then the future is likely to take care of itself.

Some twenty years ago a woman who describes herself as "an ordinary female housewife" started her research for a book. It was an ambitious undertaking, a panoramic history of the beginning of the first World War. It took temerity, for although she had completed college, she was not an historian with a graduate degree. Her husband and family "never took me seriously," she recalls.

Barbara Tuchman had passed her fiftieth birthday when *The Guns of August* was published and became a best seller. Winner of two Pulitzer Prizes since then, she was sixty-seven when her latest book, the immensely popular *A Distant Mirror: The Calamitous 14th Century* came out in 1978. She is a vital, self-confident woman, still at the peak of creative power. It would be a joke to call her elderly.

Mrs. Tuchman describes herself as a late developer, explaining that being a woman had kept her back for a long time. "My obligation was primarily toward my three children." But she and other successful women like her are not really late bloomers but persons who bloom twice, having one life as wife and mother, and then a second for themselves and society.

Although Barbara Tuchman rode out her late middle years on a wave of success, many of us are likely to be content in midlife with the inner feeling of success that attends the full realization of self. But as the birthdays pass, this second bloom does not follow automatically. Women still tend to underestimate themselves, to ask too little, to aspire too low, to esteem others beyond self. For full realization during our middle years, and for the extension of these vigorous years into the later decades, these are the points to remember:

Gain respect for yourself and your own potential. One fifty-year-old college student wears on her blouse an enormous button that says YOU CAN DO IT. It was a gift from a daughter who told her, "After ten kids, you ought to be able to manage college." This surge in confidence does not apply merely to going to college or getting a job. These are the years when one must develop a sense of mastery of all aspects of the environment: driving in a snowstorm, filling out the income tax form, managing the currency during foreign travel.

Learn to lean on yourself. Through divorce and widowhood many women are now struggling to stand alone for the first time, and those who depended most heavily on a man are experiencing the greatest pain. The achievement of inner autonomy does not mean relinquishing intimacy with a husband or a lover, or even a friend. Interdependency, a loving relationship between two persons who are certain of their own identities, is a healthier status for both.

Care about yourself. Given the gift of long life, women must learn to care for their bodies and their appearance as they would care for a piece of good machinery. Bodies atrophy through disuse. NASA studies show that for every three days a person is immobile, she loses one-fifth of her maximum muscle strength. Those who get more exercise seem to live longer and in better health. If it's hard to find time in your busy schedule, remember that you have devoted your younger years to the nurture of others; now is the time to pleasure yourself.

Get in control. Be aware of your own feelings and inner needs, and speak up to obtain them. Learn to assert yourself in your job, with your children, friends and husband. Sexual assertion is part of this. In fact, the ability to gain sexual pleasure increases a woman's confidence that she controls her own destiny.

Don't hold in your anger or be excessively concerned with being a good guy. Grouchiness, says Dr. David Gutmann of the University of Michigan, is a survival asset. The male style—keeping a stiff upper lip, bottling the emotions—is often compared favorably with the female—expressing one's feelings, crying when it seems appropriate. But we are the survivors, and our expressiveness is probably part of the reason why.

Add variety to your life. One couple in their fifties report complacently that every Saturday night they dine at the same restaurant and order the roast beef: "It's always good." This may offer the pleasure of familiarity, but there's little else such a rigid style encourages. At every age, life should be a smorgasbord of experience, of love, work, friendship, hobbies, travel. TV may be a boon, but it's also numbing. It keeps us from talking to each other.

If you hold a job, your paycheck is likely to give you a sense of independence and of status in the world outside the family. "For some there's a giddy sense of liberation just to be out of the house," says Dr. Lillian Rubin. But there is loss as well as gain, she adds, in the loss of free time. "Especially after the children are grown, women who are homemakers have the time to pursue interests and talents that until now may have remained latent . . . In doing so [a woman] develops inner resources that are independent of her role in the outer world . . . resources that may turn out to be central for living a productive and peaceful old age." Thus each path has its pluses and minuses. If financial need is not the impetus, then every woman should feel free to choose the one that best suits her basic needs.

The research studies that are now being made of the adult female's transition through life's stages stress one crucial finding: the experience of men and women is profoundly different. This is probably because we were taught different roles in childhood and we learned our lessons well. Although the drums of change may be beating loud, change takes place slowly, and decades will probably pass before boys and girls grow up with the same hopes and goals, plans and dreams—if indeed they ever do.

Right now, at least, midlife is the stage when men may suffer crisis and women experience fruition. "It's a glorious time, the point when everything is finally coming together for me," one woman says. Poised at life's midpoint, with our strengths on the rise and our weaknesses waning, these are indeed our own years.

Bibliography

Albanese, Anthony. "Problems of Bone Health in the Elderly." *New York State Journal of Medicine.* Vol. 75, No. 2 (February 1975).

Arenberg, David. "A Longitudinal Study of Problem Solving." *Journal of Gerontology.* Vol. 29, No. 6 (1974).

Bart, Pauline B. "Portnoy's Mother's Complaint." *Trans-Action.* Vol. 8, Nos. 1 & 2 (1970).

————, and Grossman, Marlyn. "Menopause." *Women and Health* (May/June 1976).

Bender, N. Judson. "Marriage in the Middle Years." *Journal of the Louisiana State Medical Society.* Vol. 126, No. 9 (September 1974).

Binstock, Robert, and Shanas, Ethel, eds. *Handbook of Aging and the Social Sciences.* Van Nostrand Reinhold, 1976.

————. "The Political Economy of Aging." *Aging in America's Future.* Hoechst-Roussel Pharmaceutical Co., November 7, 1975.

Birren, James E., and Schaie, K. Warner, eds. *Handbook of the Psychology of Aging.* Van Nostrand Reinhold, 1977.

Brecher, Edward. "Women-Victims of the VD Ripoff." *Viva* (October, November, 1973).

Breslow, Lester, and Somers, Anne. "The Lifetime Health Monitoring Program." *New England Journal of Medicine.* Vol. 296, No. 11 (March 17, 1977).

Brody, Jane E., and Holleb, Arthur. *You Can Fight Cancer and Win.* Quadrangle/New York Times, 1977.

Brooks, Barbara. "Mother Is a Freshperson." Paper delivered at the annual meeting of the American Psychological Association, San Francisco (August 1977).

Butler, Robert N. *Why Survive? Being Old in America.* Harper & Row, 1975.

————, and Lewis, Myrna. *Sex After Sixty.* Harper & Row, 1976.

Caine, Lynn. *Widow.* Morrow, Bantam, 1975.

Castelli, William P. "High Density Lipoproteins: A New Understanding of Cholesterol and Risk." *American Heart Association, 4th Science Writers Forum,* San Antonio (January 1977).

Cherry, Laurence. "Eustress; Interview with Hans Selye." *Psychology Today* (March 1978).

Contemporary Ob/Gyn. "A New Look at Barrier Contraceptives: A Symposium." McGraw-Hill, August 1977.

Cope, Oliver. *The Breast.* Houghton Mifflin, 1977.

Fidell, Linda S. "Psychotropic Drug Use by Women." Paper delivered at the annual meeting of the American Psychological Association, San Francisco (August 1977).

Finch, Caleb E., and Hayflick, Leonard, eds. *Handbook of the Biology of Aging.* Van Nostrand Reinhold, 1977.

Gilmore, Beatrice. "To Achieve or Not to Achieve: The Question of Women." Paper delivered at the annual meeting of the Gerontological Society, Louisville (October 1975).

Glick, Paul C. "Updating the Life Cycle of the Family." *Journal of Marriage and the Family* (February 1977).

―――, and Norton, Arthur J. "Marrying, Divorcing, and Living Together in the United States Today." *Population Reference Bureau,* Vol. 32, No. 5 (October 1977).

Gomberg, Edith S. "Women and Alcoholism." In V. Franks and V. Burtle, eds. *Women in Therapy,* Brunner/Mazel, 1974.

Goodman, Ellen. "Those Years in Between." Column in *Boston Globe* (September 19, 1978).

Gordon, Tavia, et al. "Menopause and Coronary Heart Disease: the Framingham Study." *Annals of Internal Medicine.* 89: 157–61 (1978).

―――. "Diabetes, Blood Lipids, and the Role of Obesity in Coronary Heart Disease Risk for Women: The Framingham Study." *Annals of Internal Medicine,* 87: 393–97 (1977).

Greenberg, Reva. *Women and Aging.* Unpublished Ph.D. thesis.

Gutmann, David. "Parenthood: A Key to the Comparative Study of the Life Cycle." Paper delivered at the annual meeting of the American Association for the Advancement of Science, Washington, D.C. (February 14, 1978).

Hamlin, Roy M. "Restrictions on the Competent Aged." Paper delivered at the annual meeting of the American Psychological Association, San Francisco (August 1977).

Howard, Lyn. "Obesity: A Feasible Approach to a Formidable Problem." *American Family Physician* (September 1975).

Janeway, Elizabeth. "Breaking the Age Barrier." *Ms* (April 1973).

Kaplan, Helen Singer. *The New Sex Therapy.* Quadrangle/New York Times, 1974.

―――. *Illustrated Manual of Sex Therapy.* Quadrangle/New York Times, 1975.

Lamport, Felicia. "A Middle-Age Spread." *McCall's* (November 1977).

Langley, Ivan J. Panel Discussion. *American Journal of Obstetrics and Gynecology.* Vol. 128, No. 4 (June 15, 1977).

LeShan, Eda. *The Wonderful Crisis of Middle Age.* David McKay, 1973.

Livson, Florine B. "Coming Together in the Middle Years." Paper delivered at the annual meeting of the Gerontological Society, New York (October 1976).

————. "Patterns of Personality Development in Middle-Aged Women." *International Journal of Aging and Human Development,* Vol. 7, No. 2 (1976).

————. "Personality Development of Men and Women in the Middle Years." Paper delivered at the annual meeting of the American Association for the Advancement of Science, Washington, D.C. (February 1978).

Lowenthal, Marjorie Fiske, Thurner, Majda, Chiriboga, David. *Four Stages of Life.* Jossey-Bass, 1975.

Mann, George V. "Diet-Heart: End of an Era." *New England Journal of Medicine,* 297, 644–50 (September 22, 1977).

Masters, William H., and Johnson, Virginia E. *Human Sexual Response.* Little, Brown, 1966.

————. *Human Sexual Inadequacy.* Little, Brown, 1970.

McNamara, Patricia M., et al. "Natural History of Menopause: The Framingham Study." *Medical Digest* (1978).

Nachtigall, Lila, and Heilman, Joan. *The Lila Nachtigall Report.* G. P. Putnam's Sons, 1977.

Nagler, Willibald. "Tennis Elbow." *American Family Physician,* Vol. 16, No. 1 (July 1977).

Neugarten, Bernice L., ed. *Middle Age and Aging.* University of Chicago Press, 1968.

————, and Datan, Nancy. "The Middle Years." In Arieti, Silvano, ed., *American Handbook of Psychiatry,* 2nd ed., Vol. 1. Basic Books, 1974.

————. "A New Look at Menopause." *Psychology Today* (December 1967).

Nowak, Carol A. "Socialization to Become an Old Hag." Paper delivered at annual meeting of the American Psychological Association, San Francisco (August 1977).

Boston Women's Health Book Collective. *Our Bodies, Ourselves.* 2nd ed. Simon and Schuster, 1976.

Palmore, Erdman, ed. *Normal Aging I.* Duke University Press, 1970.

————. *Normal Aging II.* Duke University Press, 1974.

Parlee, Mary B. "Psychological Aspects of the Climacteric in Women." Paper delivered at meeting of the Eastern Psychological Association, New York (1976).

Radloff, Lenore S. "Depression and the Empty Nest." Center for Epidemiologic Studies, National Institute of Mental Health (1977).

Ragan, Pauline K. "Cooling the Mark Out." Paper delivered at annual meeting of the American Psychological Association, San Francisco (August 1977).

Reitz, Rosetta. *Menopause: A Positive Approach.* Chilton Book Company, 1977.

Reuben, David. *Everything You Always Wanted to Know about Sex *but Were Afraid to Ask.* David McKay, 1969.

Robertson, Joan. "Socialization into Grandmotherhood." Paper delivered at annual meeting of the American Psychological Association, San Francisco (August 1977).

Robinson, Mina. "Lesbians in Later Life." *Sister Newspaper* (August/September 1978).

Romney, Seymour, et al. *Gynecology and Obstetrics: the Health Care of Women.* McGraw-Hill, 1975.

Rose, Louisa, ed. *The Menopause Book.* Hawthorn Books, 1977.

Rosenthal, Sylvia, *Cosmetic Surgery: A Consumer's Guide.* Lippincott, 1977.

Rosmond, Babette [Rosamond Campion]. *The Invisible Worm.* Macmillan, 1972.

Rubin, Lillian. *Worlds of Pain.* Basic Books, 1976.

———. "Women in Middle Life." Paper delivered at annual meeting of the American Psychological Association (August 1977).

———. "Social Class Differences among Older Women." Conference on "The Older Woman: Continuities and Discontinuities," Bethesda, Md. (September 1978).

Rush, Florence. "Woman in the Middle." In *Radical Feminism.* Koedt, Anne, Levine, Ellen, and Rapone, Anita, eds. Quadrangle/New York Times, 1973.

Sedney, Mary Anne. "Process of Sex-Role Development during Life Crisis of Middle-Aged Women." Paper delivered at annual meeting of the American Psychological Association, San Francisco (1977).

Shanas, Ethel. "Social Myth as Hypothesis: The Case of the Family Relations of Old People." Paper delivered at annual meeting of the Gerontological Society, Dallas (November 1978).

Shock, Nathan W. "Developments in Aging Research." Paper delivered at annual meeting of the American Psychological Association, San Francisco (August 1977).

Silverstone, Barbara, and Hyman, Helen L. *You and Your Aging Parents.* Pantheon Books, 1976.

Sontag, Susan. "The Double Standard of Aging." *Saturday Review of the Society* (September 23, 1972).

Tietze, Christopher. "New Estimates of Mortality Associated with Fertility Control." *Family Planning Perspectives* (March/April 1977).

Todhunter, E. Neige. "Nutrition in Menopausal and Post-Menopausal Women." In *Nutritional Impacts on Women.* Harper & Row, 1977.

Troll, Lillian, Israel, Joan, and Israel, Kenneth. *Looking Ahead: A Woman's Guide to the Problems and Joys of Growing Older.* Prentice-Hall, 1977.

Turner, Barbara. "The Self-Concepts of Older Women." Paper delivered at annual meeting of the American Psychological Association, San Francisco (August 1977).

Weissman, Myrna, and Klerman, Gerald. "Sex Differences and the Epidemiology of Depression." *Archives of General Psychiatry* (January 1977).

White, E. B. *Letters of E. B. White.* Harper & Row, 1976.

Zohman, Lenore R. *Exercise Your Way to Fitness and Heart Health.* Pamphlet published by CPC International, 1974.

About the Author

ALICE LAKE has written several hundred articles for popular magazines on many subjects, and particularly on those of interest to women. She has won a number of awards for her writing, including prizes from the American Academy of Pediatrics and the American Psychological Association. She has a grown daughter who is a lawyer and she lives with her husband, another lawyer, in Harrison, New York.